Training
Manual in
Applied
Medical
Anthropology

Edited by
Carole E. Hill

a special publication of the
American Anthropological Association

professional series

special publications of the
American Anthropological Association

Professional Series Editor
Linda A. Bennett

Published by the
American Anthropological Association
1703 New Hampshire Avenue, N.W.
Washington, D.C. 20009

Library of Congress Cataloging-in-publication Data

Training manual in applied medical anthropology / [editor] Carole E. Hill.
     p.   cm. — (A Special publication of the American Anthropo-
  logical Association ; no. 27)
  ISBN 0-913167-46-0
  1. Medical anthropology. 2. Applied anthropology. 3. Medical anthropology—Vocational guidance. I. Hill, Carole E. II. Series.
  [DNLM: 1. Anthropology. 2. Employment. 3. Medicine. GN 296 T767]
GN296.T725   1991
306.4'61—dc20
DNLM/DLC   91-26130
for Library of Congress   CIP

CONTENTS

Preface

Mark Nichter

This manual serves as a guide to the field of applied medical anthropology. As a guide, it provides information on what type of work opportunities exist, where one finds out about them, how one goes about presenting themselves to potential employers, and the range of skills necessary for the types of tasks the anthropologist may be expected to perform. In this preface, I comment on events in the 1980s which have influenced the current generation of medical anthropologists, highlight dilemmas which face anthropologists engaging in applied work, and anticipate challenges likely to engage applied medical anthropologists in the 1990s.

The Context of the 1980s

For medical anthropology, the 1980s were a time of uncertain if not scarce academic employment, but challenging new applied work opportunities. Reaganomics fostered health individualism at home, and the social marketing of technical fixes abroad. On the national scene, AIDS, drug addiction, the homeless, teenage pregnancy, malpractice litigation, rising medical costs, unnecessary surgery, organ transplants, eating disorders, and smoking frequently made the national press. The corporatization of health care; dramatic changes in the structure of insurance payments; notable drops in hospital inpatient days and rises in outpatient therapy; cutbacks in health services to the poor, the elderly, and mentally ill; a rising rate of uninsured; the closing of unprofitable clinics and the mushrooming of profitable specialty clinics were less visible in the public eye but all too apparent to practitioners.

The 1980s were a time when consumer confidence in medicine dropped and competition between health facilities gave way to prime time advertising campaigns calling attention to medical humanism as well as technical competence. It was a time when new illnesses were "textually transmitted" by the popular press (e.g., PMS, chronic fatigue syndrome, codependency), and readily accepted by the lay population, while debated among experts. Medicalization was clearly not a process simply driven by physicians in search of new life problems to appropriate (Illich 1975, 1986). Consumer demand for illness labels was complex, fostered by the commercialization of health (the myth that good health can be purchased), a "progressive" decline in discomfort thresholds (Barsky 1988), collective anxiety about aging and new threats to health, and the need for sanctioned idioms of distress.

Internationally, the discourse on primary health care shifted from community participation approaches to health to selective targeted diseases (e.g., diarrheal disease case management with oral rehydration therapy, universal immunization). Social marketing approaches to creating consumer demand became popular as did operations research as a means of creating more efficient health care delivery systems. Practitioners from both camps called upon anthropologists to develop rapid ethnographic assessment procedures to assist them in the collection of baseline data against which to plan, measure or evaluate the success of intervention programs. The 1980s were a time when donor agencies paid attention to social scientists. Anthropologists played a visible role in child survival program planning and actively participated in WHO's diarrheal disease (CDD) and Tropical Disease (TRD) programs; UNICEF's oral rehydration and nutritional status monitoring programs; and USAID's diarrheal disease and AIDS prevention initiatives (e.g., ADDR, Health Com). USAID's use of anthropologists was expanded by virtue of the New Directions Bill in 1975, which required social soundness analysis of all USAID projects.

The 80s were a time of ferment in "academia," marked by debates between advocates of critical theory, feminism, and postmodernism; renewed interest in biocultural research; studies of cultural knowledge structures and embodied knowledge; and the dramatic impact of the microcomputer, which transformed data management and analysis. As a participant observer both inside and outside the university, the 1980s appeared to me to be a time of theory posturing, a time when graduate students invested in a rising paradigm like stock in a bull market. Senior partners in the know seemed to leap nimbly from paradigm to paradigm, investing low and then quietly withdrawing when discourse became inflated.

Out of this era has emerged a generation of medical anthropologists having diverse training and theoretical orientations. Common to most is a sensitivity to the interrelationship between sociocultural and political economic factors as they impact on the distribution of health problems and health care resources. Anthropologists trained in the 1980s are aware of the legacy of development programs which have resulted in the development of underdevelopment. A majority, however, have been better trained to produce and consume anthropologically related knowledge than to participate in the process of solving health-related problems. While working in India in 1981, for example, I was struck by a quote from Robert Arnove in a local development journal which spoke to the political economy of the academy:

> Knowledge has become a commodity. There is a market mechanism for the commodity: some experts produce knowledge, other experts consume it. The production of knowledge has become a specialized profession and only those trained in that profession can legitimately produce it. Large institutions of research and training have developed as factories to produce knowledge and knowledge producers. [Arnove 1981]

On a positive note, anthropologists now pursuing applied work are more reflexive and acutely aware of reductionism (Van Willigen, Rylko-Bauer, and McElroy 1989). Interest has risen in the use of multiple methods that enable the triangulation of data, which has enhanced the trustworthiness of ethnographic reports. The current generation of applied medical anthropologists is searching for a set of operating procedures which will enable them to engage in the change process while preserving an anthropological stance which is multipositioned.

Dilemmas Populate the World of Applied Research

Dilemmas, not just job opportunities, await the anthropologist engaging in applied work. Over a decade ago, Hazel Weidman (1976) addressed the question: "Do applied anthropologists apply anthropology?" by praising the double bind that is inherent in applied work. She noted that in order to successfully apply anthropology one must have the conceptual agility to move close to the problem at hand in order to identify options, constraints, and opportunities associated with possible interventions. At the same time, the anthropologist must be able to step back and retain what she described as an alienated position, what I term a multi-positioned stance.

Stepping back is not a sign of weakness or indecisiveness. It is a strength enabling the anthropologist to shift between levels of analysis and provinces of relevance so as to retain sight of the broader context in which an individual problem is situated. This is inclusive of the incentives (motivations, stakes) of all parties involved in planned change.

Alexander (1979) and Maretzki (1976) have argued that applied medical anthropology is first and foremost systems analysis encompassing an appraisal of intervention alternatives in context over time. A primary objective of applied medical anthropology is to engage in a problem-solving process which is socially as well as culturally sensitive, responsive to corrective feedback, conducive to critical consciousness, and responsible. This entails contextualizing a specific problem and assessing what all participants in a transformation process gain and lose from intended changes and indirect consequences (Hessler, New, and May 1979).

In her 1976 article, Weidman emphasized the importance of anthropologists developing conceptual synthesizing skills as a means of retaining an alienated position necessary for applied work. A means toward that end is to practice anthropology while engaged in culturally based problem solving. This means being a participant observer *in the job,* not just *for the job,* and applying (developing) theory in one's analysis of one's work experience. This entails the generation of ethnographic data necessary for broader levels of analysis. Applying anthropology generally means working overtime beyond one's job description and situating one's work within the context of cultural change, political economic instabilities, practicalities, and contingencies.

The practice of applied medical anthropology is riddled with dilemmas which have to be addressed on a day-by-day, case-by-case basis, yet which also require more global consideration subject to comparative and historical analysis. This fosters innovative problem solving as well as critical thought. A personal example from international health may illustrate this point.

In India I faced the dilemma of whether or not to assist marketing firms contracted by international agencies to conduct research on health behavior under the rubric of social marketing. Much of this research, I feel, should be conducted by trained indigenous colleagues having the ability to contextualize individual problems and see beyond the scope of work identified by program officers.

Requested to help design a study to be conducted by non-social scientists on acute lower respiratory tract disease (ARI) symptom recognition and health care seeking behavior, I questioned whether my assistance was beneficial to the development process of India. By helping marketing firms which sell cigarettes, locally produced Barbie dolls, medicines, and infant formula, as well as public health fixes (e.g., ORS, condoms), was I helping them to become better manipulators of cultural imagery as well as competitors in the bidding process for future international health contract work? Was I undermining indigenous colleagues by helping contractors do a limited descriptive assessment of an important health problem?

Contemplating these possibilities and vocally expressing my concerns, I was told by program officers that no indigenous medical anthropologists interested in, or having experience with, this type of research could be located. Moreover, past interactions with local anthropologists had by and large been disappointing, as they did not meet work schedule expectations or know the art of data presentation.

I questioned whether funding might be directed to university programs if a demand for social science data was not being met by private contractors. Had ethnographic data become just another commodity to be purchased and used to legitimate program options which had already been decided? These questions were not so dissimilar from questions I ask myself while conducting academically oriented ethnomedical research. I have spent more than one long night contemplating the extent to which the data I have collected constitutes a form of symbolic capital extracted from the poor in the name of scholarship.

Anthropologists need to ask themselves these ethical questions. They should not immobilize us, but rather challenge us to look inward as well as outward. In the present case, I decided to offer my services to the international health agency in contracting the social marketing firm. Why? The problem of ARI in the Third World requires urgent attention as it is the second biggest killer of children. Moreover, the experience gave me an opportunity to learn more about marketing firms engaged in health research (their motivations, operating procedures), and what impressed development agencies about their data presentation techniques. It also gave me an opportunity to discuss with program officers the dilemma that faced me as an applied anthropologist as well as a professor committed to institution building and educational development in the Third World.

A set of possible development scenarios emerged from this experience which I had not considered previously and which are worth exploring. Was the university system in the Third World the appropriate place for applied research given its colonial legacy, power structure, low regard for research (merit is by seniority), competing responsibilities, and administrative difficulties? Was my gut reaction against low-level descriptive health behavior research conducted in the private sector by non-social scientists a reflection of my own professional bias? After all, I had assisted in a project to deprofessionalize anthropological skills at the local level in the name of community diagnosis (Nichter 1984). Was the contracting of social marketing firms one stage of a process, changing the image of social science research within the country and creating a demand for medical anthropological skills? Would this in turn serve to alter academic programs to meet the needs of an emerging research market primed by international agencies? Would social activist groups or private nonprofit research centers be formed to compete with social marketing firms, monitor their activities, or more broadly evaluate the impact of solutions to problems? Would better constructed studies in the private sector inspire higher quality research in the university? Would an emergent critique of the privatization of social science research and the commodification of data foster an important dialogue within the development community?

I do not know the answers to these questions, but by considering them and remaining flexible I remain open to alternatives while maintaining my awareness of core dilemmas. As an anthropologist participant in international health I cannot ignore these options or issues.

The 1990s: What is in the Cards

Let me make a few educated predictions about what the 1990s has in store for applied medical anthropology in international health. The changing demographic makeup of developing countries undergoing either moderate economic development or decline, the ravages of disease, environmental deterioration, or war, is associated with major shifts in health states. It is advantageous to consider these shifts in terms of transitions in epidemiology, health care utilization and development at large.

Epidemiological transition is defined by changing disease profiles associated with the human and environmental costs and benefits of development and underdevelopment. As Frenk et al. (1989a, 1989b) among others have noted, this transition takes several forms from epidemiological polarization (between as well as within countries) associated with distinct disease profiles concordant with economic status, to protracted transition. In protracted transition there is a mix of classic health problems associated with poverty, undernutrition, and infectious disease combined with emergent problems more characteristic of the First World (e.g., cancer, heart disease).

In some areas of the Third World (and our own periphery), deaths due to acute disease have dropped appreciably such that the burden of chronic disease has become more visible. In such contexts, a new emphasis on adult health beyond safe motherhood will emerge. Child survival will be tied more closely to adult health with increased importance given to the carrying capacity of adults in the productive years (Nichter and Cartwright 1990). There will be increased interest in controllable risk factors affecting the health of adults inclusive of accidents, occupational health, substance abuse (including tobacco use), as well as sexual behavior in the wake of AIDS. With regard to AIDS, the HIV virus has already infected between 6 and 8 million people in 152 countries, and the WHO estimates that 15–20 million will be infected by the year 2000 (Chin, Sato, and Mann 1990). The survival of entire households and communities are at stake, not just individuals (Hunter 1990; Panos Institute 1989; Preble 1990). The allocation of funds for particular disease programs could potentially polarize adult and child health priorities. Anthropologists will play an important role in directing attention to the household production of health.

In what Frenk terms counter transition, one finds a resurgence of diseases previously under control (e.g., malaria, tuberculosis). I would add to this diseases of development which involve pathogens that have adapted to a changing ecology, states of ill health associated with occupational risk and environmental deterioration, and diseases of defective modernization (e.g., diseases associated with smoking). Counter transition is an urban as well as a rural phenomena. Urban health will be the focus of attention in the 1990s inasmuch as between 44% and 51% of the worlds' population will live in urban areas by the year 2000. A significant proportion will live in densely packed unhygienic squatter settlements in 60 urban areas having a population exceeding 5 million, 80% of which will be located in the Third World (Verhasselt 1985; Yach, Mathews, and Buch 1990). Urban environments will provide breeding grounds for vectors and viruses (e.g., Japanese encephalitis, dengue hemorrhagic fever, Bancroftian filariasis) adapting to the new environment. Faced with chronic illness related to lifestyle and new diseases of development associated with urban ecology (Miller and Carballo 1989), anthropologists will be called upon to participate in the redesigning of urban environments concordant with public health priorities (Kendall et al. 1990).

Health care transition is defined by changes in the distribution and form of curative and preventive health resources as they are influenced by changing disease profiles, economics, political will, and consumer demand. A central issue facing international health in this decade will be who is going to pay for existing and newly envisioned services, and for how long? Consumer demand, community financing, and entitlement will become key issues in applied medical anthropology. Evaluations of existing services and the popularity of alternative care facilities will require an assessment of how much time and money is being spent on health care by different segments of the population in the public and private health sectors.

Anthropologists will be asked to assist in the estimation of the relative importance of predisposing, enabling, service-related, and social-relational factors affecting health service utilization. It will be important to identify what groups are or are not being served and why. Let me cite three areas where this is likely by way of examples. AIDS and family-planning research in several areas of the Third World have revealed that adolescents who are sexually active do not visit geographically accessible family planning or condom distribution centers frequented by adults. It is important to investigate whether nonuse is simply an issue of poor knowledge or "irresponsibility," or whether adolescents are interested in contraception and protection but do not visit these centers out of embarassment associated with age-cohort segregation. Health facility bypassing, leading to overcrowding at some health facilities (and high sepsis rates) while other facilities are underutilized, needs to be assessed. Self-help involving over-the-counter use of scheduled pharmaceuticals is increasing in much of the Third World. Clinical epidemiologists tracking drug resistance and lobbying for generic-drug legislation are calling for ethnographic studies of pharmaceutical-related behavior which consider factors influencing both the use and distribution of medicines. In each of these three areas new work opportunities will become available to medical anthropologists.

A more broadly encompassing health/development transition may be identified with social factors which directly and indirectly influence epidemiological and health care patterns. Increasing attention is being turned to the identification of social fixes in the form of special programs. Given the growing emphasis on health economics, questions increasingly will be raised in international health circles about the relative cost effectiveness of programs targeted at literacy, cottage industry, loans, etc., especially when they are directed toward women in the name of enhancing household health. Anthropologists will be asked to help evaluate the broad impact of transitions in women's work on the household production of health. This will require critical examination of gender relations as they pertain to resource sharing.

Let me make three final observations regarding anthropology and international health. First, in a world rapidly becoming visually literate and accustomed to the technology of cassettes and videos, it is time anthropologists explore the right mix of media to effectively convey messages in the community as well as the health ministry. We have clearly relied too heavily on the written word. Other media forms may be more effective in fostering dialogue. With regard to statistics, I would agree with my colleagues in this volume who have placed emphasis on a working knowledge of statistical analysis, but with a caveat. Quantitative skills must be used judiciously, not to mystify or alienate. In my experience, visual displays of the meaning of quantitative data are often far more powerful than the presentation of complex data sets readable only to the initiate. Those in the marketing field have learned this well. Applied medical anthropologists would profit from observing their presentation styles. Lastly, and as a tie-in to a few observations of the national scene, I think that the 1990s will be a time when applied medical anthropologists look to apply some of the lessons learned in the Third World in their own countries. This has been called for as part of a health care paradigm shift in the United States (Fregmann 1989).

The National Scene

My predictions for the United States are derived in large part from a hard look at demographics and health expenditure statistics. Boone (this volume) is correct in drawing attention to the cost of health care which currently accounts for 11% of the U.S. gross national product (540 billion dollars), or roughly $2,124 per capita (Levit, Freeland, and Waldo 1990). This is a 38% increase in real per capita expenditure over the last five years despite cost containment measures borrowed from industrial cost accounting such as the DRG (diagnostic related groups) prospective payment plan. The DRG scheme was designed to shift the monitoring of cost to the health provider so as to increase the efficiency of hospital services. In addition to fostering conflicts of interest and obligation among clinicians, it has been effectively circumvented by cost shifting and moving services to the unregulated margins of the health system (Kronenfeld, Baker, and Amidon 1989; Morreim 1988).

Cost containment and the allocation of health care resources are clearly the issues of the 1990s. Anthropologists working in clinical and community health settings may well find themselves being asked to participate in health service research aimed at identifying means of increasing health service efficiency toward the end of cost saving. It is likely that they will be asked to assist in the planning, development, and evaluation of community-based posthospital residence alternatives requiring various degrees of supervision.

The need for ambulatory home care alternatives is tremendous (Easterbrook 1987; Morrisey, Sloan, and Valuma 1988). It must be seen against a backdrop of rising rates of chronic degenerative diseases which tax social support resources (40% of American workers over the age of 40 provide some care to at least one parent), increases in the population aged 85 or older (which will triple between 1980–2010), increases in single-parent households, a growing divorce rate, and migration patterns. A push for home care must also be seen in relation to shrinking funds for care of the mentally ill. Kiesler (1982) has reported that among America's two million chronically mentally ill, 70% of funds have been spent on hospital care when there is little evidence that outcomes in these facilities are any better than lower-cost alternative care options. Insurance carriers have been searching for new alternative-care possibilities (Coursey, Ward-Alexander, and Katz 1990).

Clearly, new forms of custodial care will be required for those unable to live at home without some assistance. This will take planning and require training care providers for the chronically ill, disabled, and elderly. Care will not be limited to the physical body alone. Anthropologists may find themselves working within this community as change agents facilitating group processes and developing meaning-centered help initiatives broadly associated with the social organization of medical work (Strauss et al. 1985). For example, groups organized around the writing or telling of life narratives have the potential to reduce alienation as well as assist in the redefinition of self and community.

The development of policy for the allocation of health care resources will be of paramount importance in the 1990s. At present 12% of the population aged 65 years or older (one of nine Americans) receive 60% of federal health benefits. At the same time, their liabilities for cost sharing (on services that Medicaid covers) doubled in the 1980s. Many of the elderly have per capita incomes of $10,000 or below. They face catastrophic burdens from their share of expenses, which often

reaches 15% of their per capita income. New policy will be required and anthropologists may well be contracted to look into the real-life implications of such
policy by planners as well as lobbying groups.

Occupational health will become an increasingly important issue in the 1990s.
One in 10 workers in private industry suffers an occupational injury each year,
with 4 in 100 ending up disabled. Over 10% of workman's compensation claims
are for "mental stress," which may be the tip of an emerging iceberg given that
experts have costed the price of stress to American industry at between 50 to 150
billion dollars a year. Reviewing this data, Senator Mark Hatfield (1990) has pre-
dicted that the situation will only get worse in years to come. Ethnography of the
workplace will increasingly be recognized as an important tool for preventive/
promotive health planning by both employers and government agencies.

Another issue in the 1990s will be the growing rates of the uninsured, presently numbering over 35 million (14% of whites, 22% of blacks, 29% of hispanics). According to the Robert Woods Johnson Report (Johnson 1987) the proportion of people lacking a regular source of health care increased 65% between
1981–86, with the number of people refraining from making ambulatory health
care visits up 70%. These rates do not just reflect dire poverty. They are related
to shifts in the employment sector concordant with deindustrialization, the rising
percentage of new jobs in the service sector, rises in part-time employment, and
what Bodenheimer (1989) has termed "austerity capitalism" in reference to insurance cutbacks as a means of maintaining profit margins. Nine out of every ten
new jobs in the next decade will be in the service sector and six out of every ten
new jobs will be filled by women. High rates of uninsured people are found in
this sector, making the problem of the uninsured increasingly a women's and
childcare issue. Twenty-six percent of women of childbearing age presently have
no maternity coverage and 18 million children under the age of 13 are not covered,
although many have a parent who works (Clark et al. 1988). Anthropologists may
play a valuable role in identifying the current health care behavior of the uninsured
as a step toward the development of new policy.

Medicine has been regulated to conform to industry in the 1980s (Dolene and
Dougherty 1985; Relman 1980). In the 1990s, ethical questions increasingly will
be raised regarding regulation and equity (Oberg and Polich 1988; Powderly and
Smith 1989). An overemphasis on cost containment needs to be corrected by a
critical look at the distribution of services in relation to need. At present the middle class, despite their better health status, utilizes health services 37% more than
the poor (Johnson 1987). Longitudinal ethnographies which attend to both medical and human costs are required of the health care behavior of people deprived
of adequate primary health care. Studies that track and juxtapose acute care costs
among this population with the projected costs of adequate and timely outpatient
intervention are needed.

AIDS and substance abuse prevention/outreach programs will continue to
look to anthropologists for help with intervention programs in the 1990s. Planners
will be faced with the fact that information and "just say no" programs do not
work, requiring an assessment of cultural factors influencing behavior (Freuden-

berg 1990; Peele 1989). An area of growing concern will be adolescent lifestyle as it pertains to health and is associated with social and economic factors that influence behavior, perceptions of risk, and problem definition. As research on teen pregnancy has made evident, there are no unitary "teen problems," but rather, a complex of behavioral patterns with common visible outcomes (Hayes 1987). Patterns of teen behavior must be understood in context, not simply labelled deviant and treated as an epidemic against which youths may be inoculated by health education messages (Vinovskis 1988). Few anthropologists are currently engaged in the study of adolescent lifestyle. New job opportunities will emerge as schools struggle to remain relevant at this time of dramatic change.

Another area of applied research which may open up in the 1990s entails ethnographic studies of transactions within health and human service bureaucracies. The administrative costs in time and money to run federally regulated health insurance programs is notable. In the mid-1980s it was estimated that administrative costs account for as much as 22% (77 billion dollars) of total health care dollars and 18% (27 billion dollars) of hospital care dollars (Himmelstein and Woolhandler 1986). The rationing of health care services has required administrative monitoring systems which have increased health provider paperwork, further reducing patient-practitioner time. Systems analysis of administrative costs and procedures, efforts to circumvent rules, and reasons for doing so would benefit from applied anthropological research conducted at different points in the health care system.

A Final Note

The 1990s will present new challenges, opportunities, and dilemmas as national and international health policies change. New opportunities will arise for foreign/ U.S. collaboration in the training of applied medical anthropologists. This has the potential of either fostering colonialism or giving rise to a more global and multipositioned anthropology. The 1990s will be a time when the techniques of social science are increasingly co-opted by other disciplines. Falling rates of infectious disease, vector-borne and viral diseases for which there are no quick fixes, and chronic illness related to lifestyle will foster renewed interest in the social sciences (Amler and Dull 1987; Hinman 1990). Anthropologists will be involved in training non-social scientists in ethnographic skills and will need to demonstrate the uniqueness and vitality of their own multidimensional perspective based upon contextual problem solving. They will need to play an active role in setting agendas, not just responding to the job market.

Working within the system, applied medical anthropologists will have to remain flexible yet vigilant. While striving to make the system work better toward humanitarian ends, they will need to remain aware of efforts to depoliticize and individualize health problems which need to be assessed at different levels of analysis. To use Weidman's term, they must maintain conceptual agility in order to remain relevant as anthropologists. This requires approaching problems from a multipositioned vantage as distinct from a path of least resistance.

References Cited

Alexander, L.
  1979   Clinical Anthropology: Morals and Methods. Medical Anthropology 3:61–108.
Amler, R. W., and H. B. Dull
  1987   Closing the Gap: The Burden of Unnecessary Illness. New York: Oxford University Press.
Arnove, R.
  1981   Foundation and the Transference of Knowledge: Implications for India. Social Action 31(2).
Barsky, A.
  1988a   The Paradox of Health. New England Journal of Medicine 318(7):414–418.
  1988b   Worried Sick: Our Troubled Quest for Wellness. Boston: Little and Brown.
Bodenheimer, T.
  1989   The Fruits of Empire Rot on the Vine: United States Health Policy in the Austerity Era. Social Science and Medicine 28(6):531–538.
Chin, J., P. Sato, and J. Mann
  1990   Projections of HIV Infections and AIDS Cases to the Year 2000. Bulletin of the World Health Organization 68:1–11.
Clark, M., M. Hager, S. Hutchinson, and K. Sprinyen
  1988   Forgotten Patients. Newsweek (August 22):52–53.
Coursey, R. D., L. Ward-Alexander, and B. Katz
  1990   Cost-Effectiveness of Providing Insurance Benefits for Posthospital Psychiatric Halfway House Stays. American Psychologist 45(10):1118–1126.
Dolene, D., and C. Dougherty
  1988   DRG's the Counterrevolution in Financing Health Care. Hastings Center Report (June):19–29.
Easterbrook, G.
  1987   The Resolution in Medicine. Newsweek (January 26):40–74.
Fregmann, J. G.
  1989   The Public's Health Care Paradigm is Shifting: Medicine Must Shift with It. Journal of General Internal Medicine 4:313–319.
Frenk, J., J. L. Bobadilla, J. Sepulveda and M. Lopez-Cervantes
  1989   Health Transition in Middle-Income Countries: New Challenges for the Organization of Services. Health Policy and Planning 4:29–39.
Frenk, J., T. Frejka, J. Bobadilla, C. Stern, and J. Sepulveda
  1989b   The Epidemiological Transition in Latin America. In IUSSP, International Population Conference. New Delhi.
Freudenberg, N.
  1990   AIDS Prevention in the United States: Lessons from the First Decade. International Journal of Health Services 29(4):589–599.
Hatfield, M. O.
  1990   Stress and the American Worker. American Psychologist 45(10):1162–1164.
Hayes, C. (ed.)
  1987   Risking the Future: Adolescent Sexuality, Pregnancy and Childbearing. Vol. I. Washington, DC: National Academy Press.
Hessler, R., P. New, and J. T. May
  1979   Power, Exchange and the Research Development Link. Human Organization 38(4):334–342.

Himmelstein, D., and S. Woolhandler
  1986   Cost Without Benefit: Administrative Waste in the U.S. Health Care. New England Journal of Medicine 314(7):441–445.
Hunter, S.
  1990   Orphans as a Window on the AIDS Epidemic in Sub-Saharan Africa: Initial Results and Implications of a Study in Uganda. Social Science Medicine 31(6):681–690.
Illich, I.
  1975   Medical Nemesis. London: Marion Boyars.
  1986   Body History. Lancet (Dec. 6):1325–1327.
Johnson, R. W.
  1987   Access to Health Care in the U.S. Results of the 1986 Survey. Special Report Two. City: Robert Woods Johnson Foundation.
Kendall, C., P. Winch, P. Leontsini, and P. Hudelson
  1990   Urbanization, New Towns and New Diseases: Anthropological Contributions to the Ecology of Dengue. (Unpublished manuscript, files of the author.)
Kiesler, C. A.
  1982   Mental Hospitals and Alternative Care: Noninstitutionalization as Potential Public Policy for Mental Patients. American Psychologist 37:349–360.
Kronenfeld, J., S. Baker and R. Amidon
  1989   An Appraisal of Organizational Response to Fiscally Constraining Regulation: The Case of Hospitals and DRG's. Journal of Health and Social Behavior 30(March):41–55.
Levit, K., M. Freeland, and D. Waldo
  1990   National Health Care Spending Trends: 1988. Health Affairs. Summer 172–183.
Maretzki, T. W.
  1976   What Difference Does Anthropological Knowledge Make to Mental Health. Australian and New Zealand Journal of Psychiatry 10:83–88.
Miller, N., and M. Carballo
  1989   AIDS: A Disease of Development? AIDS and Society 1(1):1, 21.
Morreim, E.
  1988   Cost Containment: Challenging Fidelity and Justice. Hastings Center Report. (December):20–25.
Morrisey, M., F. Sloan and J. Valuma
  1988   Shifting Medicare Patients Out of the Hospital. Health Affairs, (Winter):52–53.
Nichter, M.
  1984   Project Community Diagnosis: Participatory Research as a First Step Toward Community Involvement in Primary Health Care. Social Science and Medicine 19(3):237–252.
Nichter, M., and L. Cartwright
  1991   Saving the Children for the Tobacco Industry. Medical Anthropology Quarterly (n.s.) 5(3):236–256.
Oberg, C., and C. Polich
  1988   Medicaid: Entering the Third Decade. Health Affairs Fall-Winter 83–96.
Panos Institute
  1989   AIDS and the Third World. Philadelphia, PA: New Society Publishers.
Peele, S.
  1989   Diseasing of America: Addiction Treatment Out of Control. Massachusetts: Lexington Books.

Powderly, K., and E. Smith
  1989   The Impact of DRGs on Health Care Workers and Their Clients. Hastings Center
    Report (Jan./Feb.):16–19.
Preble, E.
  1990   Impact of HIV/AIDS on African Children. Social Science and Medicine
    31(6):671–680.
Relman, A.
  1980   The New Medical Industrial Complex. New England Journal of Medicine
    303(17):963–970.
Van Willigen, J., B. Rylko-Bauer and A. McElroy (eds.)
  1989   Making Our Research Useful. Boulder, CO: Westview Press.
Verhasselt, Y.
  1985   Urbanization and Health in the Developing World. Social Science and Medicine
    21(5):483.
Vinovskis, M.
  1988   An "Epidemic" of Adolescent Pregnancy? Some Historical and Policy Consid
    erations. New York: Oxford University Press.
Weidman, H. H.
  1976   In Praise of the Double Bind Inherent in Anthropological Application. In Do
    Applied Anthropologists Apply Anthropology?, Michael V. Angrosino, ed. Athens,
    GA: University of Georgia Press.
Yach, D., C. Mathews, and E. Buch
  1990   Urbanization and Health: Methodological Difficulties in Undertaking Epide-
    miological Research in Developing Countries. Social Science and Medicine
    31(4):507–514.

● *chapter one*

Continuities and Differences in the Old and the New Applied Medical Anthropology

CAROLE E. HILL

Dramatic changes in the field of anthropology within the past decade have created a need for anthropologists to expand their knowledge and skills for the purpose of applying them to modern sociocultural and biological problems. By successfully combining traditional anthropological skills and knowledge with technical skills in research, planning, and evaluation, many anthropologists are able to make contributions outside the academic setting. These pioneers in applied anthropology are creating new employment opportunities for professional anthropologists that were rare in the past. This opening of new doors in turn affects the academic world, and their degree and training programs.

I call these recent applied anthropologists "pioneers" because they are practicing the "new applied anthropology," a term that began to be used in the 1970s, characterized by both short-term contract work in public-service agencies and long-term career jobs in public and private institutions; both may include needs assessment, program evaluation, and multidisciplinary problem solving (Angrosino 1976). This is not to say that earlier anthropologists involved in applying their knowledge and skills were not pioneers; some certainly were, but most stayed within the academic setting. Nowadays, increasing numbers of anthropologists are choosing a career outside academia. Goldschmidt (1979) details the history of the use of anthropology from the late 1800s to the present, and van Willigen (1980) has provided a bibliographic chronology of the development of applied anthropology.

The continuity between the happenings of the 1980s and the ones that laid the foundation for applied medical anthropology several decades ago are, on one hand, apparent and, on the other, seem to have been lost to our short memories. Regarding this paradox, Angrosino states that there has been an evolution toward a "new emphasis although not new concerns" (1976:1–2). The founders of applied anthropology saw the discipline as more than, although including, scholarly academic production but mostly, did not rely on or take part in setting policy for the bureaucratic structures that employed them.

In 1953, when Caudill documented government agencies' and private foundations' increased interest in the study of social aspects of health and illness, he noted that although anthropologists had been studying primitive medicine, mostly in nonliterate societies (i.e., Rivers, Field, Clements, Spencer, Harly, and Ackerknecht), none of them discussed the usefulness of their data in solving health problems (Ackerknecht 1942a, 1942b, 1943, 1945a, 1945b, 1947, 1948; Caudill 1953; Clements 1932; Field 1937; Harley 1941; Rivers 1927; Spencer 1941). Some ethnographies focused on religion and health beliefs, analyzing the coexistence of scientific and folk beliefs. Others recorded the persistence of nonscientific beliefs and the encroachment of Western medicine in to the health behavior of non-Western peoples (Leighton and Leighton 1945; Gould 1957, 1965). But these anthropologists stayed within the "abstract" boundaries of anthropology and did not venture into the "applied" aspects of the discipline (Eddy and Partridge 1987).

Applied anthropologists in international health can be traced to the 1930s and 1940s and to colonial concerns for diet and health. Foster cites the work of Sir Raymond Firth (1934), Audrey Richards (1939), and Bronislaw Malinowski (1945) as having a "practical bent" (Foster 1982). Within the United States, nutrition became a focus of attention during World War II, when the National Research Council established a Committee on Food Habits. Distinguished anthropologists such as Ruth Benedict, John Cooper, and Margaret Mead were members and contributed to the Committee's *Manual for the Study of Food Habits* (National Research Council 1945). In 1955, the Navaho-Cornell Field Health Project was implemented; it was designed to suggest culturally appropriate intervention strategies for the Navaho health system (Adair 1960; Adair and Deuschle 1958; McDermott, et al. 1960).

In the 1940s and 1950s, anthropologists were employed by governmental institutions such as the World Health Organization (WHO) and the Institute for Inter-American Affairs. Cora Dubois was the first anthropologist employed by WHO, in 1950. The Institute for Inter-American Affairs, a governmental agency established in 1942 to ensure that the United States could obtain critical raw materials for the war effort, employed George Foster, Richard Adams, Charles Erasmus, Isabel Kelly, Ozzie Simmons, and Kalvero Oberg. The program included a health and education component, and these anthropologists worked on public health projects such as environmental sanitation, health education, and control of specific diseases such as malaria (Foster 1969). World War II was a turning point for applied anthropology in general, and medical anthropology was in the forefront of this emerging field. Before then, in the 1930s, government jobs were available to anthropologists, but these jobs dealt primarily with colonial problems, i.e., with dependent peoples (Eddy and Partridge 1987). During World War II, however, the United States ended its isolationism, and anthropologists began to work jointly with the Armed Forces. In 1941, the Society for Applied Anthropology was founded, further legitimizing this curious behavior of anthropologists who worked outside of academia with agencies that attempted to solve human problems mostly through the transfer of knowledge, skills, and technology to non-Western nations. As Foster reported to the Institute of Inter American Affairs, "You cannot transplant an institution unchanged from one culture to another and expect it to function as effectively as in the place where it developed" (1969).

This task-oriented work for anthropologists that grew out of World War II remained through part of the 1950s; most jobs were within the military complex and some in public health (Angrosino 1976; Foster 1953, 1955, 1958; Simmons 1958). Research was concentrated on health problems of "target populations." Very few, however, looked at the larger setting of the bureaucracy in which solutions to such problems were evolved, a key characteristic of the new applied anthropology. In this decade, most anthropologists began to turn inward again and spend their time and efforts on abstract problems. The late 1950s and the 1960s were a very productive time for the development of theories. Few anthropologists, however, sought practical uses for this new knowledge. During this time, the largest employer of anthropologists outside academia were the technical programs of the Community Development Division of the Point Four Program (Foster 1969).

In medical anthropology we find a few exceptions to this general trend. For example, case studies put together by Ben Paul and Lyle Sanders were outstanding examples of how to combine the traditional approach with an applied focus (Paul 1955; Sanders 1954). They were concerned with the problems that arise when an indigenous community encounters Western medicine and with the problems faced by public health workers attempting to implement a health program. A more recent work using a similar approach is that of Harwood, whose case studies on the health behavior and beliefs of ethnic groups in the United States are written primarily for public health workers (Harwood 1981). Another example is the work of Steven Polgar, who sought to integrate biological and cultural variables in an epidemiological approach to solving human problems, particularly population problems. He proposed programs of "health actions which could be community based or internationally based" (Polgar 1962).

The 1970s presented the discipline with what has been called the "new applied anthropology." Partially because of the ethos of the late 1960s and the changing job market, anthropologists began to study bureaucracy and other complex social settings (studying up) with the same tools and concepts used to study smaller scale societies. This development caused internal critiques of anthropological methods and efforts to expand and refine them. The reason was that anthropologists were now being employed in bureaucracies that wanted immediate action, and most traditional anthropologists lacked the necessary skills. They had to become anthropologists *in* health rather than studying the anthropology *of* health (Hill 1984). These changes have created a very different relationship between academic social science and the multicultural world that now challenges anthropologists to make their knowledge useful in solving human health problems on the local, regional, national, or international level. Many medical anthropologists are translating knowledge into action (Wulff and Fiske 1987), especially as "health care practitioners and researchers have come to appreciate the important role played by social and cultural factors in both preventive and curative medicines" (Chambers 1985).

The effect of anthropologists practicing outside academia has created a need to systematically explore skills beyond traditional anthropology that are necessary to function in nonacademic roles. The purpose of this manual is to explore the technical skills needed to apply the knowledge of medical anthropology in settings outside academia, to describe these settings, and to identify resources in the field that are valuable to the practitioner. Furthermore, this manual should be useful to middle-level managers, supervisors, field personnel, and others whose job responsibilities include aspects of medical anthropology.

The manual is aimed at striking a balance between the skills medical anthropologists need in nonacademic settings and their career opportunities on international, national, regional, and local levels. Specifically, the authors of these chapters describe the setting in which they work—the culture, structure, and functions. Following this general description, they next place the anthropologist within the setting and explain how one can work there effectively and the contributions an anthropologist can make.

The major objective of each chapter is to delineate the skills necessary to perform the tasks, including both specific techniques such as statistical analysis, planning research, and program evaluation and analysis, and more general skills in evaluation, writing and communication, and management. Most chapters also deal with the way to obtain employment within a specific subfield: processes involved in getting a job (e.g., an internship), writing a resume, presentation of self, tapping informal networks, and so on. Finally, each author has provided a list of resources for additional information about the subfield. These are incorporated into the annotated bibliography and include texts, agency reports, case studies, and journals that can further one's understanding of practicing anthropology in a specific health setting.

The subfields represented in this volume by no means cover the entire field of applied medical anthropologists. They are the ones in which anthropologists have been successfully employed, although perhaps not in large numbers. The information and skills in each chapter, however, has a wider application to other health settings. These health settings offer future opportunities for contributions and jobs; consequently, it is important for anthropologists to know something about the skills needed to function in these settings. Each author has had experience in the particular setting he or she describes.

Theory in applied medical anthropology is touched upon implicitly in a few chapters. While the dialectic between theory and method guides the specific professional perspective of the practicing anthropologist, theory often takes a back seat to methodological skills necessary to survive in an applied setting. This neglect of theory by applied anthropologists and in this book should not be taken to mean that it is not ever-present in applied work. All practicing anthropologists apply theory. While developing a unified theoretical approach in medical anthropology has been a goal or vision of many, the fruition of this arduous task has yet to be reached. Applied medical anthropologists, whatever the level of the setting, are a part of both the macrolevel of policies and its underlining culture and structures, and the microlevel and its culture and structure. Applied medical anthropologists participate in complex systems that, through dynamic linkages, are ever reproducing and transforming people's history, culture, and institutions. The skills and techniques discussed in this book are presented as practical guides for practicing anthropologists to succeed in adjusting to and managing the morass of these complex health systems.

Public health is of paramount importance in medical anthropology, and anthropologists have been breaking new ground in federal agencies, e.g., the Centers for Disease Control (CDC). Kevin O'Reilly, by using case studies, illustrates the roles of anthropology in the CDC. Many medical anthropologists are employed in community assessment and evaluation. Linda Whiteford lays out the steps in conducting such research and the opportunities available in this area. Two major clinical settings were chosen: medical schools and nursing schools. Thomas Johnson describes in some detail his experiences and those of others in the medical-school setting and hospital setting, while nurse/anthropologist Molly Dougherty describes the opportunities in nursing education. Both emphasize the importance of understanding the context in which anthropologists work—the culture of their institutional setting. Clinical settings present anthropologists with different sets of rules from the traditional academic setting.

An additional arena in which anthropologists have had considerable impact is presented by Barbara Pillsbury who examines the roles for medical anthropologists in international health, especially through the Agency for International Development. Likewise, Margaret Boone brings together the diffuse area of health policy and planning, and emphasizes the skills needed to successfully work in it. She emphasizes that anthropologists must be aware of the human systems in which they work and take an active role in the interpretation of their work for public policy purposes.

Two chapters have been added to the present edition that directly discuss two areas crucial to practicing medical anthropology. Robert Trotter discusses the methods—old and new—that are necessary to know how to successfully apply anthropology. Problem-oriented research, with explicit policy objectives, requires systematic data collection, management and analysis that is much a way of thinking about research as it is knowledge of specific skills and techniques. Similarly, Patricia Marshall discusses ways to think about ethical problems that arise in health settings. While each case is unique, the principles involved in solving ethical problems are often ambiguous. Such issues, however, must be confronted by an applied medical anthropologist.

Several themes arise throughout all the papers that reiterate the writings of other medical anthropologists about work in nonacademic settings. Most authors discuss the marginal role of anthropologists in many medical settings and the necessity to understand the culture of the subfield in order to succeed in it. Several authors discuss personal characteristics, a topic only rarely mentioned in the literature. Nonacademic work environments generally have narrower boundaries for appropriate behavior and consequently lower tolerance for idiosyncratic behavior. An employee must fit into the system, generally a hierarchical one. This requires anthropologists to understand the structure and functioning of complex organizations. Mapping linkages from micro to macro levels allows anthropologists to fit into the system and to more appropriately delineate intervention strategies.

An important aspect of working in nonacademic settings requires anthropologists to work on interdisciplinary teams. Such collaborative efforts are crucial for the survival of anthropologists in applied arenas (Stull and Schensul 1987). They must be able to communicate, with confidence, the unique and critical skills anthropologists bring to interdisciplinary applied research; they need to assert their influence through demonstrating the relevance of social and cultural data in solving health problems. This ability is strengthened by requiring students to supplement their anthropology courses with courses that train them in the theories and methods of diverse disciplines such as social marketing, consumer research, public administration, as well as epidemiology and biostatistics.

A major necessity for practicing anthropologists is a working knowledge of statistics and of their use in program analysis and evaluation. All nonacademic settings require these skills, and when the anthropologist combines them with more traditional qualitative techniques of anthropology, he or she can make a broader contribution to the health field. Nichter, in the Preface, makes the point that anthropologists can provide culturally-appropriate interpretations of quantitative results by using their qualitative skills. Anthropologists are unique in their ability to see past the statistics and interpret or broker a health institution to the people it serves, evaluates, and teaches, facilitating communication among diverse groups. Negotiating conflicts is often required of practicing medical anthropologists.

Epidemiology is frequently mentioned by the authors. All programming and planning in health agencies begin with it to detect health problems and their causes. A working knowledge of epidemiology is imperative for anthropologists working in public health. An article in the *Medical Anthropology Quarterly* explores the need for medical anthropologists to obtain a Master of Public Health degree (Krantzler 1984).

Additional skills discussed by the authors include communication and writing. Practicing anthropologists must be able to write a report or position paper that is concise, to the point, and uses relevant data in its most condensed form. They should be able to verbally communicate effectively with a variety of subgroups in their work environment and appreciate the contributions of other disciplines and approaches to a problem. In other words, they must become experts at role playing and problem solving. These skills are related to the personal characteristics of individual anthropologists and to the training they receive in their graduate education. Indeed, perhaps a major contribution this manual could make would be to bring about a reevaluation of our system of training graduate students in applied medical anthropology (Trotter 1989), as students must be appropriately prepared for the world of the 21st century.

There are many people I wish to thank for working with me in the initial stages of planning and organizing the first manual. My advisors included George Foster (University of California, Berkeley), Benjamin Paul (Stanford University), Charles Leslie (University of Delaware), Carl Tyler (Centers for Disease Control), Joseph Westermeyer (University of Minnesota), and Thomas Maretzki (University of Hawaii). For this second edition, I wish to thank the authors of the chapters for working with short deadlines and adhering to them throughout the summer months of 1990.

The preparation of the manuscript required technical assistance from the Department of Anthropology at Georgia State University. Dana Van Tilborg and Jo Ann Taylor performed these tasks admirably, and they have my appreciation. Finally, I appreciate being asked to revise the manual for publication by the Professional Series Editor of the American Anthropological Association, Linda Bennett. Her comments, suggestions, and support were invaluable.

References Cited

Ackerknecht, Erwin A.
  1942   Problems of Primitive Medicine. Bulletin of the History of Medicine 11:503–521.
  1942   Primitive Medicine and Culture Pattern. Bulletin of the History of Medicine 12:545–574.
  1943   Psychopathology, Primitive Medicine, and Primitive Culture. Bulletin of the History of Medicine 14:30–67.
  1945a Primitive Medicine.Transactions 8:26–37.
  1945b On the Collecting of Data Concerning Primitive Medicine. American Anthropologist 47:427–432.
  1947   Primitive Surgery. American Anthropologist 49:25–45.
  1948   Medicine and Disease Among Eskimos. Ciba Symposia 10:916–921.
Adair, John
  1960   The Indian Health Worker in the Cornell-Navaho Project. Human Organization 19:59–63.
Adair, John, and Kurt Deuschle
  1958   Some Problems of the Physicians on the Navaho Reservations. Human Organization 16:19–23.
Angrosino, Michael
  1976   The Evolution of the New Applied Anthropology. *In* Do Applied Anthropologists Apply Anthropology? Athens: University of Georgia Press.
Caudill, William
  1953   Applied Anthropology in Medicine. *In* Anthropology Today. Alfred Kroeber, ed. Chicago: University of Chicago Press.
Chambers, Erve
  1985   Applied Anthropology: A Practical Guide. Englewood Cliffs, N.J.: Prentice-Hall.
Clements, Forrest E.
  1932   Primitive Concepts of Disease. University of California Publications in American Archaeology and Ethnology 32:185–252.
Eddy, Elizabeth M., and William L. Partridge
  1987   Applied Anthropology in America. New York: Columbia University Press.
Field, M. J.
  1937   Religion and Medicine of the Georgia People. London: Oxford University Press.
Firth, Raymond
  1934   The Sociological Study of Native Diet. Africa 7:401–414.

Foster, George M.
   1953   Use of Anthropological Methods and Data in Planning and Operation. Public
      Health Reports 68:841–857.
   1955   Guidelines to Community Development Programs. Public Health Reports
      70:19–24.
   1958   Problems in Intercultural Health Practice. Pamphlet 12. Social Science Research
      Council, New York.
   1969   Applied Anthropology. Boston: Little, Brown and Company.
   1982   Applied Anthropology and International Health: Retrospect and Prospect. Hu-
      man Organization 14:189–197.
Goldschmidt, Walter (ed.)
   1979   The Uses of Anthropology. Washington, D.C.: American Anthropological As-
      sociation.
Gould, Harold
   1957   The Implications of Technological Change for Folk and Scientific Medicine.
      American Anthropologist 59:507–516.
   1965   Modern Medicine and Folk Cognition in Rural India. Human Organization
      24:201–208.
Harly, George
   1941   Native African Medicine, with Special References to Its Practices in the Mano
      Tribe of Liberia. Cambridge, MA: Harvard University Press.
Harwood, Alan (ed.)
   1981   Ethnicity and Medical Care. Cambridge, MA: Harvard University Press.
Hill, Carole E.
   1984   The Challenge of Comparative Health Policy Research for Applied Medical An-
      thropology. Social Science and Medicine 18:861–871.
Krantzler, Nora J., et al.
   1984   Perspectives on Postdoctoral Public Health Training for Medical Anthropolo-
      gists. Medical Anthropology Quarterly 15:90–101.
Leighton, Alexander, and Dorothea C. Leighton
   1945   The Navajo Door: An Introduction to Navajo Life. Cambridge, MA: Harvard
      University Press.
Malinowski, Bronislaw
   1945   The Dynamics of Culture Change: An Inquiry into Race Relations in Africa.
      New Haven: Yale University Press.
McDermott, Walsh, et al.
   1960   Introducing Modern Medicine in a Navajo Community. Science 131:197–205,
      280–287.
National Research Council
   1945   Manual for the Study of Food Habits: Report of the Committee on Food Habits,
      Bulletin III. Washington, D.C.: National Academy of Sciences, National Research
      Council.
Partridge, William L., and Elizabeth M. Eddy
   1978   The Development of Applied Anthropology in America. *In* Applied Anthropol-
      ogy in America. Elizabeth M. Eddy and William L. Partridge, eds. New York: Co-
      lumbia University Press.
Paul, Benjamin D.
   1955   Health, Culture and Community: Case Studies of Public Reactions to Health Pro-
      grams. New York: Russell Sage Foundation.

Polgar, Steven
   1962   Health and Human Behavior: Areas of Interest Common to the Social and Medical Sciences. Current Anthropology 3:159–205.
   1963   Health Action in Cross-Cultural Perspectives. *In* Handbook of Medical Sociology. H. E. Freeman, Sol Levine, and Leo Reeder, eds. Englewood Cliffs, N.J.: Prentice-Hall.
Practicing Anthropology
   1981   Roles for Medical Anthropologists. Special Issue, 4:Winter 1981–1982.
Richards, Audrey I.
   1939   Land, Labour and Diet in Northern Rhodesia: An Economic Study of the Bemba Tribe. London: Oxford University Press/International Africa Institute.
Rivers, W. H. R.
   1927   Medicine, Magic and Religion. London: Kegan Paul, Trench, Trubner and Co.
Sanders, Lyle
   1954   Cultural Differences and Medical Care: The Case of the Spanish-Speaking People of the Southwest. New York: Russell Sage Foundation.
Simmons, Ozzie
   1958   Social Status and Public Health. Pamphlet No. 13. New York: Social Science Research Council.
Spencer, Dorothy
   1941   Disease, Religion, and Society in the Fiji Islands. New York: J. J. Augustin.
Stull, Donald, and Jean Schensul (eds.)
   1987   Collaborative Research and Social Change. Boulder, CO: Westview Press.
van Willigen, John
   1980   Anthropology in Use: A Bibliographic Chronology of the Development of Applied Anthropology. Pleasantville, NY: Redgrave Publishing Company.
Wulff, Robert M., and Shirley J. Fiske (eds)
   1987   Anthropological Praxis: Translating Knowledge into Action. Boulder, CO: Westview Press.

● *chapter two*

Policy and Praxis in the 1990s: Anthropology and the Domestic Health Policy Arena

MARGARET S. BOONE

Reorienting for Public Policy Work

Applied medical anthropologists work in issue areas that correspond to government programs at the local, state, national, and international levels. Medical anthropologists at all levels subdivide their pursuits into an increasingly varied set of problem areas such as nutrition, mental health, substance abuse, reproduction, epidemiology, and gerontology. These subjects organize academic pursuits, but they are not identical to the health issue areas for domestic health programs and policy. Research agendas and policy agendas differ because they develop from pressures in separate institutions—academia and government—and, while academicians often try to make their research "policy relevant," and government often acts to champion science by sponsoring research, research and policy agendas are more often different than similar.

Where and How to Refocus

An agenda of public policy issues for medical anthropologists in the 1990s recombines academic subfields under new rubrics and points to types of public programs that government officials create and administer. Applied medical anthropologists who want to affect domestic health policy in the United States need to reorient themselves beginning in their academic training, and to begin to translate scientific knowledge into practical recommendations. Medical anthropologists working in health policy in the 1990s should make three basic reorientations for public policy work.

First, medical anthropology students should begin *to refocus on the cost of health care in America.* Cost is a major problem in nearly all health care fields, and will be until well into the next century. Medical anthropologists may feel that they have little to contribute to solving the problems of cost. However, the discussion below suggests otherwise. The cost of health care looms as such an enormous issue that it dwarfs all other issues, so medical anthropologists should begin

23

to consider cost issues in their work with the poor, the elderly, women, adolescents, or any other special group. At one time or another, their public policy work will require them to make practical suggestions for improved care with some consideration of cost. Furthermore, cost became such a major issue in the 1980s that experts now predict that Americans will be required to make major ideological changes in order for the health care system to change and that the domestic health care system must change fundamentally in order to survive. Medical anthropologists could contribute significantly in helping Americans to readjust their health values and ethics.

Second, medical anthropology students should *focus on the organization and delivery of health care services.* This topic provides an opportunity to apply their broad knowledge of social structure, systems, and communications. Many of the difficulties encountered in providing quality health care in an efficient and cost-effective manner result from unplanned system failures. Anthropologists have experience analyzing organizations and need to bring this experience to bear on health care systems. In their papers and reports, medical anthropologists should practice devising, drafting, and presenting solutions to organization problems. They should anticipate the need to go an extra step beyond analysis to suggesting ways to make a health care system work better.

Third, medical anthropologists who want to impact the policy process should begin to *think in a different time frame and with a more public orientation than the academic medical anthropologist.* The time frame for most public-policy work is the future, and the action arena is the public domain. Government decision makers assess past trends—in disease rates, reproductive levels, health care demands—only so that they can predict future trends and plan programs to meet future requirements. Public-policy research usually has a very shallow time frame. Discussion of different options for health programs and policy usually occurs in a public forum. Suggestions for solutions are debated, criticized, and thoroughly altered from the initial form in which they were presented. So, an original idea eventually becomes anonymous as it is incorporated into a larger body of work: the law, a regulation, a report based on a program evaluation.

The reorientation from academic to public-policy work may often be on the medical anthropology student's own initiative. Most academic social science treats cost as a byproduct, and the shallow time frame and short memory of policy research is contrary to many essential and important aspects of traditional anthropology. Medical anthropology students may have to strike out on their own in the library. For example, the financial focus of domestic health issues can be learned in a health economics or a budget and management course. The organizational focus can be learned from journals like *Health Services Research* and *Health Management Review* or in a course on hospital administration. The public and future focus can be learned in public administration and political science courses and by examining *Futures, Policy Sciences* and *Policy Studies Journal.* Graduate courses in public health convey all three perspectives at once, as does the *Journal of Health Politics, Policy and Law.*

Setting a Health Agenda for Medical Anthropologists in the 1990s

What Is a Health Agenda?

A "health agenda" exists only at a single point in time and is subject to constant change. Different vested interests in the United States have different health agendas. However, even within a single group, a health agenda is determined by the political commitments and scientific knowledge of a wide range of people, and by the health status of the nation and its constituent subgroups vis-à-vis how that group feels it should be (which is itself an ever-changing standard determined by medical progress, change in life-styles, and changes in our natural and political environments). The setting of health agendas is a dynamic process with both long- and short-term goals and is rationalized ultimately by a balance between human values on the one hand, and cost on the other. The perfect society would have the best and most expensive health care for each and every citizen. But the United States is far from a perfect society, and there are trade-offs in terms of values, costs, and the effectiveness of health care delivery systems. The cost of health care has become a dominant issue because, while the United States is one of the wealthiest nations, it is also one of the most socially stratified. Medical advances since the end of the Second World War have been splendid but the growth rate of health-care costs has been even more spectacular, and poor Americans continue to suffer most in the face of rising costs.

Table 1 lists major domestic health issue areas that promise to dominate the health care field in the 1990s. Medical anthropology students and those medical anthropologists who want to become involved in the health policy arena should keep abreast of developments in medicine and health care through the popular press as well as academic journals in health and medicine. Research funding, course syllabi, and opportunities for public participation in hearings and committees will all depend, to some extent, on the current health agenda as expressed in the media and by politicians. The discussion that follows summarizes areas for possible involvement by medical anthropologists in the first three issues listed in Table 1: (1) The cost of health care; (2) environmental health; and (3) the health care of special populations, especially the elderly and the poor.

Health Costs: What Can Medical Anthropologists Do?

American health care costs are now the highest in the world and climbing faster than any other cost of our society. In 1988, all public and private health care consumed 11.1% of the gross national product (GNP). This is a higher proportion than for any other developed country. Federal, state, and local government spends about two fifths of this amount, and private health insurance about one third. The rest is paid by individuals (Washington Post 1990b).

Given these vast amounts of expenditures, what can anthropologists hope to do to help bring down the rate of increase for health costs? First, anthropologists can use their knowledge to help decrease costs by helping to design and operate more cost-effective programs. They can do this by applying their knowledge of human systems to increasing the compliance of patients with treatment regimens

TABLE 1.
Fifteen Major Health Issue Areas for the 1990s

1. The Cost of Health Care, Health Insurance, and Options for a Major Restructuring the American Health Care System.
2. Environmental Health and Occupational Health (including risk monitoring, risk analysis, and risk management)
3. Health Care of Special Populations (especially the elderly, the poor, and minority Americans in general).
4. Diseases and Health Conditions among the Elderly (geriatrics and gerontology).
5. Long-Term Care Programs and Facilities (for the elderly and the disabled—including AIDS victims, the mentally retarded, and the chronically mentally ill).
6. Medical Ethics (including the right to die, and implications of genetic engineering).
7. Behavioral Risk Factors for Major U.S. Killers—Heart Disease and Cancer (for example, risk factors such as sedentary lifestyle, cigarette smoking, obesity, high blood pressure, binge drinking, heavy drinking, other substance abuse).
8. Rural Health
9. Veterans Health Care
10. Epidemiology of Accidents
11. Epidemiology of Violence (homicide, suicide, physical and sexual abuse, rape)
12. Infant Mortality in High-Risk Groups; Children's Health in All Groups
13. Training and Deployment of Allied Health Professionals
14. The Organization and Management of Hospitals
15. Sexual Behavior and Sexual Health (including a possible national sex survey)

and helping them to work actively with their health care providers. Health care programs become more effective if people are empowered to take part in their own health care and if they follow the good advice of health care professionals.[1] Anthropologists can help to improve the communication process between care giver and care receiver and, for example, to reduce the number of patients who misunderstand medication instructions, or reduce the number of missed follow-up appointments, or reduce the time it takes for a nurse to complete a hospital intake interview. Anthropologists can help to design health care delivery systems that are culturally appropriate in the timing, structure, and manner in which services are delivered. In these ways and countless others, anthropologists can help health care systems operate more efficiently. Patients who have special communication problems, like Spanish speakers in an Anglo community, or elderly persons whose memories are failing, are often unable to make and keep follow-up appointments, or they omit crucial medical history data, or they forget to take their pills or even fail to give permission for needed procedures. One of the best cost arguments of all is to not increase funding or personnel at all, but to increase the effectiveness of the care that an instituted program can provide.

Second, anthropologists can also help to slow the rise in health care costs by working to reduce inpatient days. Medical treatments requiring expensive staff and equipment are concentrated in hospitals, and any overnight stay will be charged at a high rate to help offset those costs. Ambulatory surgery clinics and abortion facilities are only two examples of developments in the 1980s that now help to reduce expensive inpatient days. Because of the importance of community and home-based supports, instruction in home health equipment, follow-up procedures, and other consequences of increased ambulatory care, anthropologists can play an important role in helping to organize and deliver ambulatory services. Increased use of community and ambulatory clinics also helps to reduce overuse of emergency rooms—a problem particularly troublesome in very poor populations. Furthermore, anthropologists, by contributing their knowledge and research skills to the development of appropriate, medium to long-term care facilities, can help to keep patients in comfortable, safe, attractive, health care facilities that are less expensive than hospitals. There is an enormous gap between what the home environment can now provide and what the hospital can provide. Very few facilities fill that gap—some half-way housing, some expensive nursing homes, and some few day-care facilities. The problem of long-term, but less intensive, care will be with us for the foreseeable future, for many types of elderly, disabled, recovering, and chronically ill patients. By the time the Baby Boom Generation reaches their sixties and seventies, between 2005 to 2015, the American health care system may be unable to afford inpatient days for anything but very serious procedures. Again, anthropologists can help to plan, design, and develop model projects for long-term care facilities that are socially satisfying and culturally appropriate.

A third approach for anthropologists is by helping to reduce another high cost item, the numbers of scarce and expensive health care personnel. Physicians and other health care providers represent the single largest proportion of any health care budget. It is the presence of these health care personnel that partly determines the high cost of inpatient days. But the issue is broader than that: A great deal of care can be provided with less expert, less expensive personnel if provided in contexts that are appropriate. For example, nurse-midwives can save delivery costs for mothers who have access problems. Home nurses can reduce the costs of recovery for elderly patients. Use of paraprofessionals can allow the concentration of scarce and highly trained physicians and specialized professionals where they are needed most, thereby reducing costs.

Anthropologists can figure into the planning and implementation of these kinds of delivery systems prominently because of the importance of the social and cultural components of these systems. If the systems don't feel right, and seem right, and if they aren't right with a patient's relatives and friends, then intermediate care facilities won't work, and too many people will use too many tertiary facilities with too many well-trained, highly paid, care givers.

Environmental Health: What Can Medical Anthropologists Do?
Environmental health promises to be one of the major areas of health policy in the 1990s, and medical anthropology students should consider how their expertise and interests might intersect with this important field. Environmental health was traditionally a subfield of public health and helped to guarantee safe food and

water supplies, to control vermin, and to manage sewage earlier in the 20th century. Now, the beginning of the 1990s, environmental health is at a turning point and on the brink of a growth spurt. Environmental health is a potentially vast field that intersects with virtually all sectors of environmental science, including energy production and consumption, natural resource management, regulation of toxins and pesticides, and programs to guarantee the purity of food, agricultural products, and drugs. Environmental health also frequently overlaps with occupational health.

Participation by anthropologists in the environmental health field hinges on their knowledge of communication, education, and values, and on the central importance of human cooperation in most environmental programs. Public-policy work in the field of environmental health can propel medical anthropologists directly into debates about the scientific and political trade-offs inherent to the resolution of environmental issues. Anthropologists stand ready to play an important part in maintaining health quality in the face of a wide variety of domestic and global hazards. This is because developing technological solutions to environmental problems such as salinization, desertification, reduction of biodiversity, and overuse of pesticides will not be nearly as hard as convincing people to use them (Scientific American 1989). Anthropologists can participate fully in the development of an appropriate environmental ethos, and can help to change values, develop policies, and construct social institutions which bring about behavioral change. Nearly all experts agree that we must change fundamental human and community standards in order to maintain ''sustainable growth''—growth without a net loss in environmental quality.

For those medical anthropologists who want to delve into the more technical side of environmental health, the area of risk management is a field waiting to be exploited (Douglas 1982; Jasanoff 1986; Lave 1982; National Research Council 1983; Pet-Edwards 1989). Risk management combines the technical determination of the risk of an environmental factor (expressed often as a projection of ''excess deaths,'' and now calculated usually by a toxicologist, chemist, biologist, physicist, or mathematician), with the evaluative task of weighing risks, costs, benefits, and human values in a policy analysis paradigm (see below). Wherever there is doubt arising out of scientific uncertainty, there is a strong chance that health concerns will develop among average Americans. Medical anthropologists could not be positioned at a better time and place to help human populations understand and cope with health concerns that arise from environmental hazards— real, imagined, or potential. Medical anthropologists could play an important role as members of teams writing environmental impact statements. Environmental and social impact assessment will surely bring together both the technical and human community factors that anthropologists have always found so interesting.

Health Care for Special Populations: What Can Medical Anthropologists Do?

The two largest federal health care programs, Medicaid and Medicare, are insurance programs designed for the poor and the elderly, respectively. The federal government makes an enormous investment in providing care for these two large groups—about $32.7 billion for Medicaid and about $81.9 billion for Medicare in 1987, or about one third of the entire federal society security, health care, and health research budget for that year. During the 1980s, the "near poor" or the "working poor" who cannot afford expensive, private health insurance, and the elderly who are poorly insured by private companies also faced an increasingly unworkable system of health care in the United States, and their positions are worsening at the beginning of the 1990s.

Medical anthropologists can contribute a great deal to health programs for the poor, primarily because ethnic Americans—for example, refugees, immigrants, older residents who speak no English, or residents with a history of oppression in the United States such as blacks and Native Americans—are disproportionately represented among the poor (Harwood 1981). Minority Americans often have special problems applying for, qualifying for, and obtaining benefits from state-administered Medicaid programs. Hispanic Americans, for example, are grossly overrepresented among those with no health insurance (Washington Post 1990a). The rural and the elderly also frequently have problems obtaining entitlement benefits because of communication and interaction difficulties with the bureaucracies that administer the programs. Medical anthropologists who remain interested only in medical conditions and who fail to consider how the poor and elderly interface with government bureaucracies to obtain needed health care may succeed as anthropologists but not as expert participants in the public-policy process. For a medical anthropologist to research the social and cultural bases of a particular disease or condition is to stop short of involvement in domestic health policy The medical anthropologist must clearly outline the implications of the social and cultural factors for health care, not just for health. Again, because education and communication can play such an important part in the improvement of participation in the major federal health insurance programs, medical anthropologists have a great deal to contribute. If medical anthropologists want to become involved in policy, then they should go beyond the disease into a consideration of the system that treats it.

Medical anthropologists should also consider the degree to which, and the role through which, they want to become involved in health policy. Those who focus their research and work on minorities, on the disadvantaged, and on the elderly tend to become advocates instead of, or in addition to, expert participants. Decisions about advocacy work should be weighed carefully because an expert's credibility in the policy process often declines in direct proportion to the degree to which he or she appears to be an advocate. Strident activists help to create public pressure, but only rarely gain direct access to decision makers. Medical anthropologists may at times be more successful in their advocacy work by confining their activities to service on commissions and review panels, as expert witnesses, and as bureaucrats.

Social Science, Policy Formation, and Health: The Basis for Our Participation

Medical Anthropology and Health Policy

The rationale for participation by anthropologists in the policy process is neither self-evident nor simple. On the other hand, the relationship of economics and political science to public policy, government, and law making is more apparent. Therefore, medical anthropologists who want to impact the policy process need to work toward a clear understanding of how anthropology's research methodologies, culture concepts, and special commitments make it useful to government policy makers and program managers. If medical anthropologists want to contribute to more humane and progressive policies, better laws, and more effective programs, then they must eventually fit into the policy process rather than vice versa. In general, the same is true for all experts in other natural and social sciences. When scientists are called on by government for contributions based on their academic work, then their reports, testimony, and evaluations must be in a format and language comprehensible to nonscientists in decision-making positions.

The "Policy Arena"

The following discussion lays a foundation for the participation by medical anthropologists in the broad "policy arena" into which all sciences, including medical anthropology, must fit. For medical anthropologists, the policy arena is composed of elements from three sectors of American society that have limited ties: (1) academic social science, the training ground for pure researchers and applied scientists, (2) policy science, a burgeoning, multidisciplinary field of applied social science dominated by economists and political scientists, and (3) domestic health care, an "enterprise" composed of research, service delivery, and a changing national consciousness about health goals for the future. The fields of applied medical anthropology, health economics, applied medical sociology, bioethics, health policy research, and much of epidemiology all lie at the intersection of these three sectors of American society. All these fields combine in their approaches toward health an emphasis on empiricism (rational inquiry for bioethics), systems analysis, application, and a public orientation.

Social Science and Policy Formation

The health policy arena is amorphous, complicated, and constantly fluctuating. It is a nationwide network trailing in and out of government, academia, and the private sector. Its players are a varied assortment of politicians, journalists, bureaucrats, lobbyists, health care practitioners, staff members on Capitol Hill (or the equivalent at the state and local level), and scientific experts. They communicate primarily on the telephone, on computer networks, at national conferences, in hastily called meetings, and at lunch. They work very fast and, in general, have a short attention span for any single health issue. Therefore, the policy arena is not naturally suited to the type of work in which anthropologists (or any other scientists) engage. Nevertheless, medical anthropologists who want to impact the policy process should remember that scientific experts are indispensable to the policy process. Politicians ultimately decide how public money is spent, but their decisions have become dependent in the last half of the 20th century on the empirical studies, methods (like the survey or cost/benefit analysis), and the information-generating capacity that science has to offer. Because of important work by anthropologists in the past, the science and discipline of anthropology has become increasingly important to decision makers. Anthropological knowledge will continue to gain in importance for health-policy makers, especially if medical anthropology students become acquainted during their academic training with the complex interconnections between social science, policy formation, and health.

The science/policy relationship is a problematical one. It is widely perceived in a "two-cultures model" in which scientists and policy makers use different languages, norms, values, and styles (Bulmer 1982, 1987; Rich 1981a, 1981b). The rationale for policy work by trained anthropologists is related to changes in social science methodology, the use of social science by government, and practical problems among scientists who interact with federal bureaucrats. Normative issues in the social science/policy relationship include questions about the non-systematic use of social-science knowledge by decision makers—for example, do they pick and choose study findings for their own purposes, or for that of the current administration?—federal preferences for certain research methods—how much is government missing by relying so heavily on large-scale surveys?—and the moral frameworks in which social scientists contribute their knowledge to agencies, commissions, and hearings—who decides and how do they decide what is best for all the people or for any segment of them? Anthropologists can well understand the ethical aspects of participation in policy formation because they know from field experience that the way in which a researcher frames a problem often reflects his values and world view.

In the 1980s, with an increasing number of scientific meetings, review groups, and panels drawing members from all over the country to meet in and around Washington, D.C., the styles and purposes of the two cultures have come closer together. This trend has also been encouraged by an increase in government-sponsored "town meetings," locally held congressional hearings, and multi-site program evaluations that take place largely outside of Washington. A parallel increase in association-sponsored scientific and professional meetings has helped to decentralize government's accumulation of information and ideas. However, the integration of those ideas still takes place largely in Washington. Therefore, medical anthropologists who want to impact the policy process should plan from early in their careers to deliver papers, attend meetings, and take part whenever possible in both federally sponsored local events and Washington-based meetings. Both are indispensable. For those who want to work only on the state and local levels, the same is true on a smaller scale. The nation's state capitals and county seats are where policy is ultimately formulated, so temporary assignments in those locations are requisite.

Is Anthropology a "Policy Science"?

Social scientists have been striving to define their proper roles in the policy process throughout the 20th century, but especially since the mid-1970s. All social scientists have confronted the question of whether they should remain in the relative isolation of academia or participate fully in the policy process in order to share what they know with those who draft policy. Anthropologists—like those in sociology, economics, physics, and biology—have wondered whether they have obligations to share knowledge as a fulfillment of some "ethics of knowledge." The answer is not a simple one, but one which must be worked out by each anthropologist for himself or herself. Bermant writes, "At stake in the relation between social science and government are the issues of rights and responsibilities to influence social and political life through systematic collection and dissemination of information" (1982:141). Should an anthropologist feel an obligation to share research results to help construct better social policy? Probably so, because even in an information age with easy access to computer technology, vast information storage and search capabilities, and rapid, worldwide electronic communications, it is still the case that the values of those who collect and disseminate scientific knowledge affect its interpretation. The distinction and connection between fact and value is not as simple as once thought (Fisher 1980), and if medical anthropologists want their applied or academic work put to the best use, then they need to take an active role in the interpretation of their own work.

The question of whether anthropology is a policy science is not meaningful in today's public-policy arena, or in the context of the current policy-science literature. All empirically generated, social scientific knowledge has relevance to public policy, and all sciences have a natural legitimacy in policy formation. Modern, rational decision making is based first and foremost on knowledge generated using the scientific method. Government has a great stake in perpetuating academically based science as a relatively unbiased and inexpensive source of expert knowledge. Federal executives want to use social science, and just as many social scientists want to apply their work to solve human problems. "Policy science" is a distant discipline which developed, beginning in the 1950s, to theorize about and to explain how empirical knowledge is used to create new laws, programs, and regulations, and how public policy originates, changes, and affects social life. Policy science is an interdisciplinary field whose experts use an eclectic, yet increasingly standard, set of methods, and continue to develop a theoretical base (de Leon 1981; Lynn 1987). Anthropology, with its own method and theory, is one of the sciences that can contribute to the analysis of laws, policies, and regulations. Anthropology has contributed to policy science, for example, through use of the case-study method, through models of social change, and through values analysis. There are important ways that anthropology can continue to feed into policy science. For example, policy science has yet to develop a method, a paradigm, or a model to handle easily the evaluation of alternative values and social structures like those found in major American ethnic groups. Policy-science frameworks work best when values are given, and everyone agrees on the right social structures,—that is, where culture remains constant. Crosscultural analysis has no place now in policy science. The integration of policy science and ethnology should eventually produce a better policy science in the 21st century—one which will be increasingly useful as immigrants form an ever-larger segment of American society. Medical anthropology could serve as the mortar and pestle where the needed intellectual alchemy can take place, because of government's enormous investment in health care and because of the central importancse of health-seeking behavior in human lives.

Questions about the changing relations between academic and practicing anthropology—questions which have taken up enormous space in newsletters, textbooks, and commemorative addresses for two decades—become moot in a discusion of policy making and the utilization of anthropological knowledge by decision makers. This is mainly because participation by medical anthropologists in the health policy arena, whether indirect through published research or purposeful through other activities, is itself praxis. Anyone who publishes or speaks and finds his or her work used by others is affecting policy. The balance between academic and practicing anthropology may ultimately determine how anthropology's importance to society is expressed (through students of public policy), but the distinction matters little to lawmakers and government bureaucrats.

Medical Anthropology's Latest Contributions to Policy

The twin epidemics of substance abuse and AIDS that mushroomed in the 1980s dramatically changed the nature of the participation by medical anthropologists in health policy formation. Anthropologists found their work valued by an increasing number of federal program managers, city officials, and colleagues in the other health sciences. The social and cultural bases of behavioral risk factors have been nowhere more apparent than among drug users, gay men, and prostitutes. Furthermore, the fact that minority Americans are at greater (and increasing) risk of drug addiction and of contracting AIDS has put the work of medical anthropologists at an even higher premium (Singer et al. 1989). America's urban tragedies have ironically provided springboards for the applied careers of many medical anthropologists and a more solid place for all of medical anthropology in the policy arena. Medical anthropology students should study Table 1 carefully and begin to anticipate other opportunities both to contribute to policy and to solidify medical anthropology's position vis-à-vis government. Domestic tragedies are again the most likely areas for contribution, for example: (1) the violence and homicide epidemics in central cities, not all of which is drug-related, (2) the worsening specter of rural health in America, where old age, lack of qualified health care professionals, and tradition combine to place individuals at high health risk, or (3) the political and cultural management of the reproductive and cancer risks posed by nuclear waste, chemical effluents, pesticides, food preservatives, and industrial heat pollution—all of which routinely cross community, state, and even national boundaries. There are opportunities for medical-anthropologists to contribute substantially to these issues and others, through their knowledge of values, customs, and social change, and with their more specialized knowledge, for example, of disease classification and diagnosis, the role of the family in health care and its effect on prognosis, subjective factors in determining accessibility to services, and the behavior of health care professionals with their patients.

Nuts and Bolts: Doing Health Policy Analysis

Who Does Policy Analysis?

Medical anthropologists who are interested in applying their knowledge to policy formation will be unified by an analytical paradigm and a methodology more than a specific policy setting, or a set of roles, or an academic or practicing persuasion. The following discussion briefly defines policy analysis, explains how it is different from forms of analysis that anthropologists use more often, and summarizes its five basic steps. Applied medical anthropologists work in many types of clinical, administrative, and field settings, and all of them do policy analysis in one form or another.

Medical anthropologists are unified by their academic training and by their ability to apply social-science theory and method to human disease, health care, and the value systems underlying them. The medical anthropologist who practices at the planning and policy level—which is often described as "a higher level" with a broad view, a high degree of abstraction, and with political as well as research and service-delivery implications—usually does so as an adjunct to activities such as university teaching, consulting, basic research, or bureaucratic staff work. Practicing medical anthropology in the health-policy arena can involve, for example, library research on a current health issue, attendance and note-taking at a public hearing on a local environmental hazard, development of statistical health profiles using a computer, drafting a legislative provision or a regulation, writing a cost-effectiveness or risk-management report, or preparing a press release. Activities vary widely and the setting shifts rapidly with the issue of interest. However, all activities involve either a formal or informal type of policy analysis. Figure 1 helps to illustrate some of the terms and concepts used to explain policy analysis.

A Methodological Framework

Health-policy analysis is pursued in many guises by many types of experts in and out of government, but in its most structured format it is part of policy science. The latter was first suggested as a field of study by Harold Lasswell in 1951, but only since about 1970 have journals devoted solely to the discipline become well established. Policy science integrates the social sciences by borrowing and organizing various social theories and methodologies to study the formation of government policies and to inform the policy-making process using a technique called "policy analysis." By 1980, the policy-science literature presented a more-or-less standard method for policy analysis, and this method remains intact at the beginning of the 1990s. There are textbooks, workbooks, and workshops to teach policy analysis methodology. They introduce the student and the specialist alike to a structured policy-analysis paradigm. Case studies then illustrate the use of policy analysis methodology (a multidisciplinary social science methodology) in relation to specific health problems (Coplin and O'Leary 1988a, 1988b, 1988c; Lynn 1988). The literature usually presents examples of health policy analysis within a looser discussion of the process of policy formation, whose systematic study is basically a form of history. Policy science includes the analysis of specific cases using policy analysis, as well as broad theories about how policy forms through the interaction of special interest groups, public opinion, government, business, and the scientific establishment. Some authors find that policy develops through a "nonprocess" because of the seemingly arbitrary and therefore unpre-

FIGURE 1

Simplified Diagram for a Health Program or Policy Analysis

<u>Define</u>:

Positive Outcomes and Values to Maximize = A, B, C
Measures of the Positive Outcomes = A', B', C'

Negative Outcomes and Values to Minimize = X, Y, Z
Measures of the Negative Outcomes = X', Y', Z'

<u>Develop</u>:

A Model $f(x) = ax_1 + bx_2^2 + \ldots x_n^n + \epsilon$

<u>Diagram the Options and Their Measurements</u>:

Program or Policy Option	Option #1	Option #2	....	Option #N
Measurement, Given f(x)				
A'				
B'				
C'				
X'				
Y'				
Z'				
Summary Calculation or Statement about Option's Relative Evaluation				

THE CHOICE
(Option with
the Best Summary)

dictable nature of many system components: public sentiment, congressional interests and pressure, the progress of scientific methodology, the availability of
scientific information and trained advisors, and the interests and power positions
of all policy participants (agency executives, legislators, academicians, experts
in independent research companies and special-interest groups, program administrators, care givers, and recipients of services) (Rich 1981a, 1981b).

Policy analysis is widely referred to as an "art." However, for all practical
purposes, policy science presupposes a regularity in the policy-formation process

that makes it amenable to empirical inquiry. Policy analysts work to bring order to policy formation in all steps leading up to the policy maker's final decision to institute a regulation, pass a law, make a policy statement, approve a budget for a program alternative, establish an investigatory commission, or do nothing—which is also an option. Policy science has an interdisciplinary, applied, systems approach to the definition and evaluation of policy and program alternatives (Weiss 1980, 1988). The systems approach is familiar to all anthropologists because it views a health program or a health policy from a holistic viewpoint, and assumes that all aspects of a program or policy and its context are functionally interdependent. A policy analysis provides the decision maker with enough organized, comparative information to be able to choose an alternative (an "option") according to his or her own priorities. Choices are most often based on the fundamental political and philosophical beliefs of the party in power—although this is certainly not always the case. Policy analysis itself is apolitical but its use by the decision maker is fundamentally political.

Policy analysis relies heavily on quantitative methods and structured frameworks. It most often employs highly organized structures like matrices, webs, decision trees, taxonomies, scenarios, and other devices to organize, assess, and rank options, and apply societal values that lie at the highest levels of abstraction (see, for example, the values in Exercise #1, Question 3, at the end of this chapter). Policy analysis concretizes values in the form of program and policy options—real steps that real governments can take—and then compares them so that the policy maker can decide which steps government should take, if any. There are aspects of policy analysis that are inimical to the standard forms of analysis in ethnology, although the ethnographer often uses many of the organized structures of the policy analyst. Policy analysis combines scientific method and evaluative assessments of "good" and "bad" in a way foreign to the value-free approach of the cultural anthropologist. Policy analysts make judgments within the context of a specific society's values and therefore reason within a framework opposite to cultural relativism. Their approach toward values is similar to that of politicians or ethicists who begin an analysis with values that are assumed to be constant or "given." Policy analysis defines *a priori* a set of values and then proceeds to evaluate a program or policy accordingly. In this way, any political perspective, any view of human nature, any belief system can be "scientifically applied" to a policy or program option. Therefore, medical anthropology students will find it useful, in reviewing the health policy literature, to read both politically conservative and politically liberal health policy analyses to learn their method and style of argument. Analysts can begin with the same set of values and social goals, but arrive at very different conclusions about programs and policies through different analytical routes. Technically, that would not be possible for the ethnologist.

Policy Analysis and Cultural Analysis
Policy analysis parallels cultural analysis in several ways. Like cultural anthropology, policy science makes heavy use of the case-study method and may require collection of materials using ethnographic techniques: participation, observation,

objective analysis of values different from the analyst's, and intuitive model-building (often in a team meeting) from a combination of reflection, brainstorming, and good homework. The qualitative techniques of anthropology are often mentioned in methodological outlines for policy analysis. Many health analysts use qualitative techniques as a part of their methodological tool kit. Use of qualitative methods is especially useful when the analysis of program and policy alternatives involves important nonquantifiable variables. Like ethnology, policy analysis usually relies on development of historical background and regards a contemporary system as evolving from preexisting social, political, and environmental conditions. Unlike anthropology, its main orientation is toward the future, that is, toward decisions that determine future social conditions. Policy analysis relies on a comparative technique to contrast alternatives according to the degree to which they maximize values and fulfill predefined goals that arise from societal values. Values are not compared as in ethnology, but are held constant in any single policy analysis.

Policy analysts acknowledge with increasing frequency that the culture concept should be used to complement strict frameworks like the cost/benefit paradigm. If values vary within a single society—as they surely do in any postindustrial society—then "good" and "bad" can vary widely and still not be "crazy" or "criminal." For example, "benefits" for ethnic minorities or the elderly are often overlooked in a standard policy analysis because what those groups consider "good" is not consistent with the mainstream values that are held constant in a policy analysis. Similarly, adhering to alternatives that bolster the mainstream values that the policy analysis finds "good" can be interpreted as "costs" for the person who follows an alternative life-style. The economist's "opportunity costs" can also be widely interpreted vis-à-vis large ethnic minority populations: A "lost opportunity" that should cost the average mainstreamer dearly may provide ample opportunities for the minority person to make money and achieve intangible satisfactions.

Nowhere is culture more important to the analysis of options than with respect to health and health care. Traditional notions among ethnic minorities of what is "good health" and what is "good health care" derive so often from fundamental religious values that they can scarcely fit into a cost/benefit analysis. No matter how standardized large federal health care programs become—financially through payment systems or conceptually through DRGs (diagnosis-related groups)—there will still be widely varying definitions of good health and good health care among minority Americans. Good health and good health care can involve decreased social and physical proximity to relatives, payments for preventive health care to the detriment of "getting ahead" in a new society, and reliance on the opinions of "strangers" in matters of life, death, and propriety. These "costs" will be exaggerated as the proportion of minority residents in America rises throughout the 1990s, and as the size and density of minority population centers increase into the next century.

Health policy could be one of the most important areas for contribution by anthropologists for several reasons. Medical anthropologists have an unavoidable connection with service delivery and therefore are able to learn about health programs and health issues through practical experience. They are exposed to an array of licensed, practicing professionals who apply their academic training to practical problems every day. Medical anthropologists may be especially willing to pursue training and experience that will allow them access to the health policy arena. Health policy analysis is an area of policy science that needs anthropologists because of (1) the difficulty in measuring health costs, benefits, and effectiveness using standard quantitative measures in policy science; (2) the amount of analysis devoted to health programs for the special populations with which medical anthropologists so often work; and (3) the need for expert values analysts in the rapidly evolving synergism of technological advancement in medicine, mushrooming health costs, and resulting value conflicts in the face of limited health funds.

The following outline of a health policy analysis is a rational framework for any kind of participation in the health policy arena. It is equally useful for the executive-branch health policy analyst and the legislative-branch staffer, for the health consultant from academia, for the lobbyist, the researcher, or the medical anthropology student preparing for policy work with an exercise on a university campus.

Step 1: Determine Objectives of the Analysis

The objectives of a health policy analysis could include any or all of the following: informing a decision maker of details necessary for an option choice; self-education; talent searches for expert analysts; political aggrandizement; marking time when it is politically unwise to take any action; or as a precursor to a fully implemented program evaluation (Brewer 1981; Thomas 1985). Health programs for disadvantaged groups are often effectively shelved by appointing a commission to "study the situation." The analyst has an obligation to determine his client's true motivations. Otherwise, he or she could waste a great deal of time or simply end up not being paid! Once the true objective of the analysis is determined, the analyst organizes appropriate resources (time, money, staff) for the study, and makes an honest assessment of deadlines for deliverables.

Step 2: Determine Issues and Outline Values and Self-Interests

Public policy issues exist when there is a disagreement about how government handles a social problem. Without disagreement, there is no issue; without an issue, there can be logically no policy analysis. So, an analyst must first decide whether an issue exists, and if it does, define it. Once an issue is clearly formulated and limited, the analyst outlines the self-interest values (What is good for us) and the transcendental values (What is good for society) of all disagreeing parties as the criteria against which options are ultimately judged. There should be at least two disagreeing parties, and therefore at least two options. However, without a clear understanding of the culture-bound perspective on societal values in policy science, the anthropologist will have difficulty, and good examples are useful.

Medical anthropologists should be and will be expert health-values analysts, as they have experience manipulating abstract value concepts. They will be aided in outlining American social values related to health if, for example, they review the national health objectives for 1990, and their assessment in 1986, in the form of a "midcourse review" (Department of Health and Human Services (DHHS) 1986). It will also be useful to obtain the 1989 Public Health Service publication, *Year 2000 Objectives for the Nation* (DHHS 1990), in which the potentials for meeting objectives for different target groups are summarized.

Step 3: List Alternatives and Collect Relevant Data

The result of Step 2 is a diagram of alternative health policies or programs supported by the disagreeing parties. The health-policy analyst then collects data on health care indicators associated with each policy or program option. The analyst makes use of data from studies that monitor health care programs and policies and describe past trends, with an eye toward being able to forecast the outcome of future programs and policies by predicting trends. Sometimes a great deal of creativity is required to analyze the attainment of health objectives in uniform terms: government agencies and programs may provide data in various units, or collect the data for different purposes and therefore for different periods of time, or they may define units in different terms. All of these data collection problems potentially affect the ease of analysis. However, once various options are described in relatively equal terms, calculations or descriptions are made to determine comparability. The cost/benefit analyst assigns costs (in dollars and in scarce, expensive professionals—a factor that distinguishes health programs from others), and lists benefits in terms of health indicators (DHHS 1990), "quality of life" measures, or subjective expressions of satisfaction. The operations researcher specifies different "black boxes" (systems), which have various inputs (funds, staff, physical plant) and outputs (disease and mortality rates, health care use patterns, quality of care). At this stage of the analyst's work, his or her depth of knowledge of the health care system is extremely important, as is a capacity for absorbing large quantities of new data, that is, the ability to do the "quick study."

Many data are not readily available to the analyst because of the protective self-interests of groups affected by a program or policy. Data which do not bolster their positions are kept secret. Therefore, skills such as tact, diplomacy, political acumen, and effective interaction style are needed. Policy analysis also requires considerable financial investment in research time, facilities, and expert staff. Qualitative research skills can be particularly useful for the anthropologist-*qua*-analyst. Projection and role playing are useful methods for the policy analyst who conducts in-depth, expert interviews or Delphi panels. Qualitative techniques are very difficult for traditional analysts to use in their study of the health care of minority groups because health care effectiveness is often defined in nonquantifiable, socio-psychological terms by members of the special group. The anthropologist who works as a health analyst should be able to translate traditional anthropological methodology into effective, nonthreatening forms of investigation in the policy arena, and to use anthropological systems theory to make decisions on which data to collect.

Step 4: Build a Model

The next step involves expansion of the basic, known mechanisms operating in the health care programs or policies under scrutiny. This step makes eclectic use of social science and health care utilization theories. Disciplinary boundaries disappear and the most successful analysts are those who can draw quickly and widely from the work of many types of experts. Team work can be extremely useful in model building and academic isolation and individuality can be distinct handicaps. At the model-building stage, the cost/benefit analyst computes ratios and draws cost-effectiveness tables. Cost/benefit analysis has been used with three major types of health investments: disease-specific intervention programs, alternative methods for delivering health services, and return rates for public investments in health and training programs and in medical research. However, the analyst can use other methods. A simple flow chart can suffice, or a bar chart, or a decision-tree diagram, or a description of potential scenarios and an assessment, for example, of high-medium-low rates for the spread of a disease. An explanation can be summarized in a statistical formula using, for example, linear or multiple regression or more complex statistical models—but it need not be. Epidemiological, demographic, and sociocultural simulations on supercomputers can be derived, depending on time, money, facilities, and expertise. Quantification is not always possible or needed. Since anthropologists have experience building models with many uncertainties, contingencies, and qualitative factors, they should be ideally suited to health-policy analysis. Medical anthropologists can be especially helpful in explaining health care utilization patterns, mortality rates, and disease distribution patterns for ethnic groups and special populations like the elderly. The goal of even the most rigorous policy analysis is simplification: To simplify descriptive outcome measures of the various "options" so that a decision maker can make a rational choice between or among options. Quade observes, "An explicit model . . . provides a means for breaking a complicated decision into smaller tasks that can be handled at one time" (1975:48). It can be a challenge to translate the results of a policy analysis into meaningful terms for the policy maker. If an anthropologist fails to make this translation, he or she cannot be useful as an analyst, primarily because decision makers will not translate results for themselves. They do not have the time. Some journalists will translate results for policy makers, but it is risky to rely on journalists to translate scientific work.

Step 5: Select Preferred Alternatives (Optional Step)

The scientific phase of a policy analysis technically ends with model building and the organization of relevant information for a policy maker's perusal and ultimate decision. Recommendations are therefore an optional part of a policy analysis.

Yet, in practice, recommendations flow naturally from any policy analysis. They are an integral, implicit part of many policy analyses that do not precisely follow the steps outlined here. Ultimately, the order of the analytical steps and the reporting format are less important than the impact of a policy analysis on the policy-making process. Therefore, the ways in which knowledge is used and in which information flows, and the ethics of the use and nonuse of scientific knowledge become issues themselves, and have given rise to a separate literature (Weiss 1980). It is sometimes difficult to gauge whether a program or policy has any effect, so another form of policy analysis—evaluation—is often used. Measurement of health program effectiveness can be very tricky because of multiple, interacting factors (such as those contributing to infant mortality rates) and because of the positive, open-ended nature of health goals (such as "wellness"). Choosing quality-of-life factors to evaluate health policy alternatives requires creativity and a broad knowledge of social science and health. Efforts to use simplified, composite health indices have not been very successful in the past, but are becoming more so, especially in terms of measuring elusive concepts such as "quality of life" or "quality of care." For the medical anthropologist, evaluation research is a good place to begin work in health policy because it is often the only type of analysis mandated by state or federal law, and therefore routinely funded.

The exercises which follow this chapter include examples for completing of a health policy analysis. The medical anthropology student can begin to practice health policy analysis by examining Table 1, and for each major issue, defining: (1) a problem (probably one of many problems associated with the issue area); (2) the issues associated with the chosen problem; (3) the types of data needed to build a model that will guide comparison of program or policy options; (4) definition of at least two options; (5) an outline comparing those two or more options; and (6) choice of the recommended option that the student would make to a policy maker. This exercise can be completed for health issues at the local, state, or national level.

Roles for Medical Anthropologists in Domestic Health Policy

Three Basic Types of Work
Medical anthropologists who are committed to applying their knowledge to policy are now succeeding in combining all three types of work—government, academic, and private consulting—with increasing frequency. Academic books in anthropology are now going beyond simply appending a short "policy recommendations" section to research results; full-time consultants are teaching more frequently; and government bureaucrats are keeping in touch with their disciplinary roots and are being encouraged to do so, for example, through listings in directories of anthropologists that were once for academics only.

Two-Culture Shock
At the beginning of the 1980s, anthropologists who were active in health policy could be traced only along a loose network trailing in and out of government and

into a phantom literature. The most successful applied medical anthropologists with knowledge of how to affect health policy formation tended to "slip out of anthropology" and become government bureaucrats, successful consultants, and company vice presidents. Few stayed in teaching even on a part-time basis, so they were usually unavailable to teach students how to pursue work—as anthropologists—in health policy and program development. Their field reports and recommendations became part of the files of consulting companies and government agencies.[2] Growth in applied anthropology programs changed this somewhat. The distinction between many applied and academic activities has weakened, although the distinction remains very strong and separates colleagues in the two persuasions through different experiences, attendance at different professional meetings, and different pay scales. Academic anthropologists are now less reticent in sharing with students and colleagues lessons from their first experiences with government. These experiences are often very difficult because of the disorientation—"culture shock," for want of a better term—caused by the norm, value, and style differences between academia and government. Students in applied anthropology programs inherit only some of the applied/academic barrier. They benefit enormously from participation in the increasing number of local, university internship programs in which they gain experience in applied work before they leave school. Applied medical anthropologists should gain experience in a health service delivery setting before they leave school, even if only in a voluntary capacity. Applied students also benefit from the increasing number of courses specifically designed to teach policy studies, program evaluation, policy ethnography, health statistics, and applied skills like report writing. A variety of new anthropology and computer courses also provide applied students with needed computer skills which they will use in almost all applied work. Directories of policy research centers, ethics institutes, grants and internship programs are helpful in locating work and training experience for the advanced medical anthropology student interested in health policy.[3] Internships in Washington, D.C., and state capitals—for a congressional committee, a congressman, lobby group, or research institute—provide outstanding experience.

Training in applied medical anthropology with a policy focus should provide instruction in how to assume a particular kind of role originating in academia but played out in the world of politics, government (including public health departments), and the health care business. Objectives of a medical anthropology curriculum of this type should include the following. First, an understanding of the structure, function, and style of established health policy organizations, for example: government agencies; congressional committees; research think tanks and policy-research firms; public, quasi public, and private health planning and governing boards; and groups with a vested interest in health policy—from the American Association of Retired Persons to the American Medical Association and from Common Cause to the American Enterprise Institute. Examples of quasi public agencies are professional-standards review organizations (PSROs), which oversee medical practice in particular local areas or regions. They are nongovernmental and serve both private and public functions, sometimes applying for government funds to study specific problems and local health issues. Second, an ability to conceptualize anthropological applications in health care, to think creatively about how to bridge the gap between academic anthropology and policy-related activities, and an ability to work effectively with nonanthropologists in medicine, epidemiology, demography, statistics and computers, management, finance, economics, law, and ethics. Third, retraining in health-related skills and topics, including: survey sampling and methodology (the large-scale survey is the source of most of our knowlewdge of American health and health care); computer-assisted multivariate statistics (the medium in which most health facts are analyzed); and some basic work in epidemiology, biostatistics and/or biology (anatomy and physiology), public administration, hospital administration, business administration, public health, and/or health law. Experts in these disciplines make most of the health policy in the United States. Training in program evaluation methodology will provide the applied medical anthropology student with skills that can be used most immediately in a variety of health care settings, and will most effectively ease the transition into applied work. Fourth, work experience in the practical application of social science, for example, in an internship program.

Career Choices

After training, medical anthropologists work in a variety of settings to pursue their interest in health policy, for example: in the increasingly common, short-term, policy analysis or program evaluation research projects for contract firms; in basic health research and its interpretation for government policy makers in popular or academic publications, in government reports, or in expert testimony before congress; as federal or state health agency staff members; through service on panels, commissions, or advisory boards, and by training students in anthropology and the health professions.

Careers in the Federal Government

Many medical anthropologists who are interested in health policy will eventually work in positions as nonanthropologists. At the present time there are few, if any, positions specifically identified as "Health Science Administrator" (as at NIH) or "Health Policy Analyst" (in many federal agencies) that require training in medical anthropology. The major task of the health policy maker is to manage staff, budget, and long-term projects. He or she responds to health emergencies, presidential or congressional directives, regulatory conflicts, or value conflicts when one group must suffer because of another or when the lesser of two evils must be decided. To keep abreast of information which is potentially important to top-level health policy makers, medical anthropologists should maintain up-to-the-minute knowledge of policy issues, legislative progress, and techniques for dispersal and retrieval of information. Top health policy makers usually make their switch from academic to public-sector work before their civil service, presidential, or gubernatorial appointments, and achieve positive, widespread public notice before appointment. In interviews, they most emphasize the style differences between academia and government, especially the teamwork, anonymity, political pragmatism, and the periodic need for quick and decisive action. Top-level bureaucratic staff work in government health agencies can be discouragingly slow, and is usually poorly compensated in relation to the credentials and experience required. However, at times, rapid, difficult, and publicly unpopular choices must be made, and the policy maker must know how to make decisions and have the personal courage to do so. Good decision-making skills characterize all successful health policy makers, both on Capitol Hill and in executive branch agencies.

The "Health Policy Analyst" is usually a mid-level government bureaucrat who assists the health policy maker or high-level health program manager. Most of these positions have specific requirements for experience or training in public administration, business administration, and/or statistical methodology. The activities of the health policy analyst can be highly varied. He or she may study the health effects of private or government actions, work to develop better health services through site visits and program evaluations, or speak and write in a variety of public contexts and publications. Medical anthropologists can work directly for members of Congress as a participant in an internship program or be directly hired. As congressional staff members, anthropologists may, for example, conduct background research and help to draft health legislation, answer constituent inquiries, or attend hearings where successive versions of a health care bill are discussed and changed. Typically, congressional staff members oversee several different policy areas rather than just one. This is true for most internships and staff positions related to health policy. Staff work shifts from one set of issue areas to another set within a relatively brief period of time. Long-term projects are not as common as in academia unless they have guaranteed funding, as at the National Academy of Sciences, Institute of Medicine.

Careers in State and Local Government

Health policy work at the state and local level often involves health planning (itself a field of specialization), constant meetings, frequent travel, and consultation with the community leaders and politicians within a region. Medical anthropologists may be involved in health services research and evaluation, and therefore use some of the research skills learned in academic training. State and local health policy work often involves contact with federal offices that are established to aid state and local government. Medical anthropologists can serve as effective brokers between state, local, and federal agencies. State and local health policy work often involves collaboration with researchers at local universities. In fact, an increasing number of federal RFPs (requests for proposal) require collaboration between diverse state and community resources, including universities, private health care providers, and local public health departments. Networking is a skill needed by medical anthropologists interested in health policy work: They must be able to do it themselves, and they also must be able to encourage and cause others to draw widely from diverse sources of information and expertise.

Academic Careers

Academically based anthropologists most frequently affect health policy through attendance at conferences, service on federal and state health advisory councils, serving as members of panels that review health goals and objectives, and providing testimony as experts before Congress. Anthropologists' reports are also used indirectly to prepare testimony and government publications. They also serve on committees which review applications for grants-in-aid and for national research service awards from NIH, and thus have a role in determining the type of health research supported.

Careers in Private Business

Anthropologists who work with private companies, including hospitals and health care corporations, are often called on to draft proposals for submission to various government and nongovernment funding sources. Medical anthropologists may be involved in preparing a project proposal, for example, to develop a demonstration project to prevent substance abuse, to hold a planning conference on rural health care, or to manage a number of other subcontractors in a large-scale project for the federal government. Private contract work involves budgeting, hiring and supervising staff, reporting to the funding source, and constantly brokering information about the project in both academia and government. It usually involves travel.

A Training Exercise in Policy Ethnography

Nothing can top personal experience in preparing the medical anthropology student for work in health programs and policy. Internships are the best guided experience. An exercise called "policy ethnography" is the best way to learn about health policy as part of a university class, although to date the concept has not been well developed. The following outline describes a policy ethnography exercise that will be useful for the medical anthropology student interested in health policy work. The exercise is best pursued as part of advanced undergraduate or graduate class in medical anthropology, but it is also useful for the general applied anthropology student or the practitioner who needs an organized format for policy research. The activities involved in a policy ethnography may appear unusual to an anthropologist, but they are part of the normal, daily duties of staffers on Capitol Hill and in lobbying organizations. The notion of a "policy ethnography" was originally developed as part of my work plan to investigate the impact of social science knowledge on Southeast Asian refugee policy—although the exercise can be modified easily for health or other types of policy research.

Step 1: Identification of an Issue

Medical anthropology students may need fairly extensive practice in delineating public-policy issues because of the need to reason in a culture-bound framework and to consider vested interests in an unfamiliar, litigious model. Anthropological theory includes models of "real" and "ideal" culture, binary social structures and opposing clans, but none of these quite incorporates the notion of opposing interest groups with conflicting basic values and alternative approaches to achieving "a good society," such as the policy analyst finds in a complex, industrial society. Furthermore, anthropologists are often unfamiliar with the basic issues in domestic health policy that center on diagnostic and payment systems, reimbursement, insurance, and, in general, the issues central to the administration of the enormous federally funded "entitlement programs" in modern America. And, to date, anthropological research on services for minority Americans has not achieved a prominent place in the health care services research literature—a position it should have and hopefully will achieve in the 1990s.

Medical anthropology students should begin to define health-issue areas by following an outline modified from Coplin and O'Leary and other policy analysts. They should: (1) identify initial, potential health issues in the popular press or in the media, or use Table 1 as a starting point (sometimes there is no real issue if parties do not truly disagree); (2) narrow each health issue into two or more columns of fundamental, oppositional statements about how the program or policy option helps to achieve "a good society," or "healthy Americans" (there can be some overlap in statements, but the total set of statements must be unique for each column); (3) identify all interested parties associated with each column of statements (these are the "policy participants"); (4) list vested interests of all parties (Ask: "What is in it for each policy participant?" or, "What does each stand to gain?"); and (5) list the broad, philosophical values on which vested interests are based (Coplin and O'Leary 1988a). This type of issue definition can be achieved for any level of organization or society, from the student's own campus to the national level. Sometimes, the local community is the best place to start because "experts" are most readily accessible for personal interviews to help define the basic issues and the values behind them. Otherwise, the student must outline a set of oppositional views by reading or listening to secondary sources.

Step 2: Research the Issue

The medical anthropology student then completes quick-and-dirty library research in all academic and applied fields related to the issue. Going back more than ten years is usually a waste of time, as good references will give an adequate history of the issue. The most recent references are the most useful, especially yet-unpublished information gained on the telephone. It is important to remember that, at this point, the goal of a policy ethnography is not methodological excellence—although the student certainly requires knowledge of it and its standards. The goal is to obtain a broad overview of data sources and the potential light they can shed on the views of policy participants. Students should survey documents such as public health reports, birth and death statistics, community surveys by citizens groups, newspaper and magazine surveys, and interviews. They should make telephone calls to representatives of all interested parties and arrange for interviews to discuss the chosen issue. Some of the best work of this type is pursued on campus by students who work for the university newspaper. Enough facility should be gained on the telephone so that the "policy ethnographer" can, with little trouble, call and ask any public figure or his or her representative, about an issue. Contacts should proceed in a network fashion, using one reference to lead to another.

Step 3: Conduct Elite Interviews

Feldman (1981) provides a guide for elite interviews of the types useful in policy ethnography. Interviews must be open-ended and flexible but should focus on the same basic topics for all policy participants. The interviewer should demonstrate solid knowledge of the issues in a short, pointed list of questions. The policy ethnographer must also be sophisticated about the vested interests of the respondents, who will not be forthcoming if they suspect that they are jeopardizing their position by revealing too much. Policy ethnography involves rapid assessment because public policy issues change quickly in response to many pressures, and there is little time to assimilate relevant knowledge, analyze, write, and publish. The elite interview is the best way to achieve up-to-the-minute understanding of a controversy, and many good interviews can be completed on the telephone.

Step 4: Complete a Policy Analysis

The policy analysis can be either formal or informal, and should follow the steps described above, including: (1) determine the objectives of the analysis; (2) determine the issues, and outline the values and self-interests of all policy participants; (3) List program or policy alternatives and collect data on each alternative that is relevant to the choice between alternatives; (4) build a model to explain how the variables operate to produce outcomes in the program or policy alternatives; and (5) optionally, select the preferred alternative based on the values and self-interests of the decision maker, and explain your recommendation.

Step 5: Report

The policy ethnographer should practice reporting in a variety of formats: an article for the student newspaper, a speech before service providers, a presentation to public health officials (or a letter to them or the editors of a city newspaper), a workshop module for fellow students, or, if possible, a radio or television interview or debate at a public hearing. A formal report includes a pithy summary, a relatively brief text, and a correspondingly long documentation appendix. This format provides the best chance that policy makers will read the summary and that their staffers will have an opportunity to wade through the analysis in the text and the appendix. Few top-level decision makers have time to read more than several pages of any single report, and program managers may not read that much unless prompted.

The policy-ethnography exercise outlined here is a research form that can require a staff. Two or more students may work as a team. Once mastered, the technique facilitates all tasks requiring interaction with public-sector officials.

Conclusion

There is a long tradition in anthropology of involvement in public debates and government activities. The beginning practitioner should understand that the controversy surrounding some of this involvement is shared by other disciplines in both the natural and social sciences. However, controversy is a healthy sign of the dynamic balance between academia and government. Policy science in the 1990s will make increasing use of the policy analysis paradigm, and will prove to be useful for both academic anthropologists and practitioners as they contribute increasingly to the debate surrounding important health issues.

Practice in Policy Research

Three domestic health problem situations are described. Answer the questions that follow each exercise. (These and similar references may be helpful in your research exercises: Abt 1988; Hoaglin 1982; Rich 1981a, 1981b.)

Exercise 1: Health Policy Work at the Local Level
The Disposal of Toxic Hospital Wastes

Happyland Hospital is a 400-bed facility located in a hilly, suburban location in one of the New England states. In the past year, children at a nearby school have shown a two-fold increase in some infectious diseases, including hepatitis. A parents' group accused the hospital of negligence in disposing of their infectious hospital wastes. The parents' group paid a local laboratory to make tests of surrounding water supplies, which were inconclusive. The hospital administration wants to drop the matter because they fear the bad publicity. They stand behind the waste disposal company that they hired on the recommendation of someone on the hospital board of directors. The hospital was able to acquire the disposal company's services at a discount of 30% because it was owned by a relative of the hospital board member. The hospital claims that it will not be able to continue to stay open and offer services to the community (including treatment of several hundred indigent cases per year in their emergency room) if their administrative costs rise any further (see Crandall and Lave 1981).

1. Identify the basic issue.

2. Identify the opposing parties and possible alliances. Speculate on other local policy participants who might take a side in the controversy.

3. Identify the basic, fundamental values underlying each of the opposing parties. Consider the following positive values, and add to the list.

Fair access to education	Security of kinship ties
Free enterprise	Fair access to health care
Equality	Freedom from disease
Environmental beauty	Equal protection under law

4. What secondary sources of information would you investigate to clarify the issue? What government agencies would you contact? List the types of experts that would be useful as consultants in your investigation. What type of works in the natural sciences would you tap into, if any?

5. List in order the people that you would try to interview locally. Careful! You will not be welcomed by all of them. How would you convince the reticent ones to submit to your interview?

6. List local government's program options. Which one maximizes the health of children and is least expensive to the hospital?

7. In developing recommendations for local government, how would you approach a business education campaign that targeted disposal of toxic hospital wastes? What values would you maximize in your approach? Would a public education campaign be among your recommendations? Why or why not?

8. What approach would you take to the development of a new, local regulation of ALL health care service organizations?

9. Can we learn anything about the disposal of toxic wastes from the archaeological record?

10. Can we take any lessons on environmental health from nonhuman primates?

Exercise 2: Health Policy Work at the State Level
Air Quality in Rural America

A mountainous county in rural Appalachia has shown a puzzling rise in chronic obstructive pulmonary disease (COPD), including emphysema and asthma. The lung cancer rate has also increased. Behavioral risk factors, like smoking, are the most obvious explanation. However, evidence is growing that airborne industrial wastes have been transported from chemical plants in two other counties, and may contribute to the rise in COPD. The county government has asked the State Health Department to investigate, and the project has been assigned to you. You have one month to develop a set of recommendations.

1. List the individuals you would interview on a field trip to the rural county.

2. List the federal agencies you might contact for help. Is there any federal agency that is ideally suited to investigate?

3. Speculate on possible federal-state-local interactions in the developing a solution to the problem. Remember that you work for the state. Therefore, what are your primary objectives and your own vested interests as a bureaucrat in state government?

4. Given your knowledge of rural Appalachian cultural values, how would you approach a public education campaign against smoking?

5. Given your knowledge of economic difficulties in rural America, how would you approach the large industries which may be producing airborne toxins?

6. Outline the vested interests of the following three groups in terms of economic growth, environmental beauty, and health quality: the tourist in-

dustry in rural Appalachia; the owners of manufacturing businesses in rural Appalachia; retired coal miners in rural Appalachia.

7. Take a systems approach to COPD, and develop a model to explain its rate. Identify the major social institutions that may affect its rate; do this separately for the federal, state, and local levels. Identify major conduits of information about COPD, between the people, industry, voluntary and membership associations, the government (executive, legislative, and judiciary). Select the structural "entry point" where you would concentrate your efforts to affect change in the rate of COPD.

Exercise 3: Health Policy Work at the National Level
Health Insurance for Hispanic Workers

You work in Washington, D.C., for a special health lobbying group that has been alerted to the low rate of health insurance among Hispanic workers in the United States. Your goal is to improve the rate of coverage (see Swartz 1989).

1. You decide that your first task is to document the problem well. How would you plan an effort to collect the best statistics nationwide on health coverage of Hispanics? After you decide on the subtasks involved, budget the tasks by the approximate time required, and assign subtasks to the staff you think will be required. Do a staff-by-task-by-time chart.

2. You decide that the next step will be a research effort to discover what the problem looks like on the local level. This research will involve Hispanic workers and their supervisors. Plan a research project to investigate a selected number of workers at a selected number of sites, using a case study methodology. Ask: What will a "case" consist of?—a worker, a work location, a city, what? How will you select your cases? Will you make your selections based, for example, on proportion of Hispanic workers in a state or city? Or the size of the resident Hispanic populations? Design a plan to select your cases, and then select your cases. Then, budget staff, time, tasks (including questionnaire construction), travel, analysis and report writing. If you will need computer time budget that in too.

3. Plan and conduct a telephone survey of representatives of major health insurance companies to determine their constraints and possible incentives for them to encourage broader coverage of Hispanics.

4. Develop a mailing list of the types of individuals you would send a press release telling about the findings in your report.

Notes

1. The importance of anthropologists' role in developing patient compliance developed initially in a discussion with Robert F. Hill of the University of Oklahoma Health Sci-

ences Center, as we prepared for a season entitled, "How Can Anthropology Help Bring Down Health Costs?" at the 1988 meeting of the Society for Applied Anthropology in Tampa, Florida.

2. There are efforts to collect some of the reports and documents prepared by practicing professionals. Write and send materials to John Van Willigen, Applied Anthropology Documentation Collection, Special Collections and Archives, King Library-North, University of Kentucky, Lexington, KY 40506.

3. The *Policy Research Centers Directory* and *Policy Grants Directory* are both published by Policy Studies and edited by Stuart Nagel and Marian Neef. They are available in most large libraries. The *Directory of Washington Internships* can be obtained from the National Society for Internships and Experimental Education, Washington, D.C. Career services offices on individual campuses will be able to identify other internship directories.

References Cited

Abt, Clark C. (ed.)
    1988   Problems in American Social Policy Research. Cambridge, MA: Abt Books for the Council for Applied Social Research.
Bermant, Gordon
    1982   Justifying Social Science Research in Terms of Social Benefit. *In* Ethical Issues in Social Science Research. Tom L. Beauchamp et al, eds. Baltimore: Johns Hopkins University Press.
Brewer, Garry D.
    1981   Where the Twain Meet: Reconciling Science and Politics in Analysis. Policy Sciences 13:269-279.
Bulmer, Martin
    1982   The Uses of Social Research: Social Investigation in Public Policymaking Boston: G. Allen & Unwin.
    1987 (ed.)   Social Science Research and Government: Comparative Essays on Britain and the United States. New York: Cambridge University Press.
Coplin, William D., and Michael K. O'Leary
    1988a   Public Policy Skills. Croton-on-Hudson, NY: Policy Studies Associates.
    1988b   Public Policy Skills Workbook. Croton-on-Hudson, NY: Policy Studies Associates.
    1988c   Effective Participation in Government; A Problem-Solving Manual. Croton-on-Hudson, NY: Policy Studies Associates.
Crandall, Robert W., and Lester B. Lave (eds.)
    1981   The Scientific Basis of Health and Safety Regulation. Washington, DC: The Brookings Institution.
de Leon, Peter
    1981   Policy Sciences: The Discipline and the Profession. Policy Sciences 13(1):1–7.
Department of Health and Human Services
    1986   The 1990 Health Objectives for the Nation: A Midcourse Review. Washington, DC: Department of Health and Human Services.
    1990   Promoting Health/Preventing Disease: Year 2000 Objectives for the Nation. Washington, DC: Department of Health and Human Services.
Douglas, Mary
    1982   Risk and Culture. Berkeley: University of California Press.

Feldman, Elliot J.
    1981   A Practical Guide to the Conduct of Field Research in the Social Sciences. Boulder, CO: Westview Press.
Fisher, Frank
    1980   Politics, Values, and Public Policy: The Problem of Methodology. Boulder, CO: Westview Press.
Harwood, Alan
    1981   Ethnicity and Medical Care. Cambridge, MA: Harvard University Press.
Hoaglin, David C.
    1982   Data for Decisions: Information Strategies for Policymakers. Cambridge, MA: Abt Books.
Jasanoff, Sheila
    1986   Risk Management and Political Culture: A Comparative Analysis of Science in the Policy Context. New York: Russell Sage Foundation.
Lave, Lester
    1982   Quantitative Risk Assessment in Regulation. Washington, DC: Brookings Institution.
Lynn, Laurence E.
    1987   Managing Public Policy. Boston: Little, Brown.
    1988   Designing Public Policy: A Casebook on the Role of Policy Analysis. Santa Monica, CA: Goodyear.
National Research Council, Committee on the Institutional Means for Assessment of Risks to Public Health
    1983   Risk Assessment in the Federal Government: Managing the Process. Washington, DC: National Academy Press.
Pet-Edwards, Julia
    1989   Risk Assessment and Decision Making Using Test Results: The Carcinogenicity Prediction and Battery Selection. New York: Plenum Press.
Quade, E. S.
    1975   Analysis for Public Decisions. New York: American Elsevier.
Rich, Robert F.
    1981a (ed.)   The Knowledge Cycle. Beverly Hills, CA: Sage Publications.
    1981b   Social Science Information and Public Policy Making. San Francisco: Josey-Bass.
Scientific American
    1989   Managing Planet Earth. Volume 261(3):Special Issue.
Singer, Merrill, Peggy Owens, and Lydia Reyes
    1989   Culturally Appropriate AIDS Prevention for IV Drug Users and Their Sexual Partners. Paper presented at the First NADR Conference, sponsored by the National Institute on Drug Abuse, Rockville, MD. October.
Swartz, Katherine
    1989   Chartbook on the Medically Uninsured. Lanham, MD: Urban Institute Pres.
Thomas, Patricia
    1985   The Aims and Outcomes of Social Policy Research. Dover, NH: Croom Helm.
Washington Post
    1990a   Medicaid Standards Called a Barrier for Hispanics. March 18, p. A10.
    1990b   Spending for Health Care Takes Record Bite of GNP. May 4, p. A7.

Weiss, Carol H.
   1980   Social Science Research and Decision-Making. New York: Columbia University Press.
   1988   Reporting of Social Science in the National Media. New York: Russell Sage Foundation.

chapter three

International Health: Overview and Opportunities

BARBARA L. K. PILLSBURY

E ach year hundreds of organizations headquartered in the more affluent or technologically developed countries of the world spend hundreds of millions of dollars in projects and programs designed to improve the health of poor people in the less-developed countries of Asia, Africa, and Latin America. This is the core of the field of activity referred to as "international health." It is a field that offers important roles and challenges to anthropologists who possess the proper mix of professional training and personal skills and who are interested in combining work in the health-care field with that in developing countries.

This chapter provides some answers to the following questions: (1) What exactly is "international health"? (2) Where and how does international health work take place? (3) How does social science, especially anthropology, fit into international health? (4) What kind of employment is available? (5)What skills do anthropologists need? (6) What strategies can an anthropologist use to find work in international health? (7) What might the future hold in store?[1]

What is "International Health"?

"International health" may be defined as a multidisciplinary body of knowledge and activities pertaining to the factors that affect the health of the world's people and to the methods and techniques for providing improved health care to all people in the world. The term usually includes nutrition and population/family planning as well, since diet and childbearing are also critical determinants of health. In principle, international health means a comparative understanding of the health of all populations of the world.[2]

In actual practice, international health tends to be a more ethnocentric term, meaning essentially "factors affecting health status and health programs in all countries but my own." It particularly refers to efforts funded by organizations in developed countries to improve the health of the rural and urban poor in the developing (or "less-developed") countries. Thus it is both an intellectual body of knowledge and a form of technology transfer—usually from the richer to the poorer countries. Various programs of "technical cooperation among developing countries" ("TCDC" in United Nations phraseology) also work toward improved health in Asia, Africa, and Latin America.

The core work of international health may be summed up as: (1) problem identification and analysis; (2) interventions, or measures to remedy critical problems; and (3) evaluation of the effectiveness of the intervention. The problem is virtually always defined in terms of a specific population—for example, extremely high infant mortality (about 200 per 1000 live births) in rural Sierra Leone, a serious increase in malaria transmission in Sri Lanka, or lack of clean drinking water and sanitary facilities in the overcrowded slum areas of Cairo.

The field of international health comprises numerous areas of specialized knowledge and therefore employs people who possess such expertise. These areas require expertise concerning:

- *People and their characteristics:* geographic distribution; distribution by age, sex, ethnicity and residence; population density and fertility patterns; social and cultural characteristics; the status and roles of women; sociopolitical and economic characteristics; genetic and biological characteristics; health-seeking and other behavioral patterns.

- *Health consequences of the environment:* immediate, community, and regional environments; epidemiological investigation; direct and indirect transmission of disease; infectious disease control.

- *Planning and development:* investment in health as a factor in socioeconomic development; health planning as an element of development planning; linkages with other development sectors (especially education and agriculture).

- *Family planning/reproductive health care:* family planning information and communication; family planning services; women's health; linkages between population growth and socioeconomic development; population planning; demography; maternal health; relationships to other health problems.

- *Nutrition:* food production and distribution; food habits and their impacts (e.g., on infants, children, pregnant, and lactating women); malnutrition; linkages to infection; nutrition education.

- *Water and sanitation:* rural and urban water supply; excreta disposal; hygiene education; community management of improved systems; links to other health interventions.

- *Health education and communication:* strategies (in-school, community-based, mass media, etc.) to instruct or guide the public in such areas as improved sanitation, childhood immunization, prenatal care, family planning, and nutrition.

- *Health care financing:* resources for services (human, facilities, drugs, supplies, and equipment); alternative strategies and costs of providing health care; ability and willingness of public to pay for services.

- *Health systems and services management and administration:* of primary health care (including health, family planning, and nutrition); of additional personal health care services (including hospitals, emergency medical services, chronic disease treatment, dental health, mental health, venereal disease treatment, and rehabilitative medicine).

• *Monitoring and evaluation:* of health and nutritional status and changes therein; of fertility and population change; of project or program outcomes and impact.

The term international health is used chiefly in academic and related professional contexts, where international health is regarded as a specialization within the health field. (For example, International Health is one of several formal sections within the American Public Health Association, and a Washington DC-based organization has the name National Council for International Health.)

Operationally, outside academic circles, international health is generally referred to as one of several "development sectors"—a sort of specialization—within the field of international development, which in turn is also called economic development, foreign aid, and international development assistance.[3] (The term "foreign aid" sometimes means both *economic aid*—for socioeconomic development—and *military aid*. Here we are discussing only the former.)[4]

In the development/foreign aid context, international health work is typically referred to as "the health sector" and it competes for funds, not with other health specializations, but with other development sectors such as agriculture, education, environment, and rural development. In some cases, the health sector is referred to as "health, population, and nutrition." In other cases, nutrition and population may be treated organizationally as separate sectors, even though the direct linkages among the three are clearly recognized.

Background and Settings

The settings in which international health work occurs are thus both academic and applied, with the applied being of central importance here.

As in all international development work, the basic structure is usually one in which a wealthier "donor" (country or organization) provides funding and/or technical assistance (goods or services) to a "recipient" (country or organization) in the Third World. This may be handled as either a gift ("grant") or through a low-interest, long-term loan.

For well over a century the people of wealthier countries, through charitable (especially religious), professional, and commercial organizations have had an influence on the health and well-being of populations overseas. Their governments likewise have become officially involved in health work in other nations. During the colonial period European nations provided some health services to their colonies, but these were to protect their own citizens or they were extensions of domestic interests in overseas empires. Not surprisingly, control of communicable diseases was a major priority in those early days. The idea of "foreign aid," other than to colonies, is a recent phenomenon, arising in part from American relief efforts in Europe after the First World War but becoming institutionalized only following the Second World War. Today the scene is much changed with Japan in 1989 having become the major foreign-aid donor in total official funding amounts.

The scene is also considerably changed because of the health-improvement strategies that the donor countries now pursue. In earlier decades most assistance went to establishing and supporting hospitals and other urban-based curative facilities. In the 1970s, however, funding shifted to favor broader-based health systems, usually referred to as "basic health services" or "primary health care" (see below).

Motivations for both private and governmental programs vary widely in their blend of self-interest and altruism. The motives may include: (1) desire for goodwill, prestige, or political influence; (2) humanitarianism; (3) national protection and defense against communicable diseases; (4) willingness to respond to specific requests or pressure from other governments; (5) advancement of knowledge, research, and learning in medical sciences; and (6) support or protection of private investments. Both explicit and underlying motivations for a particular project or program will depend on the nature and priorities of the particular donor, as well as on those of the recipient nation.[5]

Current Priorities in International Health

The primary health care approach, as an alternative to physician-centered curative care, had been discussed and tested in pilot projects since the late 1960s and even earlier.[6] In 1978, however, it was resoundingly acclaimed as the preferred approach for bringing about "health for all by the year 2000." This occurred at the International Conference on Primary Health Care, sponsored by the World Health Organization (WHO) and the United Nations International Children's Emergency Fund (UNICEF) in Alma-Ata in the USSR. The "Declaration of Alma-Ata" issued by the delegates to the conference became the bible, so to speak, of the primary health care (PHC) movement (WHO and UNICEF 1978).

Primary health care, it was hoped, would be a cost-effective means to expand access to essential health-related services, particularly in underserved areas. PHC denotes a basic package of preventive, promotive, and curative services effective against major causes of death and illness. Prominently included are nutrition, family planning, and water and sanitation. At the community level, basic services are provided by minimally trained, community-based workers who are supported by a referral system of more specialized health facilities and personnel. Active community involvement is a central tenet of primary health care. All this was clearly part of the philosophical and policy orientation in international development prevailing after the mid-1970s: an approach referred to as "basic human needs," "putting people first," "development by people," and so on (e.g., Cernea 1985; Chambers 1983; Coombs 1980; and Gran 1983).

Primary health care was formally incorporated into the policies and strategies of most developing country ministries of health and of most donor organizations concerned with health in developing countries.[7] For example, in 1980 the policies dictating the use of U.S. government funds for health work in the developing countries gave first priority to "low-cost primary health care services," emphasizing maternal and child health, nutrition, and family planning, with three other specified priorities being improved water and sanitation, selected disease control, and health planning.[8] Most Western European donors also adopted this priority for primary health care. A minority of donors, however, notably Arab countries and Japan, tended to continue in the earlier "bricks-and-mortar" mode, funding construction of hospitals, clinics, and other buildings.

At the same time as the primary health care was being adopted by many developing country governments, however, it was also coming under criticism as too costly and too difficult to carry out successfully. "The goal set at Alma Ata is above reproach, yet its very scope makes it unattainable because of the cost and numbers of trained personnel required" stated one influential pair of critics (Walsh and Warren 1979). Planners had been overly optimistic too, about the interest of communities in participating in preventive health care activities and about the willingness of community health workers to work for no or little pay.[9] Furthermore, improvements in health status would be hard to achieve and document in the short term. This was becoming an especially important concern in the United States, where the Congress (which must authorize spending for foreign aid) was demanding prompt, quantifiable results.

This led to advocacy for "selective primary health care" as an alternative to broad-based *comprehensive* primary health care. Proponents of selective primary health argued that it would be more cost effective for governments and donors to invest scarce health funds on a limited number of proven interventions—e.g., measles and diphtheria-pertussis-tetanus vaccination, treatment for febrile malaria, and oral rehydration for diarrhea in children. Despite criticism, interest in selective PHC quickly evolved into more focused programs (Berman 1982; Gish 1982; Kendall 1988; Rifkin and Walt 1986, 1988).

Specifically, this evolved into "child survival," an approach which had an immediate appeal to developing country governments and donor-country policy makers alike. Every year about 15 million infants and children die, most from diseases that are no longer life threatening in developed countries and that could be prevented in developing countries by known technologies. By 1985, the United Nations International Children's Emergency Fund (UNICEF) had launched a program for a "child survival revolution" declaring that four major interventions were key to preventing childhood deaths and illness in developing countries. These were growth monitoring, oral rehydration therapy (ORT), breastfeeding, and immunization—a set of interventions dubbed "GOBI." This was subsequently expanded to "GOBI-FFF" with the addition of Female education, Family spacing, and Food supplements (Cash, Keusch, and Lamstein 1987). Saving the lives of children (especially through interventions heralded as cost effective and able to show dramatic results) also appealed to the U.S. Congress which, at about the same time, authorized substantial funding for a large child survival program to be carried out by the U.S. Agency for International Development (Agency for International Development 1990).

Women's health, especially reduction of high maternal mortality and morbidity rates, has been recognized in many countries as an important parallel priority.[10] The World Bank brought material health to the fore with its "Safe Motherhood Program" and the International Women's Health Coalition has led in developing a comprehensive approach to women's reproductive health (e.g., Germain and Ordway 1989). There has also been increased recognition that improving the status of women is essential for improving both their health and that of their children and households (e.g., Browner 1989). AIDS, of course, has also become a priority concern, especially in sub-Saharan Africa where its incidence is high.

Finally, "sustainability" has become an overriding priority in all donor-supported health, family planning, and nutrition programs. Sustainability means the ability of developing countries (governments and citizens) to carry out program activities and to continue providing benefits once donor support for a project or program has ended. There are at least three major reasons that sustainability has recently become a priority. First, by the 1980s it had become manifestly clear to the donors that many of the activities initiated and facilities built through their projects were not continued, or were grossly underutilized, after the donor's involvement had ended.

Second were drastic changes in the global economy. For roughly the first 30 years after World War II, the international economic climate for developing nations was favorable; there was rising international demand for their exports and ready sources of capital were made available by lending institutions in the developed countries. Since the mid-70s, however, the economies of developing countries have been adversely effected by drastic external shocks—violent swings in oil prices, the severe economic recession of the early 1980s, demands for debt repayment by the international banks, and demands by international agencies for major policy adjustments, including cuts in government expenditures for health and social services (Bell and Reich 1988).

A third factor is continuing rapid population growth in the developing countries—at the same time as governments and donors alike have relatively less to spend, on a per capita basis, for health care. Despite the progress family planning programs have made in reducing growth *rates* in many countries, the youthfulness of their populations means that the population size will still continue to grow well into the 21st century. This has further fueled the donors' desire that their scarce funds be invested only in activities that the recipients will be willing and able to sustain.[11]

The Donor Organizations

The many hundreds of donors involved in international health, family planning, and nutrition are of six major types, all of which employ or have employed anthropologists. They are (1) international (multilateral) agencies, (2) governmental (bilateral) agencies, (3) private and voluntary organizations, (4) universities and professional and technical associations, (5) philanthropic foundations, and (6) private and commercial firms.

International (Multilateral) Organizations. International organizations are official bodies directed and funded "multilaterally," that is, by a number of nations working in collaboration, often on a regional basis and, in many cases, as a "specialized agency'' or other affiliate of the United Nations. Primary among the UN specialized agencies working in health is the World Health Organization (WHO), which has headquarters in Geneva, six regional offices (for Africa, Southeast Asia, the Eastern Mediterranean, the Western Pacific, the Americas, and Europe), and numerous field projects. (The official functions of WHO are listed in Figure 1.) WHO policies are established by the World Health Assembly, which consists of delegates from well over 100 member nations. This body convenes annually in Geneva and directly influences the health work of member nations and of organizations.[18]

FIGURE 1

**Functions of the World Health Organization
(as specified in WHO Constitution, Article 2)**

1.   To act as the directing and coordinating authority on international health work.

2.   To establish and maintain effective collaboration with the United Nations, specialized agencies, governmental health administrations, professional groups, and such other organizations as may be deemed appropriate.

3.   To assist governments, on request, in strengthening health services.

4.   To furnish appropriate technical assistance and, in emergencies, necessary aid, on request or acceptance of governments.

5.   To provide or assist in providing, on the request of the United Nations, health services and facilities to special groups, such as peoples of trust territories.

6.   To establish and maintain such administrative and technical services as may be required, including epidemiological and statistical services.

7.   To stimulate and advance work to eradicate epidemic, endemic, and other diseases.

8.   To promote, in cooperation with other specialized agencies, the prevention of accidental injuries.

9.   To promote, in cooperation with other specialized agencies where necessary, the improvement of nutrition, housing, sanitation, recreation, economic or working conditions, and other aspects of environmental hygiene.

10.   To promote cooperation among scientific and professional groups that contribute to the advancement of health.

11.   To propose conventions, agreements, and regulations, and make recommendations with respect to international health matters and to perform such duties as may be assigned thereby to the Organization and are consistent with its objective.

12.   To promote maternal and child health and welfare and to foster the ability to live harmoniously in a changing total environment.

13.   To foster activities in the field of mental health, especially as affects the harmony of human relations.

14.   To promote and conduct research in the field of health.

15. To promote improved standards of teaching and training in the health, medical, and related professions.

16. To study and report on, in cooperation with other specialized agencies where necessary, administrative and social techniques affecting public health and medical care from preventive and curative points of view, including hospital services and social security.

17. To provide information, counsel, and assistance in the field of health.

18. To assist in developing an informed public opinion among all peoples on matters of health.

19. To establish and revise as necessary international nomenclatures of diseases, of causes of death, and of public health practices.

20. To standardize diagnostic procedures as necessary.

21. To develop, establish, and promote international standards with respect to food, biological, pharmaceutical, and similar products.

Another UN specialized agency, the United Nations Fund for Population Assistance (UNFPA) similarly serves a central role in supporting the family planning programs crucial to improving women's and children's health and well-being. UNICEF is the lead UN specialized agency working in child health programs and has been a leader in efforts to train and collaborate with traditional birth attendants. Both organizations are headquartered in New York City. The United Nations Educational, Scientific, and Cultural Organization (UNESCO) also plays important roles, especially in health education. The Food and Agriculture Organization (FAO) and World Food Programme are important in the nutrition sector.

The giant of the funding agencies working in international development is the World Bank (formally, the International Bank for Reconstruction and Development [IBRD]), headquartered in Washington, DC. The Bank traditionally provides large loans to governments, as opposed to grants and personnel-intensive technical assistance, and thus has concentrated more on "bricks and mortar" (construction) activities. Recently, however, it has also become more concerned in its health, nutrition, and population projects with human, quality, and utilization issues (see Akin, Birdsall, and de Ferranti 1987).

Other international agencies, or "multilaterals," active in international health work are listed in Figure 2.

FIGURE 2

International Multilateral Organizations Having Interest in International Health (partial listing)

ACAST	Advisory Committee on the Application of Science and Technology to Development (a)
ADB	Asian Development Bank
AfDB	African Development Bank

AfDF	African Development Fund
ASEAN	Association of Southeast Asian Nations
CACM	Central American Common Market
CEEC	Committee for European Economic Cooperation
CFNI	Caribbean Food and Nutrition Institute
CIEC	Conference on International Economic Cooperation
CGIAR	Consultative Group on International Agriculture Research
CIAP	Inter-American Committee on the Alliance for Progress
DAC	Development Assistance Committee of the OECD
ECA	Economic Commission for Africa (a)
ECLA	Economic Commission for Latin America (a)
ECOSOC	Economic and Social Council (a)
ECWA	Economic Commission for Western Asia
EDF	European Development Fund
EEC	European Economic Community
ESCAP	Economic and Social Commission for Asia and the Pacific (a)
FAO	Food and Agriculture Organization (b)
GATT	General Agreement on Tariffs and Trade (c)
IAEA	International Atomic Energy Agency (c)
IARC	International Agency for Research on Cancer (WHO)
IBRD	International Bank for Reconstruction and Development (the World Bank) (b)
IDA	International Development Association (b)
IDB	Inter-American Development Bank
IFAD	International Fund for Agricultural Development
IFC	International Finance Corporation (b)
ILO	International Labour Organization
IMF	International Monetary Fund (b)
INCAP	Institute of Nutrition of Central America and Panama
LAS	League of Arab States
OAS	Organization of American States
OAU	Organization of African Unity
OECD	Organization for Economic Cooperation and Development
PAHO	Pan American Health Organization (WHO) (b)
PASB	Pan American Sanitary Bureau (OAS)
UN	United Nations
UNCTAD	United Nations Conference on Trade and Development (a)
UNDP	United Nations Development Programme (a)
UNESCO	United Nations Educational, Scientific and Cultural Organization
UNFDAC	United Nations Fund for Drug Abuse Control (a)
UNFPA	United Nations Fund for Population Activities (a)
UNGA	United Nations General Assembly (a)
UNHCR	United Nations High Commissioner for Refugees (a)
UNICEF	United Nations International Children's Emergency Fund (a)
UNIDO	United Nations Industrial Development Organization (a)
UNIFEM	United Nations Development Fund for Women
UNRWA	United Nations Relief and Works Agency for Palestine Refugees in the Near East (a)
WFC	World Food Council

WFP	World Food Programme (FAO) (b)
WHO	World Health Organization
WMO	World Meteorological Organization
(a) = part of the United States	
(b) = U.N. specialized agency, or subsidiary thereof	
(c) = Agency in special relation to the United Nations	

Governmental (Bilateral) Agencies. Whereas "multilateral" means multiple donor governments collaborating to extend aid, "bilateral" refers to a relationship in which the government of one country extends aid directly to the government of another country. Most health aid is channeled to the recipient government's ministry of health to support programs agreed on by the ministry and the donor. In each donor country, its government has established a special agency with primary responsibility for "programming" such assistance. In the United States this is the Agency for International Development (AID, called USAID in developing countries), which is the major employer of American behavioral scientists for international health work, either directly or through the many organizations it funds for this work. In Canada, it is the Canadian International Development Agency (CIDA) which is assisted by the International Development Research Centre (IDRC); in Sweden it is the Swedish International Development Authority (SIDA), assisted by the Swedish Agency for Research Cooperation with Developing Countries (SAREC); in Japan it is the Japan International Cooperation Agency, and so on.

In addition, various sections of other government agencies become involved. For example, in the United States, the Peace Corps, the National Institutes of Health, the Centers for Disease Control (CDC), the Department of Health and Human Services, the Institute of Medicine at the National Academy of Sciences, the Department of Agriculture, the Bureau of the Census, and even Army and Naval research units all play selected roles, often funded by or in other types of collaboration with AID. In addition, significant proportions of the funds of numerous multilateral organizations (including WHO, UNFPA, and PAHO) come from the U.S. government; this may be upwards of 15%–30% of these organizations' budgets.

AID has its headquarters in Washington, DC, with resident field missions in over 50 countries around the world. Central responsibilities for health, family-planning, and nutrition programs are lodged in AID Washington's Office of Health, Office of Population, and Office of Nutrition, respectively, but a tremendous amount of additional health-related programming also takes place in regional bureaus and policy offices in Washington and operationally in the field missions, as well as through the U.S. government's Food for Peace program that works largely through AID.[13] U.S. government expenditures for health work in the developing countries currently amount to more than $300 million annually, although the exact amount is difficult to determine as it includes many different "accounts."

Private and Voluntary Organizations.   These are charitable and humanitarian organizations, often collectively referred to as "private voluntary organizations"
(PVOs) in the U.S. and "nongovernmental organizations" (NGOs) in the UN
system and in developing countries. The hundreds of such groups active in inter-
national health range from denominational religious organizations (e.g., Catholic
Relief Services and Seventh Day Adventists) to those with more muted religious
orientation (e.g., Medical Assistance Programs International and American
Friends Service Committee) to purely secular groups (e.g., Save the Children
Foundation, CARE, Rotary International, and the International Women's Health
Coalition). PVOs and NGOs range from large *international* NGOs, such as the
International Planned Parenthood Federation, which has affiliates and activities
in over 100 countries, to *national* NGOs working only in a single developing
country, to *local* grass-roots NGOs which may work only in a single community
in that country.

In contrast to government programs, PVO programs are smaller in scope and
are usually implemented in developing countries by their own field personnel or
by "indigenous NGOs" (i.e., host-country voluntary organizations). PVOs typically provide direct "people-to-people" aid rather than government-to-govern-
ment (and only then to-the-people) aid. Many PVOs, however, also work directly
with host-country governments in expanding and supplementing their health,
family planning, and nutrition programs. Finally, many PVOs do depend heavily
on government funding as well as on voluntary contributions. Most U.S.-based
PVOs working in health are members of the American Council of Voluntary
Agencies for Foreign Service and of the National Council for International
Health, which periodically collect and publish summaries of POV activities.
Globally, the International Council of Voluntary Agencies plays a similar role.[14]

Universities and Professional and Technical Associations.   Dozens of academic,
professional, and technical associations are funded by and work under contract or
in loose collaboration with the various official agencies. Their most important
functions include provision of technical specialists, training, and fellowships.
They also disseminate technical information, maintain professional standards,
and at times implement field projects. A major example has been the American
Public Health Association (APHA), headquartered in Washington, DC, which
has an International Health Section, maintains a consultants' roster, and has produced several useful state-of-the-art analyses in international health. The National
Council for International Health (NCIH), also located in Washington, provides a
somewhat similar brokering function.

Dozens of universities provide training for participants from overseas projects, conduct applied research on international health topics, and occasionally
provide technical assistance overseas as well. For example, Columbia University's Center for Population and Family Health has been working with Senegal's
Ministry of Health on an important study and strategy for reducing that country's
very high maternal mortality rates (Gueye et al. 1989). Some universities have
departments of international health (such as Harvard University and Johns Hop-

kins University, which now has a Center for International Community-Based Health Research and a new Social Science and Public Health doctoral training in International Health). Land-grant colleges or universities, through Title XII, often participate in food and nutrition work.

Philanthropic Foundations. Numerous philanthropic foundations have long been active in international health work, each having developed a specific field of interest and expertise in which it hopes to make a meaningful contribution toward solution of particular health-related problems. Preeminent among those that recognize the importance of behavioral-science contributions are the Rockefeller Foundation, the Ford Foundation, the Milbank Memorial Fund, and Carnegie Corporation (all headquartered in New York), and the Pathfinder Fund (based in Boston). Grantmakers in Health, in New York, serves as a clearinghouse for data on the activities and priorities of foundations, and also of corporations, working in health.

Private and Commercial Firms. Two types of private firms also play roles in international health. Of primary importance are the numerous *consulting firms* established chiefly to assists governments (donor and recipient) in project design and implementation. Examples include Management Sciences for Health (MSH), John Snow, Inc., Westinghouse, Medex, and Family Health International, based in Boston, Washington, Honolulu, and Chapel Hill, North Carolina, respectively. In contrast are the larger, profit-seeking *commercial firms,* including multinational corporations, notably pharmaceutical and medical-supply firms. In many cases the profit motives of such corporations prevail over concern for health improvement—a most dramatic example being the promotion of infant formula in the developing countries. However, they do also provide much-needed commodities, certain useful research training, and other development opportunities.[15]

Among the six types of organizations presented here, there is often healthy cooperation, but, occasionally, counterproductive overlap, competition, and jurisdictional disputes or "turf-battling." This is as true within the health sector as it is throughout the "aid community" in general—unfortunately. Often funds must flow from one organization (e.g., AID or WHO) through several smaller and more specialized, or local, organizations before they begin to reach the intended beneficiaries. Some organizations are restricted by their legal or organizational mandates from certain activities and thus must call on others to carry out functions critical to their own goals but which they themselves cannot fund. Personnel also move among organizations at a fairly high rate of turnover. The picture is a rather dizzying one, and a beginner may need several years to map it out clearly.[16] Understanding this complex scene, however, permits the participant in it to be significantly more effective.

Social Sciences, Especially Anthropology, in International Health

It is now quite well-recognized throughout the international health field that the enormous and complex task of improving health on a community-wide level requires not only medical but also social science (or behavioral science) expertise—that of anthropologists and others. From the social science perspective, this general recognition and the consequent hiring of larger numbers of social scientists does not yet go far enough, and the biomedical model remains too dominant. Nevertheless, the present situation represents significant improvement over earlier years.

In those early international health activities, program planners and field personnel operated on the basis of two assumptions: (1) that the most advanced Western medical practices and their institutional framework are absolutes that should function equally well in all settings, and (2) that people in developing countries will immediately perceive the advantages of adopting the new health practices and give up their old ones. Thus early workers in international health tended to see their task in simplistic, easily definable terms: transplant the Western medical model and health goals will be achieved.

By about 1950, international health specialists began to recognize that improving health conditions in developing countries would require more than this silver-platter approach. Slowly a new assumption supplanted the old ones: health programs in developing countries will be more successful if they take into consideration, in both design and implementation, the social, cultural, psychological, and economic characteristics of the intended beneficiaries (the so-called "target group"). It was believed that people in the developing countries want better health and will therefore give up deleterious health-related behaviors but must first be helped to recognize the advantage of doing so.[17]

Increasing numbers of behavioral scientists, including anthropologists, were brought in to work on the design of health projects during subsequent years. Initially their mandate was to identify the cultural, social, and psychological barriers inhibiting acceptance of new health measures so that health programs could be designed and introduced in accord with cultural expectations. Much anthropological work, not surprisingly, concerned traditional practitioners, especially birth attendants.[18] Where "community participation"—involvement of a project's intended beneficiaries in its design and implementation—was regarded as important for project success, anthropologists were increasingly asked how to bring about such participation.

Today the contributions of anthropologists in international health are significantly broader.[19] As anthropologists became more widely accepted in the field of social and economic development during the 1970s (in large part because of the emphasis on basic human needs and primary health care—approaches philosophically close to anthropological convictions) anthropologists assumed a wider range of roles. For a beginning anthropologist, the primary task may still be the description of the health behavior (including nutritional and fertility-related) behavior of specific population groups in a developing country. Once having gained such experience, however, many anthropologists now play more central roles in the design, implementation, and evaluation of projects intended to improve the health of those populations.

Another recent contribution by anthropologists has been the streamlining and adaptation of anthropological methods for use (by anthropologists and others) in program development and evaluation. This includes such areas as rapid rural appraisal, social marketing, and focus group research.

"Rapid rural appraisal" methodology has been an important contribution. Since the late 1970s, rural sociologists and agronomists had been using qualitative research methods for a process known as rapid rural appraisal. Anthropologists have now introduced this in the health field. It is called "rapid" because it does not call for the usual year in the field, but instead uses data collection guidelines and checklists to focus on a specific problem area for a period as brief as a few months or even only a few days. Time, complexity of the problem, and human and financial resources all combine to influence the actual length of field work.[20]

Finally, many medical anthropologists have become full-time staff members of development organizations and a good number hold or have held important policy and management positions.

Behavioral scientists who have succeeded in establishing a track record in some aspect of international health often feel very much a part of the interdisciplinary effort. In large organizations this interdisciplinary effort necessarily includes such colleagues as health planners, physicians, nurses, nutritionists, demographers, economists, sociologists, and policy analysts. When a team is brought together for activities such as project design or evaluation, the division of labor will depend on the nature of the particular activity. Larger teams tend to include four types of personnel: a physician, a nonphysician health specialist (e.g., nutritionist, health educator, or family planning specialist), a management specialist or health planner, and behavioral scientist (e.g., economist, anthropologist, or sociologist). Depending on the anthropologist's technical expertise, experience, and especially interactional skills, he or she may be directed to focus only on the cultural and community aspects of project work, or may be asked to join in the overall planning and negotiating stages as well.

Kinds of Employment

The tasks a medical anthropologist performs in international health depend, among other factors, on whether he or she is employed part- or full-time and on a short-term, long-term, or permanent basis. The most common arrangements are outlined in the following sections.

Short-Term Contract

"Short-term" usually means anywhere from about two weeks to about six months duration. Under such contracts the anthropologist (sometimes referred to as a "contractor") is hired to provide very specifically defined services, the terms for which vary from one organization to another. The four following kinds of work are typical.

First is *project design* work. This typically calls for travel to a developing country as part of a project design (or "feasibility") team whose task is to produce a document outlining the structure of the project being contemplated. The anthropologist may be required to write a part of the document describing the health-related behavior of the intended beneficiaries and how that would affect, and be affected by, the envisioned project. This is often called the "social analysis" or "social-soundness analysis."[21] Anthropologists are also occasionally hired as a team member for a *health-sector assessment* in a developing country.[22]

Second, the anthropologist may be contracted to join an *evaluation* (or "assessment") team that travels to the field to investigate and prepare a collective report detailing the strengths and shortcomings of an ongoing or already completed project or program.[23]

Third, and in contrast to such team efforts concerned with the actual mechanics of project work, anthropologists are contracted to do analysis that comes closer to being research, although it is still much more problem focused and time constrained than traditional academic research.[24] Often too, an anthropologist may be asked to produce a technical report (occasionally referred to as a "desk study") on cultural aspects of a particular health issue using available documentation rather than field visits.[25]

Fourth, several anthropologists may be brought into a large, applied research project. For example, each does an independent study in his or her country of expertise; all studies are on the same subject and follow the same research design, and everyone's findings are eventually put together in a joint report.[26]

A person working on a short-term contract may be referred to as a "contractor," "consultant," "temporary advisor," or "expert." This depends both on the hiring organization and on the individual's level of expertise. A first step is to get one's name placed on a "consultants' roster," which many organizations maintain. Being on the roster does not constitute work and does not even ensure actually being called on for work, but it may lead to such a request, especially if the right kind of interaction is maintained with professionals in the organization.

Often a consultant works on contract to a private consulting firm that in turn is working on contract to a governmental agency such as AID. A direct short-term with AID is usually referred to as a "personal-services contract" or even a "purchase order." A consultant may be required to produce a lengthy technical report or simply to provide sound, reliable professional advice, usually in the form of a short, strategically composed memo. Successful performance on one contract is likely to lead to additional ones or to other work with the same firm or agency.

Long-Term Contract

Occasionally an anthropologist is asked to join the staff of an organization for a period of one to three years. In contrast to short-term work, the anthropologist on a long-term contract has an office at the organization and works there rather than at home or out of a suitcase. In this case, one becomes involved in a much broader array of activities, ranging from mundane administrative chores to more glamorous policy work, and often has responsibilities for managing the work of others, including short-term contractors. WHO/Geneva, for example, hired an anthropologist on a three-year contract with its Special Programme in Human Reproduction; another social scientist recently headed the Social and Economic Working Group of WHO's Special Programme for Research and Training in Tropical Diseases; an anthropologist is Associate Director of the Water and Sanitation Project in Washington, DC.[27]

Permanent Employment

This public-sector equivalent of university tenure is offered by U.S. government agencies (such as AID and the Department of Health and Human Services) and by international organizations (e.g., the World Bank and UN agencies such as WHO, FAO, UNICEF, and UNFPA). Such employment is usually referred to as "career," "direct hire," "civil service," "foreign service," or "foreign service national" and carries the expectation of lifelong employment unless the employee's work is grossly unsatisfactory. Usually only U.S. citizens are eligible for U.S. government career appointments; multilateral organizations hire citizens from many countries. Some organizations have internship programs through which junior anthropologists have a chance to enter the career service—e.g., AID's International Development Intern (IDI) program or the intern program at the World Bank.

With career employment, the anthropologist enters into the daily business of the organization and may attain a high position in it. For example, in AID at least two anthropologists have recently served as mission directors, the position within AID analogous to that of ambassador, and medical anthropologists hold or have held such positions as senior health policy advisor in the Bureau for Program and Policy Coordination, Coordinator of the Child Survival Program, Director of the Office of Nutrition, and Chief for Research and Evaluation for Asia.[28]

To illustrate the specific tasks for which anthropologists are responsible in international health work and the skills required for carrying them out, two actual "position descriptions" (also called "job descriptions") are provided in Figures 3 and 4 below. One is for a headquarters position, the second for a field position in a developing country. The position description in Figure 3 was prepared for a full-time staff position in Washington, DC. Tasks and skills specified in this job description are characteristic of "headquarters" work. Central among them is understanding and being adept at bureaucratic politics.

The position description shown in Figure 4 was written to recruit a female anthropologist to a 2½-year field position with UNICEF in Pakistan. As is apparent, many of the skills required are similar to those for headquarters work. A field position, however, involves more contact with developing-country people—both officials and ordinary citizens.

FIGURE 3

Position Description for Chief of Applied Research Division, Office of Health, U.S. Agency for International Development, Washington, DC.[a]

Part I—Introduction

Incumbent serves as Chief of the Division of Applied Research in the Agency Directorate for Health, Bureau for Science and Technology. The incumbent is responsible for technical leadership for activities related to the Office of Health's applied research portfolio and the direction, allocation of resources, development, and administration of a global program of applied health research that contributes to sound sector planning and effective field programs of health services delivery.

Part II—Duties and Responsibilities

1. Directs an Agency-wide program of applied health research addressed at priority health problems of the developing world with special attention to the creation of effective, sustainable health services directed at the health and survival of children and mothers.

2. Supervises a professional multi-disciplinary staff with advanced degree training in public health, demography, epidemiology, other social sciences and related disciplines.

3. Conceives, plans, and oversees the implementation and evaluation of complex projects and programs involving multiple disciplines and a variety of academic, international, governmental and other public and private institutions as implementing agencies. Identifies critical research needs and key issues in developing countries and formulates Agency-wide goals and objectives for responding to those needs, taking into account and coordinating with research activities of other agencies. Determines the appropriate allocation and levels of funding among competing areas of applied health research, making modifications or adjustments when needed.

4. Provides the Agency with professional leadership and technical liaison to bring to bear the research capabilities of the Agency, the U.S. and international scientific community, industry, universities and other centers of excellence on the priority health problems of the developing world. Encourages centers of excellence in the U.S. and abroad to perform needed research and to strengthen their capacity and commitment to carry out relevant research on priority topics.

5. Establishes firm cooperation and collaborative efforts with research programs of concern and relevance to the Agency's policies and strategies in the health sector among international, governmental and non-governmental interests. Encourages joint efforts of the public and private sector.

6. Exercises a leadership role in the dissemination of relevant data and findings to field missions, projects and host country counterparts and other colleagues. Seeks innovative ways to disseminate key information and promote its use to strengthen health sector planning and programs.

7. Provides professional and technical leadership, advice and assistance on research matters to the Office of Health, regional bureaus and USAID missions on the formulation, implementation, design and evaluation of sound scientific and technical projects and on the use of research funding.

8. Establishes and maintains communications with professional organizations in the public and private sector with related expertise, such as professional associations, commissions and task forces, universities, international organizations and so forth. Among the concerned related organizations are: the Department of Health and Human Services and its agencies (e.g. Centers for Disease Control, National Institutes of Health); National Science Foundation; National Academy of Sciences; Institute of Medicine; Rockefeller Foundation; Ford Foundation; Social Science Research Council; National Council for International Health; American Medical Association; foreign and international organizations such as UNICEF and WHO.

9. Represents the Agency at governmental, inter-governmental, and non-governmental meetings concerned with needed research and the application of research findings.

10. Has responsibilities for staff development and training.

---

[a]This position was filled by Anthropologist Pamela Johnson.

And now, in contrast, a position for a field anthropologist:

FIGURE 4.

Position, Description for Anthropologist with UNICEF in Pakistan[a]

Post Title: Anthropologist (Female)
Organizational Unit: Programme Section Unit for Baluchistan
Duty Station: UNICEF Sub-office, Quetta
Purpose: Development of baseline ethnographic data on traditional patterns of culture in Baluchistan to assist Project Staff in establishing rapport and gaining community support for objectives of the Baluchistan Integrated Area Development (BIAD) Action Plan.

Identification and interpretation of social and cultural constraints, especially regarding mother and child health and attendant problems (e.g., nutritional habits) which may inhibit implementation of programme objectives.

Preparation of material to guide Project staff in familiarizing themselves with indigenous Baluchistan lifestyles, thus promoting awareness of regional diversity and sensitivity to local perceptions of felt-needs and ensuring community participation on objectives achievement.

Major Duties and Responsibilities:

1. Advise BIAD staff on research methodology, fieldwork techniques, sampling design and analysis/interpretation of statistical and other field data.
2. Participate as a team member to assist with:
    (a) Compiling representative village profiles with a view to gaining comprehensive perspectives on the social and cultural components which may enhance/retard implementation of the BIAD programme.
    (b) Carrying out in-depth studies into indigenous ethnomedical concepts and practices which appear to have substantial influences on or relevance to the development and operation of the BIAD programme at cluster level (for example: customary child rearing practices; use and influence of traditional health practitioners, e.g., *hakims, pirs, duis,* and *shamans;* belief systems regarding the nature of good and bad health, the causality diagnosis, and curing of diseases; and socially sustained concepts concerning food, water, sanitation, and cleanliness.
    (c) Integrating ethnographic factors into the overall strategy of the Programme and its implementation especially regarding the education/motivation inputs and evaluating the performances of these approaches.

(d) Developing a research scheme for the mobile teams and others involved with community activities so that these activities harmonize with the diverse felt needs and wants of the individual target communities and also with their local level social organization.

(e) Preparing a course of study for training field staff, that will readily be understood by them, allow them to interact in a sensitive manner with villagers, and permit feedback into the Programme design.

(f) Selecting and training interviewers required for anthropological and health studies.

(g) Developing a simplified method for tabulation and analysis of data that can be readily intelligible to mobile technical teams carrying out social anthropological research components and will take account the diverse backgrounds and specific experience of the different members of the team.

(h) Supervising the tabulation and analysis of social and cultural data and recommending methods and techniques for utilizing the findings to promote the goals of the Programme, in accordance with the data and as new shifts of emphasis within the Programme dictate.

3. Undertake any other duties and responsibilities which may be assigned by the Programme Office pertinent to the activity components outlined above.

Supervisory Responsibility: Supervises one assistant anthropologist officer and one secretary (shared).

Personal Contacts:

(a) Internal:
- All staff of the Programme Section, Water Supply and Environmental Sanitation Section, Information and Programme Support Communication Section, and other technical staff as required. (Frequent.)
- Representative staff on the Planning, Supply Administration, Finance, Personnel Sections. (Occasional.)

(b) External:
- Secretarial and Directorate staff of Planning and Development, BIAD, Health, Education, Irrigation, Social Welfare Department, Local Government, district level elected representatives, and administration in the province. (Frequent.)
- Secretaries and Directors of line departments Provincial and Divisional elected representatives and administration. (Occasional.)

Working Conditions: Involves frequent travel throughout province to programme clusters to carry out or monitor anthropological research activities and efficacy of recommendations selected for implementation.

Job Statistics. Though not directly responsible for the management of resources, the financial impact of technical advice on the UNICEF-assisted BIAD Project can be significant. The total UNICEF-assisted BIAD Project can be significant. The total UNICEF assistance to the social section of BIAD is approximately U.S. $10 million.

Minimum Qualification Requirements Essential to This Post:
Education: Ph.D. in Anthropology
Language(s): Fluency in English and working knowledge in Urdu.

Specialized Training: Medical Anthropology.
Experience: Minimum 5 years of field experience.

---

^aPamela Hunte filled this position

What Skills Do Anthropologists Need?

As the above position descriptions illustrate, a wide diversity of skills is asked of the anthropologist working in international health. Some are more essential than others, and, understandably, more skills are expected at a senior level than for an entry-level position.

Required, Expert Skills

The following list includes those essential skills that the medical anthropologist must have to be effective in international health work.

1. Detailed familiarity (including field experience) with one major geographical region (Africa, Asia, Latin America, or the Middle East) and with at least one country (preferably a significant one).
2. Language fluency (French, Spanish, and Arabic are most sought after).
3. Knowledge of traditional/indigenous health (including fertility and food) beliefs, behavior, specialists, and systems.
4. Knowledge of how traditional health systems and behavior change under the impact of modernization.
5. Knowledge of how cultures work in general and under the impact of modernization, with special attention to economic and rural/urban issues.
6. Expertise in social science data-gathering and analysis techniques, ideally including social survey and longitudinal research methods in addition to open-ended interviewing and microresearch.
7. A network of contacts (or at least a repertory of names) among leading social scientists, in developed and less-developed countries, who work in health-related fields.

General Knowledge Areas

In addition to expert skills required, medical anthropologists working in international health should be familiar with the following general areas of knowledge regarding the context of international health projects and programs.

1. International development in general.
2. International health and health care systems in general.
3. Principles of project design, implementation, and evaluation, including familiarity with impact measures and socioeconomic indicators of development.

International Health Specializations

While no medical anthropologist is necessarily conversant with all areas of specialization within international health, familiarity with one or more of the following specialized areas of knowledge greatly increases one's effectiveness.

1. Epidemiology and communicable diseases.
2. Demography and family-planning programming.
3. Nutrition and food production and distribution.
4. Evaluation of health programs and their impact.
5. Economics, particularly the principles of microeconomic theory and the theory and principles of cost/benefit, cost-effectiveness, and financial analyses.

Operational and Bureaucratic Skills

In the bureaucratic setting one soon discovers that there is a difference between knowledge of a subject and knowing how to communicate that knowledge effectively. The following skills must be learned by anthropologists, many of whom master these skills "on the job" if they have not been acquired through previous experience in complex organizational settings.

1. Ability to perform as a team member during data-gathering and related field activities, as well as during other phases of project work.
2. Good verbal self-expression in individual and group situations.
3. Ability to function (and write) well under severe time constraints.
4. Ability to understand and function within complex organizations (bureaucracies), in both Western and less-developed countries.
5. Ability and willingness to produce conclusions based on short (e.g., three- to eight-week) field trips.
6. Ability to write well and quickly in jargon-free English, presenting clear arguments, conclusions, and constructive recommendations in a format easy for decision makers and program implementors to act on. (This requires topical headings, subheadings, and frequent enumeration or "bullets" rather than solid prose throughout as is typical in academic writing.)
7. Ability to manage (or implement) projects and to supervise others (including contract negotiation and management).
8. Ability to design and manage research projects.
9. Ability to gather up-to-date academic work on selected topics and condense findings into a single, jargon-free report that project planners and implementors can easily use.
10. Ability to interact on an ongoing basis with organizational personnel so that one's contributions are used as intended.
11. Ability to understand policy and decision-making processes.
12. Ability to communicate effectively with, and speak the technical language of, other specialists (e.g., doctors and engineers).
13. Ability to act as a bridge between development agencies on one hand and project participants and intended beneficiaries on the other.
14. Knowledge of when and how to generalize from one community or country to others.
15. Flexibility and creativity in surmounting "impossible" situations.

16. Tact and diplomacy, patience (but not passivity), and perseverance (without being abrasive).

Finding Employment in International Health

Finding work requires developing a strategy based on three elements: professional qualifications, personal contacts, and careful self-marketing.

Qualifications

Rarely are positions labeled: "for medical anthropologist." The anthropologist seeking work in international health usually competes not just with other anthropologists but with a broad range of behavioral scientists and public health specialists. Although there is no fixed set of qualifications for employment in international health, the following are important.

"LDC" experience in health is probably the most useful qualification, although often a person with strong skills in other areas may get hired without developing country health experience and then learn on the job. *Technical training in health, at either the graduate or postgraduate level, is probably the second most important qualification.* A Ph.D. in medical anthropology, although very desirable, is not essential; even a doctorate in anthropology is not always essential. (For example, the employee responsible for producing AID's "Health Sector Policy Paper" had an M.A. in anthropology and a Master of Public Health.[29] Nevertheless, to succeed against increasingly stiff competition, some formal training in health is very important. A third very useful qualification is *successful prior experience in complex organizations,* especially in the public health and development fields. Whether publications are important depends on the job and its level. A long publication record is not essential, but publications may help, especially if they include reports prepared for nonacademic audiences. Teaching experience is not essential either, although it may help in many ways once on the job. *A strong combination of skills and knowledge bases outlined in the preceding section* will probably be the determining factor in getting hired.

There are now numerous training opportunities for anthropologists interested in international health. These include programs offering a Master of Public Health (M.P.H.) degree as well as other programs in which anthropology is a or the lead discipline.[30] For anthropologists lacking adequate experience or formal training, measures for closing the gap might include working as a volunteer for a PVO (especially overseas), or at least reading through recent WHO journals and documents (collections located at the Pan American Health Organization in Washington, DC, and at the United Nations in New York) as well as the international health and international development holdings of the Applied Anthropology Documentation Project at the University of Kentucky.

Personal Contacts and Self-Marketing

In addition to the qualifications an employer lists in a job announcement or position description, considerable entrepreneurial ability and political sensitivity may also be necessary for actually getting the job. For large organizations, it may be necessary to find an "in-house" professional (one on the staff of the organization being approached) and to interact with this contact person in such a way that he or she becomes convinced that having you working for the organization would be worth personally investing time and energy to help you get hired. Just as an academic rarely secures a teaching position by writing to the personnel office of a university or by answering an advertisement, so does hiring in the applied world depend on research and contacts. It is smart to find out the basic information from the personnel office of a large organization (e.g., does the organization have an internship program? Is a hiring freeze on?) However, often it is virtually useless to try getting hired by the personnel office without first finding an inside professional supporter.

To develop such an inside supporter or supporters, it is necessary to start well in advance to establish a wide circle of professional contacts in agencies and firms working in international health. The contacts can be made while doing fieldwork, through various professional meetings, visits to those agencies and firms, and follow-up letters and phone calls. Ask your supporters for suggestions on documents specific to your areas of mutual interest to learn about relevant aspects of the organization's work; read them quickly and follow up with intelligent questions and observations on what you've read.

Two points of consideration are essential in this interaction. First, reciprocate. Be useful to these supporters—for example, by supplying them with material and information that you've come across elsewhere. Second, be aware that people in these organizations work under severe time constraints and respect their time. Academics often think in terms of semesters and years—bureaucrats (more like clinical doctors) in terms of hours, today, and next week. Do not become an imposition. Be specific about what you want but do not make excessive requests; be appreciative.

While developing this network of contacts, it is essential to market oneself as a product that potential consumers (i.e., employers) need. Many of the principles involved have been amply discussed elsewhere (e.g., in issues of *Practicing Anthropology*).[31] Here are additional suggestions related specifically to contacts and to learning to market oneself.

1. *Begin early market research.* Understand the general market—in a sense, develop an ethnography of the international health market. Read "The Innovating Organization" in George Foster's *Applied Anthropology* (1969:91–113). Identify your target "customer" and its felt and unfelt needs. Acquire a working ethnography of the organizations you are particularly interested in. For a large agency, start with its telephone directory and the organizational charts contained therein, and read policy statements, annual reports, earlier publications, and so on. Learn the jargon of the field as well as terminology specific to individual organizations.

2. *Package your product persuasively.* Get advice from people with jobs you would like. Reorganize your curriculum vitae into a resumé that emphasizes nonacademic and other action-oriented experience and expertise. Even prepare sev-

eral alternative resumés for customers with different needs. Read books on getting jobs (e.g., *Go Hire Yourself an Employer* [Irish 1978]).

3. *Put yourself on consultants' rosters and placement lists.* At a minimum, try the International Health Placement Service of NCIH, the American Public Health Association's international health roster, and the consultants' roster of the Institute for Development Anthropology. Try to become personally acquainted with the individuals who maintain these rosters and stay in frequent contact.

4. *Attend professional meetings where international health specialists gather.* Attend NCIH's annual meeting in Washington—where everyone present is in the international health field. Try also the annual meeting of the American Public Health Association, which has an International Health Section.

5. *Create a specific task for yourself.* Even if no specific opening exists (usually none do), ask your insider contacts if they are involved with or responsible for work that you might be able to assist with. Or, once you are sufficiently familiar with their needs, submit a proposal outlining work you would like to do on a short-term contract. Often this should simply be a short (two- to three-page) but very well written statement, or "scope of work," marked "Preliminary" and "For discussion purposes only." Then, if your idea meets your insider contact's needs, use his or her suggestions to work this into a longer, formal proposal or scope of work. If your contact decides to support it, do not haggle with him or her over payment and contract details. Save as much as this as possible for personnel departments and contract officers so that your relationship with your contact remains professionally collegial, rather than tarnished by money matters. To get a foot in the door, be prepared to settle for a small contract (but with as high a daily rate as possible) and to invest extra personal time to turn in a superb product. Also, if full-time employment is a possibility, suggest to your contact that you sketch out a preliminary job description outlining what you might do, thus making it as easy as possible for that person to help get you hired.

What Might the Future Hold?

What will happen in health care in the developing countries as humanity marches toward the 21st century? What opportunities will it hold for anthropologists? At Alma-Ata in 1978, WHO and member developing countries adopted the goal of "health for all by the year 2000." Will there be "health for all"?

Many countries have made great progress during the past decade in eliminating the diseases of poverty and in reducing malnutrition and too-high fertility rates. In many countries of Asia and Latin America, and in parts of the Near East, disease patterns are becoming more like those of a developed country: communicable diseases have been largely brought under control, being replaced by the "diseases of civilization" as populations in those countries become more elderly, urban, and subject to pollution and stress. These are countries and populations that are passing through epidemiologic and demographic transition (Frenk et al. 1989).

Certainly the phenomena of epidemiologic transition are well worth academic study. But what does this mean for international health programs? For giving, lending, and technical assistance by international donors? Given that international health assistance has, in the past, been premised in large part on humanitarian aid to those less fortunate, will this rationale still exist?

The answer is that the job is not yet done. In all developing countries there remain large segments of the population that do not yet have access to affordable basic health care. One thinks, for example, of Northeast Brazil, where "mother-love" sometimes means simply letting one's baby die.[32] Even in countries that are passing through the epidemiologic transition, as their populations continue to grow during the next few decades (and many even to double), provision of even basic health care for the disadvantaged sectors of those populations will remain a daunting task. Financing and management of health resources, and understanding health-seeking behavior and payment for care, become increasingly important.

Elsewhere, in sub-Saharan Africa and in poor countries such as Nepal and Bangladesh, communicable disease rates and maternal and infant mortality rates remain unacceptably high. Here the needs for technical and financial assistance from foreign donors remain similar to those of the past decade, further complicated in much of Africa by AIDS.

As practitioners, we have come a long way from the days when our role was often seen simply as reconciling traditional healing models with those of the West. The needs and challenges today are far more complex, involving new issues of financing and sustainability and based on clearer knowledge of what works and what doesn't. Increasingly the diseases of the 1990s and the 21st century will be ones of life-style, changing ecology, and urbanization. These are problems with social and behavioral dimensions that medicine alone cannot solve. More than ever, this calls for anthropologists to get involved, to become more activist, and for the discipline of anthropology to play a more leading role in working to improve health and health care systems throughout the world.

Notes

1. International health is a major and exciting area for anthropological intellectual involvement and theory building. This essay, however, focuses on *employment* in international health (following the guidance for this training manual). Nor, unfortunately, does space permit adequate discussion of the various subfields within international health or citation of all key literature and institutions. The author is grateful for helpful comments on earlier drafts to: Abby Bloom, Ann Brownlee, David Dunlop; Mary Elmendorf, George Foster, Pamela Hunte, Pamela Johnson, Carl Kendall, and Soheir Sukkary-Stolba.

2. A classic introduction to the field is John Bryant's (1969) *Health and the Developing World.* Another leading introduction is Paul Basch's *Textbook of International Health* (Basch 1989). Especially helpful for the anthropologist is Ann Brownlee's *Community, Culture, and Care: A Cross-Cultural Guide for Health Workers* (Brownlee 1978). *Health, Culture, and Community: Case Studies of Public Reactions to Health Programs,* edited by anthropologist Benjamin Paul (1973), remains another classic that should be read by all anthropologists interested in this field, along with a valuable series of articles by anthropologist George Foster (1977, 1982, 1984, 1987a and 1987b). One of the most accessible sources of state-of-the-art thinking on issues in

international health is the journal *Social Science and Medicine*. Work by anthropologists figures prominently in this interdisciplinary journal, thanks to the many years of thoughtful and determined efforts by Charles Leslie, former Senior Editor for Medical Anthropology. The many publications of the World Health Organization and the National Council for International Health are also valuable resources.

3. For a general introduction to international development, see Partridge (1984) and, on the role of anthropologists therein, also Pillsbury (1986).

4. U.S. government spending for military aid far outstrips that for economic aid. The United States ranks embarrassingly low, compared to other developed countries, in terms of the percentage of its gross national product that it gives in foreign socioeconomic aid—less than 1% of the federal budget. At least 15 other countries surpass the U.S. in terms of per capita spending (although the U.S. was, until 1989, the largest donor in terms of the *total* amount of money spent).

5. An important distinction is often made between the terms "project" and "program." Typically, "project" refers to an activity of limited duration—e.g., three years—carried out in a particular location by a designated organization. A "program" refers to a group of projects or other activities, all of which have something in common—e.g., a donor's communicable disease control program spanning several countries or a health program in one country that operates in numerous localities.

6. See Djukanovich and Mach (1975). Three of the best known pilot (research and demonstration) efforts were Narangwal in India, Danfa in Ghana, and Lampang in Thailand (Faruqee 1982).

7. On donors, see Joseph (1980). For anthropological analyses of primary health care, see especially Coreil and Mull (1990), Bloom and Reid (1984), Bloom (1987), and Buzzard (1984).

8. Agency for International Development (1980:10).

9. See, for example, Parlato and Favin (1982), Berman, Gwatkin, and Burger (1986), Goldsmith, Pillsbury, and Nicholas (1985), Mandl (1982), and Nichter (1986). A factor in both the blossoming and then waning of enthusiasm for primary health care was the Chinese barefoot doctor. In the 1970s, China's rural health care system, based on the minimally remunerated barefoot doctor, was a model studied and admired by almost all health planners who sought a strategy for providing affordable health care in the rural areas. By the 1980s, however, China itself had begun backing away from its earlier barefoot doctor model.

10. See Leslie and Gupta (1989); Pillsbury, Brownlee, and Timyan (1990); Population Information Program (1988).

11. For work by anthropologists on sustainability; see Buzzard (1987) and Yacoob (1990). See also Akin, Birdsall, and deFerranti (1987), Parlato and Favin (1982); Leslie and Gupta (1989).

12. See Foster's keen analyses (1987a and 1987b) of the bureaucratic workings of WHO and other international agencies.

13. The *Guide to U.S. Government Agencies Involved in International Health* (National Council for International Health 1982) presents program descriptions, organizational charts, addresses, and phone numbers of 20 major government agencies working in this field. See also Pease (1984).

14. The *Directory of U.S.-Based Agencies Involved in International Health Assistance* (National Council for International Health 1980) contains information on more than 300 private-sector agencies, including PVOs, civic groups, professional associations, labor unions, universities, small-business groups, and transnational corporations. A

similarly useful directory is *Medicine and Public Health: A listing of U.S. Non-Profit Organizations in Medical and Public Health Assistance Abroad* (American Council of Voluntary Agencies for Foreign Service [TAICH] 1979). A second TAICH directory, *U.S. Non-Profit Organizations in Development Assistance Abroad* (American Council of Voluntary Agencies for Foreign Service 1983) is more general but also useful. A fourth important reference is *Voluntary Foreign Aid Programs: Reports of American Voluntary Agencies Engaged in Overseas Relief and Development Registered with the Agency for International Development* (Agency for International Development 1980b). For further discussion of PVOs, see Cernea (1988) and Tendler (1982).

15. See Basch (1989) from which this outline derives.

16. See Foster (1987b) and, on the general bureaucratic culture of international development, Hoben (1980) and Partridge (1984).

17. See Foster (1977 and 1982) as well as Paul (1973).

18. See Cosminsky and Harrison (1983) and Pillsbury (1982).

19. See Nichter (1989) and Coreil and Hull (1990). The work of many anthropologists in the area of child survival is brought together in a monograph series, ''Behavioral Issues in Child Survival Programs'' (Brownlee 1990a, 1990b, 1990c), Pillsbury (1990), and Sukkary-Stolba (1989a, 1989b). Anthropologist Mark Nichter also maintains an extensive bibliography on international health topics which can be made available to interested scholars and practitioners.

20. One important set of guidelines is the field manual, *Rapid Assessment Procedures for Nutrition and Primary Health Care: Anthropological Approaches for Improving Programme Effectiveness* (Scrimshaw and Hurtado 1987). Also known as ''RAP,'' these guidelines have now been adapted to other health areas such as AIDS (published by WHO's Global Programme on AIDS). A companion manual for use in training workshops has also been developed by Scrimshaw and her colleagues (Scrimshaw, Cummins, Novaes da Mota, and Nyamwaya 1991). Anthropological methods have also been adapted for nutrition education by Nichter and Nichter (1981) and for studying diarrheal disease (Bentley et al. 1988; Brown and Bentley 1988), infant feeding (Griffiths et al. 1988), immunization (Coreil et al. 1989), and acute respiratory infection, ARI (by Gretel Pelto and Sandy Gove, forthcoming from WHO). See also Kendall (1983a, 1983b); and Huntington, Berman, and Kendall (1989).

21. See, for example, Harrison (1976).

22. ''Terms of reference'' for such an assignment with the World Bank are presented in Perrett et al. (1980)

23. For example, Bloom (1984) and Mailloux et al. (1980). For an anthropological overview of evaluation work, see Pillsbury (1982). Also valuable are guidelines by anthropologist Polly Harrison and colleagues (LeSar, Mitchell, Northrup, and Harrison 1987).

24. For example, Bastien (1988), Bender and Macauley (1989), Blanchet (1989), Enge and Harrison (1987), and Green (1985).

25. For example, Elmendorf and Isely (1981); Yacoob and Porter (1988); Buzzard (1987); and Pillsbury, Brownlee, and Timyan (1990).

26. An example was WHO's Task Force on Indigenous Fertility-Regulating Methods, brought together through the efforts of anthropologists John Marshall and Lucile Newman (Newman 1985).

27. These are John Marshall, Patricia Rosenfield, and May Yacoob.

28. The latter are, respectively: Abby Bloom, Pamela Johnson, Norge Jerome, and Barbara Pillsbury.

29. This was Abby Bloom (Agency for International Development 1980a).
30. Training opportunities include programs at the University of California at San Francisco and Berkeley, UCLA, Case Western Reserve University, the University of Connecticut, Harvard University, Johns Hopkins University, University of Kentucky, and the University of South Florida, in addition to M.P.H. programs and programs in applied anthropology (see van Willigen 1987). International health is applied anthropology par excellence.
31. See, for example, Minoff (1982:53–77); Louis and Atherton (1982:20–21).
32. The phenomenon exists in many countries, but is forcefully depicted by anthropologist Nancy Scheper-Hughes (1987 and elsewhere).

References Cited

Agency for International Development
    1980a   Health Sector Policy Paper. Washington, DC: U.S. Agency for International Development, Office of Health.
    1980b   Voluntary Foreign Aid Programs: Reports of American Voluntary Agencies Engaged in Overseas Relief and Development Registered with the Agency for International Development. Washington, DC: Agency for International Development, Bureau for Food for Peace and Voluntary Assistance.
    1986   A.I.D. Policy Paper: Health Assistance (revised). Washington, D.C.: U.S. Agency for International Development, Office of Health.
    1990   Child Survival: A Fifth Report to Congress on the USAID Program. Washington, DC: U.S. Agency for International Development, Office of Health.
Akin, John, Nancy Birdsall, and David deFerranti
    1987   Financing Health Services: An Agenda for Reform. Washington, DC: World Bank.
American Council of Voluntary Agencies for Foreign Service, Technical Assistance Information Clearing House (TAICH)
    1979   Medicine and Public Health: A listing of U.S. Non-Profit Organizations in Medical and Public Health Assistance Abroad. New York: American Council of Voluntary Agencies for Foreign Service.
    1983   U.S. Non-Profit Organization in Development Assistance Abroad. New York: American Council of Voluntary Agencies for Foreign Service.
Basch, Paul F.
    1989   Textbook of International Health. Revised edition. New York: Oxford University Press.
Bastien, Joseph W.
    1988   Cultural Perceptions of Neonatal Tetanus and Programming Implications, Bolivia. Resources for Child Health Project for USAID/La Paz. Arlington, VA: John Snow.
Bell, David E., and Michael R. Reich, eds.
    1988   Health, Nutrition, and Economic Crises: Approaches to Policy in the Third World. Dover, MA: Auburn House Publishing.
Bender, Deborah, and Rose Macauley
    1989   Immunization Drop-Outs and Maternal Behavior: Evaluation of Reasons Given and Strategies for Maintaining Gains in the National Vaccination Campaign in Liberia. International Quarterly of Community Health Education 9(4):283–298.

Bentley, Margaret, et al.
    1988   Rapid Ethnographic Assessment: Applications in a Diarrhea Management Por-
        gram. Social Science and Medicine 27(1):107–116.
Berman, Peter A.
    1982   Selective Primary Health Care: Is Efficient Sufficient? Social Science & Medi-
        cine 16:1054–1063.
Berman, Peter A., Davidson E. Gwatkin, and Susan E. Burger
    1986   Community-Based Health-Workers: Head Start or False Start towards Health for
        All? Population, Health and Nutrition Department PHN Technical Note 86-3. Wash-
        ington, DC: World Bank.
Blanchet, Therese
    1989   Perceptions of Childhood Diseases and Attitudes towards Immunization among
        Slum Dwellers—Dhaka, Bangladesh. Resources for Child Health Project. Arlington,
        VA: John Snow.
Bloom, Abby L.
    1984   Prospects for Primary Health Care in Africa: Another Look at the Sine Saloum
        Rural Health Project in Senegal. A.I.D. Evaluation Special Study No. 20. Washing-
        ton, DC: Agency for International Development.
    1987   Where There Are No Data: The Evolution of Primary Health Care. Ph.D. Dis-
        sertation. Faculty of Medicine, University of Sydney.
Bloom, Abby, and Janice Reid, eds.
    1984   Anthropology and Primary Health Care in Developing Countries. Special issue,
        Social Science and Medicine 19(3).
Brown, K. H., and M. E. Bentley
    1988   Improved Nutritional Therapy of Diarrhea: A Guide for Planners and Decision-
        Makers involved in CDD Programs. Arlington, VA: PRITECH.
Browner, Carole H.
    1989   Women, Household and Health in Latin America. Social Science and Medicine
        28(5):461–473.
Brownlee, Ann T.
    1978   Community, Culture, and Care: A Cross-Cultural Guide for Health Workers. St.
        Louis: C. V. Mosby.
    1990a   Breastfeeding, Weaning, and Nutrition: The Behavioral Issues. Office of
        Health, Behavioral Issues in Child Survival Programs Publications No. 4. Washing-
        ton, DC: Agency for International Development.
    1990b   Breastfeeding, Weaning, and Nutrition: Expanded Bibliography. Office of
        Health, Behavioral Issues in Child Survival Programs Publication No. 5. Washing-
        ton, DC: Agency for International Development.
    1990c   Growth Monitoring and Promotion: The Behavioral Issues. Office of Health,
        Behavioral Issues in Child Survival Program Publication No. 6. Washington, DC:
        Agency for International Development.
Bryant, John
    1969   Health and the Developing World. Ithaca, NY: Cornell University Press.
Buzzard, Shirley
    1984   Appropriate Research for Primary Health Care: An Anthropologist's View. So-
        cial Science and Medicine 19:273–277.
    1987   Development Assistance and Health Programs: Issues of Sustainability. Program
        Evaluation Discussion Paper No. 23. Washington, DC: Agency for International De-
        velopment.

Cash, Richard, Gerald Keusch, and Joel Lamstein, eds.
  1987   Child Health and Survival: The UNICEF GOBI-FFF Program. London: Croom Helm.
Cernea, Michael
  1985(ed.)   Putting People First: Sociological Variables in Rural Development. New York: Oxford University Press for The World Bank.
  1988   Nongovernmental Organizations and Local Development. Washington, DC: World Bank, Discussion Paper No. 40.
Chambers, Robert
  1983   Rural Development: Putting the Last First. New York: Longman.
Coombs, Philip H., ed.
  1980   Meeting the Basic Needs of the Rural Poor: The Integrated Community-Based Approach. New York: Pergamon Press.
Coreil, Jeannine, and J. Dennis Mull, eds.
  1990   Anthropology and Primary Health Care. Boulder: Westview Press.
Coreil, Jeannine, Antoine Augustin, Neal Halsey, and Elizabeth Holt
  1989   The Use of Ethnographic Research for Instrument Development and a Case Control Study of Immunization Use in Haiti. International Journal of Epidemiology 18(4):901–905.
Cosminsky, Sheila, and Ira Harrison
  1983   Traditional Medicine: An Annotated Bibliography of Latin America, Caribbean and Africa. New York: Garland Press.
Elmendorf, Mary, and Raymond Isely
  1981   The Role of Women as Participants and Beneficiaries in Water Supply and Sanitation Programs. Arlington, VA: Water and Sanitation for Health Project.
Enge, Kjell I., et al.
  1987   Maternal-Child Health Providers in Guatemala: Knowledge, Attitudes, and Practices: Research Findings and Suggestions for Application. Arlington, VA. Management Sciences for Health, PRITECH Project.
Faruqee, Rashid
  1982   Analyzing the Impact of Health Services: Project Experience from India, Ghana, and Thailand. Staff Working Paper No. 546. Washington, DC: World Bank.
Foster, George M.
  1969   Applied Anthropology. Boston: Little, Brown and Co.
  1977   Medical Anthropology and International Health Planning. Social Science and Medicine 11.527–534.
  1982   Applied Anthropology and International Health: Retrospect and Prospect. Human Organization 41:189–197.
  1984   Anthropological Research Perspectives on Health Problems in Developing Countries. Social Science and Medicine 18(10):847–854.
  1987a   World Health Organization Behavioral Science Research: Problems and Prospects. Social Science & Medicine 24(9):709–717.
  1987b   Bureaucratic Aspects of International Health Agencies. Social Science and Medicine 25(9):1039–1048.
Frenk, Julio, Jose Bobadilla, Jaime Sepulveda, and Malaquias Lopez Cervantes
  1989   Health Transition in Middle-Income Countries: New Challenges for Health Care. Health Policy and Planning 4(1):29–39.
Germain, Adrienne, and Jane Ordway
  1989   Population Control and Women's Health: Balancing the Scales. New York: International Women's Health Coalition.

Gish, Oscar
    1982   Selective Primary Health Care: Old Wine in New Bottles. Social Science and
        Medicine 16:1049–1054.
Goldsmith, Arthur, Barbara Pillsbury, and David Nicholas
    1985   Community Organization. Primary Health Care Operations Research (PRICOR)
        Monograph No. 3. Washington, DC: University Research Corporation.
Gran, Guy
    1983   Development by People: Citizen Construction of a Just World. New York: Prae-
        ger.
Green, Edward C.
    1985   Traditional Healers, Mothers and Childhood Diarrheal Disease in Swaziland:
        The Interface of Anthropology and Health Education. Social Science and Medicine
        20(3):277–285.
Griffiths, M., E. Piwoz, M. Favin, and J. Del Rosso
    1988   Improving Young Child Feeding During Diarrhea: A Guide for Investigators and
        Program Managers. Arlington, VA: PRITECH.
Gueye, Abdoulaye, Alpha Boubacar Diallo, Amadou Dia, and Patrick Kelly
    1989   Raport de la deuxieme mission d'identification pour la reduction de la mortalite
        maternelle au Senegal [Project for the Prevention of Maternal Mortality in Senega].
        Dakar: Ministry of Public Health, United Nations Development Program and Colum-
        bia University Center for Population and Family Health.
Harrison, Polly Fortier
    1976   The Social and Cultural Context of Health Delivery in Rural El Salvador: Im-
        plications for Programming. San Salvador: Report prepared for USAID/El Salvador.
Hoben, Allan
    1980   Agricultural Decision Making in Foreign Assistance: An Anthropological Anal-
        ysis. In Agricultural Decision Making: Anthropological Contributions to Rural De-
        velopment. Peggy F. Barlett, ed. Pp. 337–369. New York: Academic Press.
Huntington, D., P. Berman, and C. Kendall
    1989   Health Interview Surveys for Child Survival Programs: A Review of Methods,
        Instruments and Proposals for Their Improvement. Institute for International Pro-
        grams, Occasional Paper Series, No. 6. Baltimore: Johns Hopkins University.
Irish, Richard K.
    1978   Go Hire Yourself an Employer. Garden City, NY: Anchor Books.
Joseph, Stephen C.
    1980   Outline of National Primary Health Care System Development: A Framework
        for Donor Involvement. Social Science and Medicine 14:177–180.
Kendall, Carl
    1983a   Operational Research Guidelines. Geneva: Diarrhoeal Diseases Control Pro-
        gramme.
    1983b   Techniques for Small-Scale Operational Research. Geneva: Diarrhoeal Dis-
        eases Control Programme.
    1988   The Implementation of a Diarrheal Disease Control Program in Honduras: Is It
        "Selective Primary Health Care" or "Integrated Primary Health Care"? Social Sci-
        ence and Medicine 27(1):17–23.
LeSar, John, Marc D. Mitchell, Robert Northrup, and Polly F. Harrison
    1987   Monitoring and Evaluation of Child Survival Programmes. In Child Health and
        Survival: The UNICEF GOBI-FFF Program. R. R. Cash, G. Keusch, and J. Lam-
        stein, eds. Pp. 173–204. London: Croom Helm.

Leslie, Joanne, and Geetz Rao Gupta
    1989   Utilization of Formal Services for Maternal Nutrition and Health Care. Washington, DC: International Center for Research on Women.
Louis, Suzanne, and Joan Atherton
    1982   The Secret Life of Anthropological Training: A Job Search Strategy. Practicing Anthropology 5(1):20–21.
Mailloux, Laurier, et al.
    1980   Evaluation of the Primary Health Care Project in Nepal. Kathmandu and Washington, DC: Agency for International Development.
Mandl, P.-E., ed.
    1982   Community Participation: Current Issues and Lessons Learned. Assignment Children (special issue) Vol. 59/60. Geneva and New York: UNICEF.
Minoff, Iles, ed.
    1982   Stalking Employment in the Nation's Capital: A Guide for Anthropologists. Washington, DC: Washington Association of Professional Anthropologists.
National Council for International Health
    1980   Directory of U.S.-Based Agencies Involved in International Health Assistance. Washington, DC: National Council for International Health.
    1982   Guide to U.S. Government Agencies Involved in International Health. Washington, DC: National Council for International Health.
Newman, Lucile, ed.
    1985   Women's Medicine: A Cross-Cultural Study of Indigenous Fertility Regulation. New Brunswick: Rutgers University Press.
Nichter, Mark
    1986   The Primary Health Center as a Social System· PHC, Social Status, and the Issue of Team-Work in South Asia. Social Science and Medicine 23(4):347–355.
    1989   Anthropology and International Health: South Asian Case Studies. Dortrecht: Kluwer Academic Publishers.
Nichter, Mark, and Mimi Nichter
    1981   An Anthropological Approach to Nutrition Education. Newton, MA: Educational Development Center.
Parlato, Margaret B., and Michael N. Favin
    1982   Primary Health Care: An Analysis of 52 A.I.D. Assisted Projects. Washington, DC: American Public Health Association.
Partridge, William, ed.
    1984   Training Manual in Development Anthropology. Washington, DC: American Anthropological Association.
Paul, Benjamin, ed.
    1973   Culture and Community: Case Studies of Public Reactions to Health Porgrams. Revised edition. New York: Russell Sage Foundation.
Pease, Clifford A., Jr.
    1984   U.S. Bilateral Health Programs—An Historical Perspective. International Health News 5(4):2, 7.
Perrett, Heli, et al.
    1980   Human Factors in Project Work. Staff Working Paper No. 397. Washington, DC: World Bank.
Pillsbury, Barbara, Ann Brownlee, and Judith Timyan
    1990   Understanding and Evaluating Traditional Practices: A Guide for Improving Maternal Care. Washington, DC: International Center for Research on Women.

Pillsbury, Barbara L. K.
  1982   Policy and Evaluation Perspectives on Traditional Health Practitioners in National Health Care Systems. Social Science and Medicine 16:1825–1834.
  1984   Evaluation and Monitoring. *In* Training Manual in Development Anthropology. William Partridge, ed. Pp. 42–63. Washington, DC: American Anthropological Association.
  1986   Making A Difference: Anthropologists in International Development. *In* Anthropology and Public Policy. Special Publication No. 21. Walter Goldschmidt, ed. Pp. 10–28. Washington, DC: American Anthropological Association.
  1990   Immunization: The Behavioral Issues. Office of Health, Behavioral Issues in Child Survival, Monograph No. 3. Washington, DC: Agency for International Development.
Rifkin, Susan B., and Gill Walt
  1986   Why Health Improves: Defining the Issues Concerning "Comprehensive Primary Health Care" and "Selective Primary Health Care." Social Science and Medicine 23(6):559–566.
  1988(eds.)   Selective or Comprehensive Primary Health Care? Special issue. Social Science and Medicine 26(9).
Scheper-Hughes, Nancy
  1987   Culture, Scarcity, and Maternal Thinking: Mother Love and Child Death in Northeast Brazil. *In* Child Survival: Anthropological Perspectives on the Treatment and Maltreatment of Children. Pp. 187–208. Boston: D. Reidel.
Scrimshaw, Susan, and Elena Hurtado
  1987   Rapid Assessment Procedures for Nutrition and Primary Health Care: Anthropological Approaches for Improving Programme Effectiveness. Los Angeles: University of California, Latin American Center and United Nations University.
Scrimshaw, S., L. Cummins, C. Novaes da Mota, and D. Nyamwaya
  1991   Training Manual in Basic Anthropological Techniques. Los Angeles: University of California, Latin American Center and United Nations University.
Sukkary-Stolba, Soheir
  1989a   Oral Rehydration Therapy: The Behavioral Issues. Office of Health, Behavioral Issues in Child Survival Programs Publication No. 1. Washington, DC: Agency for International Development.
  1989b   Oral Rehydration Therapy: Expanded Bibliography. Office of Health, Behavioral Issues in Child Survival Programs Publication No. 2. Washington, DC: Agency for International Development.
Tendler, Judith
  1982   Turning Private Voluntary Organizations into Development Agencies. Program Evaluation Discussion Paper No. 12. Washington, DC: Agency for International Development.
Walsh, Julia A., and Kenneth Warren
  1979   Selective Primary Health Care: An Interim Strategy for Disease Control in Developing Countries. New England Journal of Medicine 301(18):967–974.
van Willigen, John
  1987   Becoming a Practicing Anthropologist: A Guide to Careers and Training Programs in Applied Anthropology. NAPA Bulletin No. 3. Washington, DC: National Association for the Practice of Anthropology.

World Health Organization and United Nations International Children's Emergency Fund
    1978   Primary Health Care: Report of the International Conference on Primary Health
    Care, Alma-Ata, USSR, 6–12 September 1978. Geneva: World Health Organization.
Yacoob, May
    1990   Community Self-Financing of Water Supply and Sanitation: What are the Prom-
    ises and Pitfalls? Health Policy and Planning 5(4):358–366.

chapter four

Applied Anthropology and Public Health

Kevin R. O'Reilly

The health field in America today is divided, though not equally, between two branches, medicine and public health. The two branches represent very different approaches: medicine is concerned with treatment of disease and with healing, while public health is concerned with prevention of disease and promotion of health. Medicine represents the greatest amount of money expended and individuals involved; public health is practiced by relatively few professionals and with a much smaller budget but probably directly affects more peoples' lives around the world.

Public health and medicine have common roots. The former, however, has been more influenced throughout its history by social science and a concern with social issues. In the 1850s, Rudolph Virchow wrote "Medicine is a social science . . . anthropology in its widest sense, whose greatest task is to build up society on its physiological foundation" (Rosen 1958). While Virchow was commenting on all medicine at the time, history shows that only public health has embraced his philosophy to any appreciable degree.

By its nature, public health dictates that health problems be viewed behaviorally, as well as medically. In fact, the roots of the leading causes of death or years of potential life lost (heart disease, cancer, accidental or violent death, and AIDS) are all or largely behavioral; as such, only their symptoms or sequelae can be helped by traditional medical practices. Prevention of mortality from these causes must involve not just physicians but also specialists from the social sciences who are trained in the study of human behavior, the relationship between behavior and health, and theories of behavior change.

Public health is recognized as a discipline that requires teamwork from people of different professional backgrounds (Hasan 1975). Applied anthropologists should be on that team; with increasing frequency, they are. Anthropologists fit especially well in the public health endeavor because they share with health professionals an interest in the biological approach to health problems as well as an interest in a broadly conceived ecological approach (Paul 1956a, 1956b). Along with their colleagues in other behavioral sciences, they bring with them a tradition of exploring the determinants of human behavior, and the relationship between beliefs and behavior, that challenges epidemiologists and public health physicians to expand their explorations (hypotheses and investigations).

There is a tradition of anthropologists working in public health, and some of the more important figures in the development of medical anthropology worked for a time in schools of public health (Paul 1955, Polgar 1962). Today, many medical anthropologists work primarily in, or in a collaborative fashion with, schools of public health. In this chapter, I will draw on examples from my experience as an applied anthropologist at the Centers for Disease Control (CDC), where over 4000 people from more than 150 different professional backgrounds work to improve domestic and international public health.

The CDC is an agency of the U.S. Public Health Service of the Department of Health and Human Services. The CDC, charged with conducting research and disease surveillance and providing technical assistance to the United States and other countries in their public health programs, is composed of six individual centers. While the boundaries among the centers are not immutable, their responsibilities are generally as follows:

1. The Center for Infectious Diseases investigates outbreaks of infectious disease and conducts surveillance, epidemiological, and laboratory research.
2. The Center for Environmental Health and Injury Control monitors exposure to hazards from environmental sources, such as toxic-waste sites, and investigates the epidemiology of accidental injury and death.
3. The Center for Prevention Services is responsible for control programs intended to reduce sexually transmitted diseases and tuberculosis, as well as to increase immunization coverage and reduce vaccine-preventable diseases.
4. The Center for Chronic Disease Prevention and Health Promotion is charged with family planning, nutrition, health education and promotion, and investigates the epidemiology of chronic disease.
5. The National Institute for Occupational Safety and Health conducts research in occupational safety and health, trains professionals in this field, and provides recommendation to the Department of Labor for regulation of workplace safety and health.
6. The National Center for Health Statistics is the government's principal vital and health statistics agency. The center produces a wide array of data on the health of the nation.

The Actors in Public Health

Public health work takes two broad forms. The first involves research on the causes of disease or risks to health and on the distribution of diseases; this is the task of epidemiology. The second is the application of that knowledge to target populations, in the form of disease intervention strategies. These can be adult and childhood immunization programs for vaccine-preventable diseases. They can also be health-education programs that promote modification and elimination of behaviors that may adversely affect health or the adoption of behaviors that may promote health. Epidemiology traditionally has been practiced by physicians with special training in the field or with experience in the scientific method. This was particularly true when the greatest public health problems were infectious diseases, usually the result of a single infectious agent, perhaps in conjunction with already poor health status. Now, however, the most important public health problems in the developed world, when defined as the leading causes of death, are either chronic disease resulting in part from smoking, diet, and/or sedentism (e.g., heart disease or cancer) or involve other complex behavioral issues (AIDS, homicides, suicide, and accidental death, often in conjunction with substance abuse). The causes of these public health problems are complex. Consequently, epidemiological methods necessarily have become more sophisticated and analytic techniques have become complicated. The Ph.D. epidemiologist, with extensive training in research design and multivariate statistics, is increasingly in demand.

The growing focus on chronic disease has also opened the way for greater contributions to the process of epidemiological investigations by anthropologists. Earlier studies of infectious disease tended to focus on a narrow range of possible etiologies, but current investigations of chronic disease must include many social, cultural, and behavioral characteristics of the population under study. Thus anthropologists, and other social scientists, need to be involved in the entire investigative process, from hypothesis generation to data analysis and interpretation findings.

Many disease-control programs, such as those aimed at sexually transmitted diseases, could not function without the efforts of public health advisors. These are specialists in many fields, ranging from case finding (as in sexually transmitted-disease or tuberculosis-control efforts) to logistics (assuring that vaccines or other supplies are available when needed) and general program management. It is the public health advisor, then, who makes most programs function properly.

Health promotion and education is a somewhat newer field than epidemiology. Briefly, it involves bringing public health knowledge to bear on changing behaviors that expose people to unnecessary risks of morbidity or mortality. In recent years, health promotion and education has become increasingly scientific. Current approaches blend qualitative and quantitative methods to determine the areas of greatest potential impact from a health-education program and the methods of health education best suited to particular target populations (Green et al. 1980). Although epidemiology has had a number of notable triumphs since the beginning of the century (for example, the control of malaria, tuberculosis, and polio in this country and the eradication of smallpox worldwide), the real measure of the effectiveness of health education and its new approaches will be in the years to come with respect to changes in behaviors related to public health problems.

Public health consists of policy-relevant or action-oriented research and the application of research in the form of public health programs. Anthropologists' public health research uncovers the sociocultural origins of health-promoting or health-threatening behaviors. In the design of intervention programs, anthropologists encourage consideration of the culture of the target populations.

The Anthropologist in Public Health

Although anthropologists work in collaboration with physicians, it would be naive to assume that the working conditions in medical schools and in schools of public health are similar. Public health is by nature multidisciplinary; while physicians still hold the more powerful positions, for the most part they also recognize both the strengths and the weaknesses of their profession and the need to collaborate with other disciplines. Public health physicians' experiences, avocations, and commitment to public service usually set them apart from physicians in medical schools or clinical practice. They function, for the most part, as team members in the public health effort. Public health is historically socially oriented; its professionals are typically committed to public service. These features make public health a more hospitable environment for social scientists. It should be even easier for the anthropologist than for other social scientists, because both anthropology and public health are more interested in groups than in individuals and both have heavy commitment to other cultures (Paul 1956a:51).

The exact nature of the anthropologist's day-to-day activities in public health largely depends on the setting in which he or she works. Anthropologists can be employed full-time, part-time, or as consultants by federal, state, local, or private public-health agencies, by schools of public health, or by individual communities. The activities in these different settings can be varied and either international (as Barbara Pillsbury explains in her chapter) or domestic.

Applied anthropologists can contribute to both research and application. The role that the anthropologist plays in public health research covers the entire scientific process, from generation of hypotheses and operationalization of concepts to statistical analysis and interpretation of results (Janes, Stall, and Gifford 1986). This is substantially similar to what most anthropologists do throughout their professional careers. Important differences distinguish anthropological research, however. Public health research (epidemiology) tends to be highly quantitative. While anthropologists are accustomed to evaluating a host of relationships among variables, often not quantified and/or involving observations on relatively few people, epidemiologists test relationships among relatively few variables, always quantified and involving large numbers of people, with data frequently collected through disease-surveillance systems. Although the rich qualitative data collected through the anthropological approach may more readily suggest associations and casual relationships among health-related behaviors and disease, the sample's representativeness poses a problem. Representativeness is less often a problem in public health research, but the relatively limited amount of information available on each observation is a common frustration. The narrower conceptualization of problems in epidemiology often excludes factors that the anthropologist would be quick to include. The anthropologist doing public health research is likely to be continually searching for more information on the research subjects or for creative ways to infer causal relationships when that additional information is impossible to obtain.

Although standard anthropological research might ultimately further our understanding of culture, public health research (like any applied anthropological research) is focused on a problem and should result in action or policy to ameliorate that problem in a relatively short time.

Anthropologists can also contribute to most of the current efforts in public health programs: health-education programs, risk-reduction and health-assessment programs, comprehensive vaccination programs, family-planning programs, maternal and child health programs, and programs to control sexually transmitted diseases, to name a few. All of these public health activities have similar requirements and components. The following description of the essential elements of good public health programs shows the range of possibilities for an anthropologist's input.

Program Development Stage

1. Assessment of public health needs of a community or identification of a health problem through disease surveillance and discovery of its causes through careful epidemiologic investigation.
2. Assistance in determining the actual target for a program's activities—often not the same as the at-risk group. For example, programs to improve the health of children usually must focus on their parents.
3. Assessment of a community's perceptions of its health needs.
4. Education about the particular public health problem under consideration, if it is not recognized as serious by community members.
5. Careful consideration of the dominant culture of the community (including identification of the community's political structure, leadership, and particulars of community history that might affect program implementation and/or success) as well as consideration of minority cultures and subcultures likely to be encountered.

Implementation Stage

1. Clear exposition to the community of the objectives and operation of the program.
2. Development of community support and input for the program.

Operation of the Program

1. "Troubleshooting" to investigate quickly problem areas where programs do not function as planned.
2. Evaluation of a program to determine if it has reached its target population and attained its stated goals.
3. Assistance in incorporating evaluation findings into future program operation.

An anthropologist may be involved with any or all of these activities, depending on the nature of his or her employment. Those working full-time in a public health agency will have more opportunity for involvement in all stages of a program, while anthropologists employed in a school of public health would be more likely to be contacted for consultant work. Anthropologists who function as consultants are less likely to affect the entire range of program development and operation and may be contracted for a specific purpose, perhaps as a program evaluator. In any case, the opportunities for anthropological input may exist in any stage of the public health endeavor.

Examples of Public Health Work

In the following sections I will describe two of my tasks as a full-time employee in a federal public health agency, one domestic and one international, to illustrate the type of work an applied anthropologist may be called on to do.

Reducing the Risk of AIDS Among Hard-to-Reach Groups

The AIDS epidemic has posed many challenges for public health. When originally discovered, the AIDS epidemic affected primarily homosexual men. These individuals were exposed to the agent that causes the disease, human immunodeficiency virus (HIV), through sexual activity that exposed them to infected body fluids, especially semen. A broad community-based effort in the gay community, coupled with public health resources and a health education campaign, has greatly decreased the prevalence of the behaviors that originally fueled the epidemic. While challenges still remain in that community, the rate of new infections with HIV is probably higher in other communities, particularly the inner cities where drug abuse, coupled with sexual activity, places young people at risk. The new challenge for public health, then, is to intervene to change the behavior of populations that have characteristically not availed themselves of public health information or activities.

With this in mind, we have begun a series of projects to change the risk-taking behaviors of five hard-to-reach groups: men who have same-sex contacts but who do not identify themselves as homosexual or gay; intravenous drug users not in treatment programs; women who may knowingly or unknowingly be the sexual partners of men in these first two groups; prostitutes; and high-risk adolescents (runaway youth, throwaway youth) who may be at risk through intravenous drug abuse or through prostitution. Clearly, the first step in an endeavor like this is to discover why these individuals behave the way they do and what can be done to persuade them to change and to help them to do so. To this end, we have completed a rapid and targeted ethnography of the groups under study, focusing only on information that we hypothesize will be useful in forming and evaluating interventions.

Based on those qualitative results, we have developed interventions informed by theories of behavior change. A careful reading of those theories, derived primarily from social psychology, revealed that a great deal of conceptual similarity existed among them. Pooling their key factors, we derived six cognitive components that should be addressed in an intervention, as well as structural or cultural components. We also adopted a model called the "Stages of Behavioral Change" that allows us to describe communities and individuals within them in terms of their readiness to change. Thus, we can target interventions appropriately, allowing communities and individuals in them to progress along a continuum until they reach the point of long-term consistent avoidance of HIV risk behaviors.

This group of projects, still underway, represents a new approach to HIV interventions in a number of ways. First, carefully collected qualitative information is being used in the formation of interventions. Second, all interventions are developed based on theories of behavior change, allowing modification of those interventions as indicated by evaluation results in directions that are understandable. Third, evaluation takes place using brief street intercept questionnaires which monitor sexual and drug-related risk behaviors and prevailing opinion and belief in these communities frequently and randomly. Fourth, all interventions are staged to allow for community progression along a continuum of readiness to change. This allows stage-appropriate outcome evaluation goals to be set, including consideration of the risk involved in those behaviors, contemplation of changing those behaviors, intention to change, and commitment to change. Finally, each step in the research process is documented, described, and measured carefully to allow replication of these multicenter results elsewhere or to allow application of this community intervention strategy to other health problems.

Traditional Birth Attendants in Rural Kenya

In rural areas in the developing world, a traditional birth attendant or midwife may be the only source of health care delivery many women will ever see. As such, they represent a unique channel through which contraceptive supplies can be made available to rural women. Their suitability for this task, however, depends on a number of factors, including the acceptability of birth limitation in that culture, the midwives' attitudes about family planning, their ability to learn the new skills and concepts required, and the community's perception of the appropriateness of the midwives for this new task.

In recent years, programs to train traditional birth attendants in safe delivery techniques and basic hygiene have been conducted in several places. A number of organizations have conducted these programs in Kenya; one has been conducted with four different tribes by the national family planning organization. Through CDC, I was part of a team (composed of an anthropologist, an obstetrician, and a public health advisor specialized in community health) charged with evaluating that program and with determining the possibility and acceptability of having trained, traditional midwives provide some family planning and maternal and child health care services. In conjunction with Kenyan family-planning officials, we were to design the evaluation, pretest, and field the necessary data-collection instruments; assist in data analysis; and facilitate incorporation of the results into program planning and operation. Careful consideration of many cultural differences among the tribes and between the Kenyan program operators and the Western donor agencies that provided funds and technical assistance was obviously required.

The evaluation we designed consisted of three surveys, one for each major focus of the program: (1) health care professionals in the regional and provincial health facilities, (2) trained and untrained midwives, and (3) women in the villages served by those two groups of midwives. The first survey was designed to determine the willingness of health care professionals to collaborate with traditional midwives in bringing family planning to rural villages and to receive referrals of difficult deliveries from the midwives. The second survey was to compare trained midwives' attitudes on family planning, knowledge of delivery skills and sterile-delivery technique, and willingness to deliver family planning methods with those of a matched group of untrained midwives. The third survey compared responses of women in villages served by trained and untrained midwives to questions on contraceptive use, prevalence and duration of breastfeeding and postpartum abstinence, details of the last midwide-assisted delivery, and attitudes about family planning and midwives as family-planning distributors.

Most village women believed that midwives are an acceptable if not preferred source of family-planning methods, most midwives were willing to act as distributors, and most health care providers were willing to help in the effort. The message seemed clear: a mechanism already existed for community-based distribution of contraceptive supplies.

These results became available at a time when population planners in Kenya were considering implementing a community-based distribution system, using village women as distributors. Some agencies conducting midwife training were also then reevaluating their programs. To gain the maximum impact from our evaluation, we reported the research results in a two-day workshop, to which the family-planning organization invited all the other agencies that trained midwives, all the organizations that funded such activities or provided technical assistance, and representatives of the population planners at the Ministry of Health. The workshop had three goals: (1) to provide the client agency and other programs training midwives with the results of the evaluation; (2) to help the client agency incorporate those results into future planning activities; and (3) to prompt discussion on the future role of midwives, including their potential for community-based distribution of contraceptives.

The workshop proved very successful. At the conclusion, an advisory panel on midwife training was appointed from among representatives of the organizations present, and discussions were begun with the Ministry of Health on allowing midwives to distribute contraceptive supplies (especially oral contraceptives) and on incorporating them into any plans for community-based distribution.

This evaluation is a good example of an international public health endeavor in which a collaborative team, working closely with local professionals, uses quantitative methods to generate recommendations that can be quickly implemented as program or policy to improve health care.

Skills Needed in Public Health

Many features of the traditional graduate education in anthropology would not help the applied medical anthropologist to function in public health projects like the ones just described. Many courses that could make the anthropology graduate student more prepared for applied work are not part of the traditional graduate program, and some skills not generally taught in graduate programs of any nature are important to public health. In this section, I will outline the essential skills for an applied medical anthropologist working in public health. In the last section, I will suggest some pointers for finding a job.

Degree Programs

Students who wish to work in public health would enhance their chances of finding employment by obtaining a Ph.D. Opportunities are developing for M.A. applied anthropologists, and programs offering that degree are becoming more common. The Ph.D., however, will bring the job applicant more immediate recognition, especially given the large number of people in public health with M.D. degrees. Although many people in public health have master's degrees, especially a Master of Public Health (M.P.H.), they are often appended to other professional degrees. Students who wish to stop with Master's-level training in anthropology may wish to consider an additional degree in public health, perhaps even an M.P.H. This degree is immediately recognized and understood in public health circles. Though designed more for health professionals than for social scientists, an M.P.H. degree may be a useful credential even for the Ph.D. anthropologist (Krantzler et al. 1984). Students may also want to combine a master's degree in epidemiology or biostatistics with a Ph.D. in anthropology. While not all doctoral programs would cooperate with students desiring this course of study, many, especially those training applied anthropologists, would welcome students with this goal.

Content Areas for Coursework

Apart from additional training in public health, however, anthropology students should begin by studying medical anthropology. A broad subfield that includes ethnomedicine, health care delivery, social epidemiology, and disease ecology, medical anthropology provides students familiarity with the theoretical issues involved in health and illness. Although all topics of medical anthropology are important in public health, students should pay particular attention to social epidemiology and to issues of health care delivery. Courses in epidemiology will teach them the concepts and methods of that discipline. Familiarity with theory and operations of health care delivery systems (acquired through coursework, work experience, or research experience) will contribute to the student's understanding of the setting in which he or she aspires to work.

The student should be well-grounded in social science research methodology, understanding the nature of social inquiry and the research paradigms that are commonly used and able to evaluate critically, on a methodological basis, the findings of research reports.

Survey research and quantitative methods, including multivariate analysis, are becoming more accepted by anthropologists, but in general, anthropology lags behind other social sciences and far behind epidemiology in this regard. As practiced by the epidemiologist, research methodology has become very involved and highly specialized. Quantitative skills are important for applied anthropologists, whose interdisciplinary work often requires that statistics be used as a common language. This is particularly true of public health, where the population-based studies of epidemiology are usually carefully constructed and meticulously executed and analyzed. Thus experience with all phases of survey research, from conceptualization of hypotheses to analysis and report of findings, is an important qualification for employment in public health.

In addition to learning those multivariate techniques which typify the work of quantitative anthropologists, students should also learn those of the epidemiologist and how they are related: What is the difference between p-values and confidence intervals? What are the relative risks? How are they similar to the measures of association anthropologists use? The answers to these questions are not complex but significant, and knowing them will help the anthropologist speak the same language as public health colleagues. Even though the anthropologist may not be hired to conduct multivariate epidemiological research, knowing survey research and quantitative methods will certainly provide research credentials, facilitate interdisciplinary collaboration, and establish the anthropologist as a scientist in the public health sense.

Many anthropologists who work in public health (and other applied settings) engage in evaluation research. This is especially true of anthropologists who act as consultants. Students who wish to do this type of work should be well-grounded in evaluation methods (as other chapters in this book also indicate). A knowledge of basic evaluation methods, both quantitative and qualitative, when coupled with multivariate analysis skills will strengthen the student's chances of finding employment in public health.

Other important tools not usually taught in graduate school can increase a student's chances of gaining employment in public health. Among these are basic communication skills, both written and verbal. In public health agencies, where written and verbal reports are often the basis of policy decisions, data must be summarized clearly and ideas communicated succinctly. In many ways, how the information is presented is as important as its content. An outline form of writing that highlights important points for quick reading and summary is commonly used in public health reports. A one- or two-paragraph executive summary at the beginning of a document is often all that is read. Reviewing evaluation reports, research summaries, other public health reports will help the student adjust to this style of writing. He or she should practice both writing and speaking skills. Attending public health meetings will familiarize the student with the succinct way in which research reports are presented verbally.

Many anthropologists working in the health field make little or no attempt to adapt their style to it. Health professionals and anthropologists are trained in very different ways. The graduate anthropology student is required to study and assimilate ideas, with new concepts evaluated in light of previous knowledge. This process ultimately results in a conceptual framework and theoretical orientation. In medical school, however, students must memorize an enormous amount of facts, from which basis they are to make quick decisions in a clinical setting. It is therefore inappropriate to present anthropological information to physicians in the same way as to anthropologists. We must recognize these differences and adapt our style accordingly as we do when we work in other cultural settings; we do not expect people of other societies to deal with us on our own terms. Similarly, we should present information to health professionals in the concise, factual manner to which they are accustomed, outlining implications of the results for public health or medical practice.

Another important skill for work in public health is the ability to function as part of a team. This involves accommodating different points of view and methods while assuring that one's own contributions are heard and incorporated. This skill usually comes with experience and increasing confidence; at the outset it is helpful at least to realize that this skill is needed.

The real test of an applied anthropologist, however, is translating anthropological knowledge, theory, and data into action or recommendations for action. This is a difficult task for many anthropologists so schooled in the complexity of culture that they can see no way to recommend action. In the action-oriented public health arena, the applied anthropologist is often asked to help formulate policy-relevant recommendations, even though he or she may not have had firsthand field experience with the particular topic or with the group affected. In such a case, one must draw on anthropological theory, existing knowledge, and the perspective gained from education to arrive at a decision or recommendation. Willingness to work from existing knowledge without the addition of new information specific to the problem is rare in published anthropological works. However, it is practically a requirement in many applied settings, where time to gather new data quickly enough to meet deadlines is limited.

Another important skill for all applied anthropologists, therefore, is the ability to work quickly but carefully. Policy-relevant work is done in public health, and information the research provides may influence decisions. This information must be reported in the specified, often very short time. In fact, a notable difference between academic and applied settings is the relatively frenetic pace of the latter. The luxury of reexamining a problem or attempting to reframe it in an ever broader cultural matrix is usually not afforded the applied anthropologist. However, keeping in mind that small amounts of carefully derived and documented facts are more appropriate in the public health or medical arena should help the beginning applied anthropologist feel less concerned about time.

This section has outlined the skills needed to work in public health. Many of these can be learned from applied or medical-anthropology courses, in schools of medicine or public health, or in other social-science departments. In addition to coursework, students can learn from the experiences of applied anthropologists through interviews, especially with those working in public health. The experiences of many applied anthropologists are documented regularly in *Practicing Anthropology* and the occasional *Profile of an Anthropologist* section of the *Anthropology Newsletter*. These provide excellent insight into the variety of work and responsibilities of nonacademic anthropologists.

How to Obtain a Job in Public Health

Unlike academic jobs, for which anthropologists with specific interests and expertise are sought, those in the applied sector rarely specify "anthropologist." However, positions for "social scientists" and "behavioral scientists" are often listed, and anthropologists should not hesitate to apply. Job openings for nonspecified research personnel with expertise in social or behavioral research are also common, and an anthropologist could meet the requirements.

Public health positions, many of which are suitable for applied medical anthropologists, are usually announced in the *American Journal of Public Health*. The American Public Health Association also maintains a list of persons interested in international consulting positions. In addition to short-term employment, the list may provide opportunities for experience in public health that an anthropologist seeks.

Although the job seeker should certainly respond to position announcements, networking may be a more productive strategy. Public health agencies often have budget and personnel constraints that make creation of new positions difficult and time-consuming. Many agencies' directors are more motivated to make that effort when they know the candidate they want to hire. The person familiar to the agency and whose skills are appreciated is more likely to find a position than is an unknown individual.

The value of contacts cannot be overestimated in locating a job, either full-time or as consultant, in a public health agency. Job seekers must build recognition for themselves and for their potential contribution as anthropologists. Finding a contact inside the agency is the first step of this strategy. It is only successful, however, when the job seeker has firm ideas and suggestions about how he or she can contribute and fit into the public health agency as an anthropologist, and this in turn entails a detailed knowledge of the structure, operation, and goals of the agency. Much of this information is available in published documents; in fact, this research is analogous to the archival study conducted before regular ethnography. An even better source of information, though, is a contact within the agency (a key informant). Learning about the agency through research and contacts is the best way to begin building the necessary network.

This approach has resulted in initial consultant jobs for many anthropologists and ultimately in full-time employment for anthropologists who performed well as consultants. The strategy also has worked for students who gained employment in public health agencies after working as an intern. Some applied anthropology programs emphasize this practical aspect of a student's education, others do not. In the latter case, students should attempt to arrange an internship as independent study. The experience will benefit the agency, the anthropology department, and the student, and it may result in employment. Even if it does not lead directly to employment, it will at least establish a network of contacts in public health, a network that will be useful in identifying opportunities and securing employment in the future.

Often, initial employment for these former consultants or student interns has been less anthropological in nature. It is the responsibility of the new employee to create an appreciation for the contribution the discipline can make and to re-shape their job. I have seen many examples of this successful reformulation and believe that, with time and patience, most anthropologists can convince their public health employers of the benefits to the agency from having a real applied anthropologist on board.

Conclusion

Applying anthropology in a variety of settings is a challenging task. It usually requires some modification of the methods an anthropologist uses, which can be intellectually challenging. The application also requires modification of the roles the anthropologist may be accustomed to playing in academic settings, which can be emotionally challenging. But in public health, the task is certainly worth the effort. The goal of public health is important, and anthropology's contribution to it is so valuable as to make the challenges worthwhile.

Some familiarity with various public health settings and the roles anthropologists play in them may make the anthropologist's adaptation somewhat easier. I hope these reflections provide a basis for understanding and a starting point for further exploration of applied anthropology in public health.

References Cited

Green, L., et al.
  1980   Health Education Planning: A Diagnostic Approach. Palo Alto, CA: Mayfield Publishing.
Hasan, K. A.
  1975   What is Medical Anthropology? Medical Anthropology 6(1):7–10.
Janes, C. R., Stall, and Gifford
  1986   Anthropology and Epidemiology: Interdisciplinary Approaches to the Study of Health and Disease. Boston: Kluwer Academic Publishers.
Krantzler, N. J., et al.
  1984   Perspectives on Postdoctoral Public Health Training for Medical Anthropologists. Medical Anthropology Quarterly 15:90–101.
Paul, B.
  1955   Health, Culture and Community. New York: Russell Sage Foundation.
  1956a   Anthropology and Public Health. In Some Uses of Anthropology: Theoretical and Applied. Joseph B. Casagrande and Thomas Gladwin, eds. Pp. 49–57. Washington, D.C.: Anthropological Society of Washington.
  1956b   Social Science in Public Health. American Journal of Public Health 46:1390–1396.
Polgar, S.
  1962   Health and Human Behavior: Areas of Interest Common to the Social and Medical Sciences. Current Anthropology 3:154–205.
Rosen, G.
  1958   A History of Public Health. New York: MD Publications.

● *chapter five*

Need Assessment and Program Evaluation in Community Health

LINDA M. WHITEFORD

The tremendous growth in the field of medical anthropology in recent years has resulted in more medical anthropologists than ever before working in the field of community health. Today, anthropologists are employed in public health departments, in state and federal health programs, in community mental health agencies, in rural health programs, and in metropolitan hospitals. They serve as planners, policy makers, providers, brokers, administrators, and re-searchers. They are often cross-disciplinary hybrids, combining anthropology with training and/or experience in public health, nursing, social work, psychol-ogy, or medicine. The work in which they are involved combines the humanistic skills used in cultural brokerage and the scientific skills of research and design.

Community health has been defined as "the coordinated efforts of all indi-viduals and groups in the community to promote, maintain, and improve the health and well-being of the people" in the community (Osborn 1966:12). It dif-fers little from public health except that "public" health often suggests a health system based on an enduring legal authority and supported through taxes. "Com-munity" health is broader in implication and is based on the concept that there are organized cooperative efforts made by community agencies to assess, protect, and improve the health of members of the community. Community Health Cen-ters (CHCs) most recently stemmed from Neighborhood Health Centers begun around 1965 during the War on Poverty. Their purpose was to "provide care to the medically underserved, improving health status, reducing frequency and length of hospital in-patient stays, reducing inappropriate emergency room use, providing a full range of community health services, fostering community eco-nomic development, and establishing community participation in their adminis-tration" (Wood, Hughes, and Estes 1986:139).

This chapter discusses the critical area of community health assessment and evaluation, and the unique contributions applied medical anthropologists make to it. It is organized around four questions central to an understanding of the role medical anthropology can play in community health assessment and evaluation:

1. How is community health defined, and how does one assess it and eval-uate community health programs?

101

2. What kinds of activities might a medical anthropologist be expected to perform in the field of community health assessment and evaluation?
3. How can a medical anthropologist get a job with an agency?
4. What unique contributions do medical anthropologists make to community health?

Community Health

Ideally, community health should refer to the health status of the community as a whole and of diverse groups within. It can also refer to the ability of health care providers to meet the community's perceived health needs and to make health services equally accessible to all members of the community. Community health, however, is a broad field and the ideal of a uniformly healthy community is seldom, if ever, fully achieved through community health programs. Applied medical anthropologists are often involved in community needs assessments and program evaluations, each critical to providing appropriate services to the community. The first step is to reach agreement on what constitutes health, the second is to assess the community's health needs in terms of that definition, and the third is to design, implement, and evaluate programs that will meet those needs.

Definitions of the term "community health" are as elusive and varied as those of the term's constituent words. Community health indicators are devised to measure the physical and mental well-being of groups within a community. Some rates that are often used are those of infant mortality, homicide, mental illness, child abuse, teenage pregnancy, childhood diseases, and divorce. The reduction or eradication of these social and physical ills is the principal aim of community health agencies. Implementation of these aims and the agencies that pursue them vary considerably depending in part on the resources of local agencies which are at least partially determined by the regional and national contexts within which they operate.

Regardless of the divergent foci among agencies, one element they share is the need for regular program evaluations, and assessments of the state of health of the communities they serve. Medical anthropologists bring to community health assessment and evaluation a long-standing respect for cultural diversity and humanistic values, combined with a thorough knowledge and rigorous application of the scientific method. Medical anthropologists are typically trained in a variety of theoretical orientations and methodologies. They are sensitive to the significance of cultural relativism, dedicated to a systemic or processual view of cultural phenomenon, and concerned with the holistic view to the diverse forces directing community health. These qualities distinguish them from other behavioral and social scientists.

The field of community health was developed by people who were not medical anthropologists. It reflects the beliefs and methods of its founding disciplines: Western medicine, social psychology, environmental sciences, and social work. Community health agencies necessarily exist within a bureaucratic framework and must share a bureaucratic subculture. To the medical anthropologist, this creates both obstacles and opportunities, as will be discussed in this chapter. Health assessments and program evaluations, the focus of the chapter, lie at the heart of community health concerns. Those concerns remain defined today by the founding disciplines, but must also meet the bureaucratic needs of the organizations that create, fund, and supervise them. For the medical anthropologist who plans to work in community health evaluation, familiarity with the fundamental concepts of these founding disciplines is as essential as knowledge of the cultural rules and the local language in studying a foreign society. The medical anthropologist working in a community health setting must demonstrate his or her competence as a member of that community without losing the anthropological perspective, a perspective that can enrich community health programs themselves.

Anthropologists can help reduce community health agencies' isolation from the populations they are supposed to serve by forming new links or strengthening existing ones between health care providers and the patient population. Medical anthropologists such as Merrill Singer and Stephen Schensul working with the Hispanic Health Care Council in Hartford, Connecticut, have clearly demonstrated how anthropological knowledge can enhance communication among community health planners, providers, and the patient population, each of whom were previously isolated from the others.

While most medical anthropologists in community health agencies work at middle management levels where they use skills in research design and evaluation, they may also contribute their special expertise to developing social policy, designing data bases, managing quality assurance programs, or directing the agency (Angrosino 1981; Hill 1984). Anthropology has a potential role in community health at every level, from designing intake forms; incorporating ideas and information from target populations into needs assessments; developing interagency and agency-community linkages; to program development and formulation of responsible and responsive social policy.

While the relationship between anthropology and medicine has often been marked by distrust and misunderstanding arising from lack of a common basis for discussion and from anthropologists' failure to treat medical doctors with the degree of respect they expect, the field of community health has responded positively to anthropologists' work. Noel Chrisman, Thomas Johnson, Marilyn Poland, and countless others work successfully in community health settings and write about their techniques for minimizing conflict. Chrisman writes that his positive relations with medical personnel resulted from applying a cultural analysis to the world of the physician, learning the physicians' worldview and how to integrate his own ideas into the physicians' frameworks (Chrisman 1982).

Anthropologists' involvement in community health programs has expanded beyond program evaluation, assessment of health status, and cultural brokering. Anthropologists now combine traditional marketing techniques with theories and skills from anthropology to create socially conscious health messages designed to reach particular target populations, as for instance, Carol Bryant's work to encourage young mothers to breastfeed their infants (Bryant 1990). Since the early 1980s, health care providers have been concerned with the increasing levels of infant mortality and morbidity among portions of the population in the United States. While middle-class women are returning to the practice of breastfeeding, many young, socioeconomically disadvantaged, first-time mothers are not. The positive physical health consequences derived from breastfeeding are well-documented. Less well-documented but no less significant are the emotional benefits of breastfeeding which include creating a bond between mother and infant and involving the parents in an active, physical role. Committed to the importance of breastfeeding, Bryant collaborated with local health departments and community groups to develop brief, informational videos to be played in the waiting rooms of public health departments. The issues raised in the videos were elicited from young women of the target population who discussed the benefits of breastfeeding their babies in a series of focus group interviews. The videos are powerful and effective because Bryant went to the young women themselves to learn how they evaluated the issues and then used their words and ideas to communicate with other young women.

Medical anthropologists in community health settings apply their academic training to collaborate with professionals of other disciplines to increase effective communication *within* health care institutions, as well as *between* agencies and the populations they serve. In an assessment of pediatric emergency room use, an anthropologist and several physicians conducted research together at a large county hospital (Whiteford 1984). We found that too often pediatric patients were seen too early or too late in the course of the illness to maximize the effectiveness of their interactions with the health care system. Lack of regular access to medical care deprived patients of information they needed to evaluate the severity of their medical situation. Based on personal interviews both in the hospital and in patients' homes, and reviews of medical charts and hospital observations, we learned that in the absence of reliable biomedical information, families brought their children into the hospital either in crisis or needlessly. As a result, providers felt that their services were being misused, and the clients felt that the providers ignored the information they offered and treated them rudely. Both groups felt cheated from being able to provide or receive good, community-based health care.

The patterns of utilization errors were not exclusive to the patients. We also saw emergency room intake forms that rarely elicited information about the circumstances leading to the patient's decision that emergency care was needed. Lacking details of the patients' perception of the onset of symptoms, hospital staff could not make appropriate recommendations to parents for their future use of medical services. Our assessment documented the inappropriate use of resources and the lack of primary medical care. To remedy this situation one of our recommendations was the creation of a telephone line available to parents seeking medical advice. While the recommendation was not immediately instituted, there now exists a hospital-based, open telephone line any concerned parent can call for referrals, reassurances, and uncomplicated explanations (Whiteford 1983). In both of these cases, anthropologists elicited information from the client population and the provider population, then used the information to help facilitate more effective delivery of community health services. These are but brief examples of ways in which medical anthropologists contribute to the understanding of community health problems. The following section discusses some of the approaches and techniques medical anthropologists use.

Tasks Expected of an Anthropologist Involved in Community Health Assessment and Program Evaluation

Need assessment and program evaluation are two basic research tools which occur before, during, and after any community health intervention. An assessment occurs before the intervention and should take into consideration the needs perceived both by members of the community and by local practitioners, and should gather information comparable to national indicators. Program evaluations such as periodic program monitoring occur at the beginning of a community health intervention, as it proceeds, and again at the end of the intervention to determine its effectiveness. Aside from needs assessments and program evaluations, two other orientations are used to measure community health. Before assessment and evaluation are discussed in greater detail, the epidemiological and health program classification approaches will be introduced.

The multiple approaches are not mutually exclusive, but in combination provide techniques for assessing the health of the target population (in this case, the community), cataloging the provision of health-care services, and evaluating the impact of various health-care programs. While each of these perspectives will be discussed, greatest emphasis will be on program evaluation.

Epidemiology

Epidemiology is often defined as the study of the distribution and determinants of diseases and injuries in human populations (MacMahon and Pugh 1970). Primary sources of data used in epidemiology are censuses, vital statistics and morbidity data, and associated health records. Descriptive and analytic epidemiological studies *describe* and *explain* disease occurrence. Descriptive epidemiological studies focus on general observations concerning the relationship between patterns of disease and human population. These studies are often referred to as person, place and time studies because they take as their primary foci those characteristics. Age, sex, race or ethnic group, marital status, social class or socioeconomic status, religion, and occupation constitute the attributes of greatest concern describing persons. Place is where disease occurs. Place can be a room, a restaurant, a church picnic, or even a continent. The third variable in person, place and time studies is time. Time reflects occurrence and is an extremely informative variable. Time trends can be short-term, periodic, or long-term and can be used to anticipate disease cycles. Sometimes, however, projecting future epidemics can be misleading. The anticipated 1976 swine-flu epidemic never occurred, but was expected because the conditions were similar to those that existed during the 1918–19 influenza pandemic. That the epidemic did not occur reflects the complications in anticipating illness outbreaks. When epidemics do occur they are described in terms of a careful tabulation of the distribution of disease-onset times of the afflicted members of the population. This is referred to as the "attack", or incidence rate. Incidence and prevalence rates of illness and death (morbidity and mortality) are expressed as "crude," "specific," and "adjusted" rates, depending on the nature of the study. (See Table 1 for a list of the most common measurements and indices used in epidemiology.)

When epidemiologists, particularly social epidemiologists who focus on the social origins of disease, seek causes of unusual features in morbidity and mortality rates, they usually look for associations among environmental, social, or behavioral characteristics of populations and the high or low rate of occurrence of illness. Most epidemiological research uses aggregated statistical data, although the use of in-depth interviews is increasing, particularly among social epidemiologists and among medical anthropologists like Craig Janes or Kevin O'Reilly. O'Reilly works for the Centers for Disease Control, applying anthropology to gain better comprehension of social factors influencing the spread of AIDS, while Janes used epidemiological anthropological skills to ascertain the

---

TABLE 1

Measurements and Indices Commonly Used in Epidemiology

Age-specific death rate	$\dfrac{\text{Number of persons of a given age dying during the year}}{\text{Population in specified age group at midyear}}$	× 1000
Case-fatality rate	$\dfrac{\text{Number of deaths from a specified disease}}{\text{Number of cases of that disease}}$	× 100
Crude birth rate	$\dfrac{\text{Number of live births during the year}}{\text{Population at midyear}}$	× 1000
Crude death rate	$\dfrac{\text{Number of deaths occurring during the year}}{\text{Population at midyear}}$	× 1000
Infant death rate	$\dfrac{\text{Number of deaths of children under 1 year of age during the year}}{\text{Number of live births during that year}}$	× 1000
Maternal (puerperal) death rate	$\dfrac{\text{Number of deaths from puerperal causes during the year}}{\text{Number of live births during the year}}$	× 10000
Neonatal death rate	$\dfrac{\text{Number of deaths of children under 28 days of age during the year}}{\text{Number of live births during that year}}$	× 1000
Perinatal death rate	$\dfrac{\text{Number of fetal deaths and infant deaths under 7 days of age during the year}}{\text{Number of live births and fetal deaths during the year}}$	× 1000

relationship between migration and levels of hypertension of Samoan migrants to California (Janes 1986).

Epidemiological research designs may be retrospective or prospective (Friedman 1980). That is, epidemiologists examine past occurrences (retrospective), where rates and factors are known, using extant data. An analysis of changes in rates of adolescent pregnancies between 1950 and 1970 based on birth records would be a retrospective analysis. Prospective epidemiological research is based on the collection of new data, usually to test the consequences of some change in the system. A prospective study might follow a cohort of adolescents after their initial exposure to a school health clinic dispersing contraceptives to see if the rate of adolescent pregnancies changed. Both retrospective and prospective studies are basic tools of epidemiology and are used separately, or in conjunction with one another. Marilyn Poland effectively combines both retrospective and prospective formats in her research on barriers to prenatal care by utilizing patient records of women delivering at a large Detroit hospital (retrospective), with postpartum interviews conducted with the women before they leave the hospital (prospective) (Poland et al. 1990).

An advantage of assessing community health through epidemiological indicators and survey research is that the resultant health indices may be compared readily with those of other communities. The most frequently used indices are birth and death rates, and rates of infant mortality and morbidity. Other community health indices used are cause-specific summaries such as death rates due to particular causes, for example, traffic accidents, coronary disease or cancers. Cause-specific indices can be summarized to show change over time, within specific populations, and before and after interventions. Cause-specific rates can also draw attention to secondary or contributing health factors. For instance, childhood diseases such as measles and mumps are not usually associated with high mortality rates in healthy children. Communities reporting high rates of child mortality due to measles should stand out like a red flag, signaling to community health researchers that children in these communities are at high risk of premature death. During a recent measles epidemic in the Dominican Republic, 10% of all the children admitted to a major pediatric hospital with measles died (Whiteford 1990). This unusually high cause-specific mortality rate signalled the need for further investigation of two secondary health issues affecting the health of Dominican children: the low rate of immunization and the high rate of child malnutrition.

Changes in the health status of a community can be traced by charting incidence and prevalence rates for populations in the community. Incidence rates are derived from the number of new cases of a particular problem or condition reported in a specific locale at a given period of time, divided by the total number of people exposed. Prevalence rates are created by counting the number of existing cases of a condition in an area at a given time, and dividing that number by the number of individuals at risk of the condition. The category "at risk" is composed of people susceptible to an illness, exposed to a condition, or vulnerable to the condition being addressed. They are "at risk" of contracting the disease. Fertile women who are exposed to pregnancy are "at risk" of becoming pregnant. Both infertile women and those not exposed to pregnancy would be excluded from the "at risk" category. The incidence rate of pregnancy is composed of each woman whose pregnancy is first recorded during the study period; prevalence rates of pregnancy record the cumulative number of pregnant women during the study time, not just the initial recording of the pregnancies.

Health Program Index

While epidemiology concentrates on morbidity and mortality rates and ratios in a population, a health program index focuses on the health services actually provided for a population. A health program index is a listing of the various health-related programs available in the community, the relations among their administrative and financial organizations, and the explicit aims and goals of the various programs. It provides the researcher with a conceptual model of the health care delivery system.

To develop a health program index, researchers need to identify local agencies involved in health care delivery, health programs in the planning process, locus of responsibility for administration, the local health care priorities. The health program index should include information on health problems that are specific to particular portions of the population, the data used to justify and develop new and existing programs, long-range goals, eligibility requirements limiting the number of people who can receive the services, and the number of cases that each program is capable of serving.

Creation of a health program index gives the researcher an overview of the services offered, the reasons used to justify the programs (i.e., local needs, legislative mandates), and the formal interrelationships among various agencies. It also focuses on local administrators' perceptions of local needs. Compiling such an index is an excellent way for the medical anthropologist working in community health to learn about local agencies and programs. In 1981 we began such a project with support from the Children's Defense Fund and local community participation (Whiteford 1984). This research was a regional portion of a national project to determine the provision of health care to indigent children. The project was called "ChildWatch," and through the use of a health program index we documented the lack of health services for poor children and the consequences of changes in program provision and eligibility. The use of this technique clearly demonstrated the "holes in the safety net" and the number of children whose lives were at risk due to the inability of community health providers to deliver care.

Community Health Needs Assessments and Program Evaluation

Models

Community need assessments and program evaluations form critical and central parts of the development of any effective and appropriate health intervention. Because community assessment and program evaluation require a set of skills for medical anthropologists employed in community health settings, evaluation techniques will be described in greater detail later in the chapter. For the moment, however, several basic comments need to be made. Program evaluation is based on both common sense and conceptual sophistication. It is simultaneously straightforward and complex, and sounds easier to do than it is. Good program evaluation requires that the following basic conditions are met: (1) the research design actually provides means to answer the questions being asked; (2) the sample appropriately represents the population being studied; (3) the data-gathering techniques fit the research goals; and (4) the sample, time, and personnel available for conducting the study are realistic (Popham 1975). Many program evaluations, however, must be conducted under less-than-ideal conditions and still succeed in providing the requisite information.

The following section of this chapter will discuss the most frequently employed evaluation and assessment models. These models include: (1) context evaluations (needs assessments); (2) formative evaluations; (3) summative evaluations; (4) pilot (feasibility) studies; (5) unit testing; (6) periodic program monitoring; (7) single-group time series; (8) control group with post-test; (9) nonequivalent control group; and (10) before-and-after comparison (see Table 2).

The first step is to design a research strategy matching the agency's goals with the kind of results rendered by particular research techniques. The researcher is responsible for establishing standards of reliability, validity, and utility, and for selecting the valuation procedure to be employed.

Techniques. The first step in any evaluation is clarification of its goals, purpose, and scope so the research design and sample can be appropriate to those ends. There are four facets of that clarification, each of which must be negotiated with the sponsor. These include determining: (1) the focus of the evaluation; (2) the information considered credible and pertinent by both sponsor and researcher, and the research design and measurement instruments; (3) the form in which results will be presented (formal reports, brief notes, technical analyses, development of intervention strategies, staff training, or a single-page executive summary); and (4) whether the research can be accomplished within the limitations of time, budget, and political climate.

Once the anthropologist and community health agency have agreed on the kind of evaluation to be undertaken, the form of reporting, and the information to be sought, the program itself must be examined. Not all programs are equally amenable to evaluation; some program goals cannot easily be translated into measurable outcomes. The anthropologist must assess whether or not the program has measurable objectives, recognizable elements for assessment of program implementation, and an identifiable target population. Often federal programs are difficult to assess because their goals are stated in ambiguous terms such as "to promote greater use of health educational materials," leaving the question of how to measure the "promotion" to the researcher.

One of the most difficult tasks in program evaluation is the selection of appropriate research design. However, the success of the project is impossible if the wrong design is chosen. If time is spent carefully during the design period, the evaluation itself should proceed smoothly. The preliminary and background re-

TABLE 2
Summative Evaluation

Design	*Notation*
1. Single-group time series (longitudinal design)	$Y_1 \quad Y_2 \quad X \quad Y_3 \quad Y_4$
2. Time series with nonequivalent control group (Program A, Group A) (Program B, Group B)	$\dfrac{-R \quad Y_1 \quad Y_2 \quad X \quad Y_3 \quad Y_4}{-R \quad Y_1 \quad Y_2 \quad -X \quad Y_3 \quad Y_4}$
3. True control group (classical experimental design)	$Y \quad R \quad \dfrac{X_1 \quad Y_b}{-X \quad Y_b}$
4. True control group with posttest only	$R \quad \dfrac{X \quad Y_b}{-X \quad Y_b}$
5. Before-and-after comparisons	$Y_a \quad X \quad Y_b$
6. Nonequivalent control group	$M \quad \dfrac{Y_a \quad X \quad Y_b \text{ (experimental)}}{Y_a \quad -X \quad Y_b \text{ (control)}}$

R refers to the random assignment of subjects to groups.
$-R$ refers to groups composed of subjects nonrandomly assigned (nonequivalent groups).
M refers to subjects assigned to groups matched on one or more attributes.
_____ separates experimental group from control group.
X refers to exposure to the program.
$-X$ refers to lack of exposure to the program (or exposure to a different program).
Y refers to the groups tested, either both experimental or one a control.
Y_a refers to the group tested before exposure to the program.
Y_b refers to the group tested after exposure to the program.

search is time-consuming but necessary. Background research should focus on program characteristics such as: (1) how long the program has been in operation, its planning documents, and its history; (2) the size of the program; (3) characteristics of program recipients; (4) characteristics of the program staff; and (5) methods used in the program.

Once the goals of the evaluation are agreed on and the program's objectives are determined, the evaluation procedure can be selected. Depending on the goals, the anthropologist may choose among three types of evaluations: a needs assessment or context evaluation, a formative evaluation, or a summative evaluation. *Needs assessments* try to determine the target populations' needs so programs can be designed or redesigned to meet them. *Context evaluations* are used in determining a community's readiness to accept a particular program. *Formative evaluations* are conducted during the course of program activities to obtain information for program improvement. Formative program evaluation (sometimes called "process evaluation") helps conceptualize what the program is and what it does. *Summative evaluation* (also referred to as "outcome evaluation") on the other hand, focuses on the total impact and outcomes of the program. Needs assessments, formative evaluations, and summative evaluations differ by when they occur in the course of a program, and by the audience to which they are directed.

Concepts. Needs assessments and program evaluations, like any research design, are of value only to the extent that their results are *reliable, valid,* and *useful.* Each of these three concepts has a specific meaning useful in the understanding of community health program evaluation and needs assessment.

Reliability is one aspect of research measurement (Bohrnstedt 1970). A measure (or indicator) is considered reliable to the extent that it always produces the same score for the same element being measured. For example, when a bathroom scale is accurately calibrated to give the same reading for the same weight, it is reliable. A measure is reliable, then, when its application to a particular situation produces the same results repeatedly, assuming that the situation being measured does not change between measurements. An unreliable indicator will obscure or dilute any real differences that exist. In general, indicators based on counts are more reliable than those based on people's memories of an event or of how they felt when something occurred. People rarely forget how many children they have, although they may forget the exact conditions surrounding the birth of each child. Self-administered questionnaires often have reliability and validity problems because the context in which they are answered varies. Although reliability can be estimated without great difficulty, validity presents a more complex problem.

An indicator is considered valid to the extent that it actually measures what it is intended to measure. For instance, the number of pediatric patients at a county hospital's emergency room may reflect less about the absolute health status of children in the county than it does about the number of indigent families with young children who have no regular pediatrician and therefore seek health care through Medicaid access to the county hospital (Whiteford 1983). In this case, rates and ratios of children's use of the county hospital's emergency room would be invalid indicators of the health status of children in that community. The concept of validity is not hard to understand, but developing valid social indicators is difficult. Concepts such as socioeconomic indicators and quality of life are difficult to prove universally valid. Most social variables are invalid to a degree. Because of the lack of shared standards for social variables, we must often rely on indicators we know are somewhat invalid but for which no more accurate indices have been found.

As an example, it might be assumed that birth rate would be a good indicator of future school population size. However, if sociocultural factors are ignored, exclusive reliance on birth rates would be an invalid indicator on which to base future classroom estimates. Let us say that school officials planned to use county birth records to assess future school population in the primary grades. However, even if valid and reliable estimates of county immigration and emigration were possible, birth rates might not be valid indicators of future population growth for many places. Counties along the U.S.-Mexican border, for instance, use birth rates to estimate future grade school populations. But as a valid indicator, birth rates are inappropriate because many women from Mexico have their babies in U.S. hospitals or the many "birthing clinics" that line the border. Simultaneously, women from the United States go to Mexico to have their children because it is less expensive, they have family there, or they prefer the birth practices (Whiteford 1979). A count of children born in the U.S. side of the border county would be an invalid predictor of future classroom size, since many of those children will not attend school in the United States, but in Mexico. However, the county has no other mechanism by which to estimate classroom age cohorts; therefore, although birth rates are to a degree invalid measures on which to base estimates of future classroom occupancy, they are often used.

Utility. The third criterion for selection of indicators builds on both reliability and validity. One aspect of utility is the ability of the indicator to communicate a concept to an audience. Both the validity and reliability of the indicator must be high if it is to have any significant utility. Indicators with clarity and simplicity of expression have greater impact and ability to communicate than those composed of long lists of complex relationships with which the audience is not familiar.

Needs Assessment

A needs assessment is a discrepancy analysis that examines the difference between the ideal situation and the status quo. It is conducted during the planning of a health intervention program so the program can be made responsive to the needs of the target population.

Anthropological skills are particularly suited to the assessment of health needs in a community because assessments are most effective when they are based on realistic appraisals of perceived needs and organizational constraints. Needs assessments may be conducted by a community survey, interviews with key individuals in a target population, public forums, and analysis of existing records. Needs assessments often focus on the health needs of a specified segment of the population. Information for that segment may have to be disaggregated from more comprehensive data for analysis. This may not be possible without primary research such as surveys or open-ended interviews. After the target population is delineated, special attention is paid to developing indices reflective of the needs specific to that population and to highlighting health risks pertinent to the program under consideration. Such risk factors may be specific to cultural, ethnic, genetic, age, or socioeconomic groups; they might include, for instance, rates of adolescent pregnancy, incidence of low birth weights, exposure to work-related hazards, or lack of access to health care facilities.

Donna Rose, an anthropologist planner/evaluator for a community Mental Health Board, conducted a needs assessment for a program to deinstitutionalize clients (Rose 1981). She identified the target population of the program being planned and examined the use of the state mental health facilities by that population. In her needs assessment, Rose identified key demographic characteristics of the target population through a review of client records, conducted interviews with key-informant clients awaiting discharge from the state hospital, and analyzed the target population's use patterns of the hospital. Creation of a client profile gave program planners a clear view of the care, backgrounds, and medical histories of the people most directly affected by the program. The key-informant interviews elicited patients' concern with their lack of vocational and recreational skills needed to live successfully in a residential community outside the hospital. Rose's primary recommendation to the planning board for the program of deinstitutionalizing the patients was:

> In planning a residential treatment program for this population, special attention needs to be directed to the holistic requirements of the individual, with provisions being made for their educational, vocational, recreational, and personal needs, in addition to the residential and psychiatric needs outlined in a community residential treatment program. [1981:vii]

The consumer model of needs assessment is most often employed to focus attention on the users or potential users of a program. The consumer is the major source of information on priorities of need for additional services by target population, age group, and physical area. Within the consumer model, five groups are included:

1. Health-care agencies local agencies and individuals who directly or indirectly treat people with health problems.

2. Secondary, related agencies those that make referrals to the primary health-care givers.

3. High-risk individuals—people who may or actually do experience a high level of need for the programs being considered. Their identification may be based on the histories of those individuals or on characteristics they share with others who frequently use the services. Adolescent mothers are such a high-risk group, even though not all experience difficulties during pregnancy and not all infants born to such mothers are in the "failure-to-thrive" category. However, because of the high percentage of difficulties experienced by adolescent mothers and their newborns, they are placed in a high-risk category.

4. Community and civic groups—groups organized around a central, health-related goal.

5. The community at large—all people living in the program area. The population may be represented by a sample drawn at random or stratified to represent groups with special health problems related to the program being considered.

Following a recent increase in immigration of Southeast Asian refugees, a county health department was mandated to assess the health status of the refugees and to develop programs to meet their needs. The assessment was complicated because of the diversity of national, ethnic, and linguistic backgrounds of this population—a problem greatly compounded by the variety of interactions its members had with U.S. officials since they left their home countries. Clinic personnel, already overworked, understaffed, and without special expertise in the language, culture, health practices, and beliefs of this population felt overwhelmed and confused by the new population. Lack of understanding resulted in physical markings from indigenous medical practices (rub medicine) being misconstrued as child abuse and patients' noncompliance with drug regimens were perceived as lack of need.

County health personnel turned to anthropologist Margaret Anderson and asked her to conduct the necessary needs assessment (Anderson 1981). Out of approximately 700 refugee cases, Anderson analyzed a random sample of 240 individuals. These cases were used as a data base for statistical analysis and for comparison with data from personal interviews Anderson conducted. Among the 18 health parameters used to describe the population were age, sex, ethnic group, time spent in a holding camp, escape route (e.g., boat), family size, results of tuberculosis testing, hemoglobin value, and results of parasite screening. Along with the collection of health status indices, Anderson interviewed refugee sponsors, clinic personnel, and other clinic patients.

Anderson's consumer population was a heterogeneous group with unusual health histories, distinctive health beliefs and practices, and no common language; yet they were being treated by the providers as if they were a single, relatively homogeneous population. Anderson, because of her anthropological training, was cognizant of the role cultural differences play in health practices. Acting on that awareness, she incorporated into her needs assessment a crosscultural comparison of health statistics by national origin.

The Indo-Chinese population Anderson assessed showed patterns of positive test results that varied systematically with country of origin. Vietnamese, Cambodians, Laotians, and ethnic Chinese each demonstrated different responses to the various health screenings administered. Anderson concluded that variation in tuberculosis test response and parasitic burdens were a result of cultural differences in food habits in the native countries (preparation, eating style), means of escape (sea voyage or overland), and the area of encampment (Malaysia, Indonesia, Hong Kong). The relation between cultural or subcultural practices and health status is too often overlooked in assessing community health. As this case shows, cognizance of diversity within a population as it relates to health care and the use of health services can allow providers to be more responsive to their clients' needs by uncovering culturally specific descriptive categories.

In another case, Patricia Long also took advantage of her liminal position as an anthropologist among social workers, psychiatrists, and physicians to develop a needs-assessment strategy that combined anthropological techniques and community health indices (Long 1980). In addition to the standard survey and analysis of social indicators, Long's assessment included the best estimates of a group of key informants (Delphi method). She found that none of the three methods by itself provided sufficient information to allow the planning board to respond to community needs. However, her research, combining both emic and etic data, supplied the board with valid information about community needs and was sufficiently quantitative to justify future programs. Long exemplifies the medical anthropologist's creative use of multiple methodologies to make a unique contribution to community health.

Formative Evaluation

Formative evaluations are conducted during the early stages of a program and provide data used to modify the ongoing program. The results may be reported informally as a speech or in conversations with the project director or staff. Such an evaluation monitors implementation of a program or of pilot tests in the preliminary phases of the program's execution. Formative evaluations can supply program personnel with immediate feedback on such elements as materials being used, format of delivery, recruitment of clients, and client responses. Pilot and feasibility studies, unit testing, and periodic program monitoring are approaches commonly used in formative evaluations.

Pilot and Feasibility Studies. Pilot studies and feasibility studies are usually experimental designs conducted to evaluate the relative quality of two or more formats of a particular aspect of the program. For instance, a pilot study might be undertaken to determine the most effective order in which to present information to women attending a family planning clinic. Two groups of women would be randomly selected; in one, the women would first see the family planning practitioner alone and receive physical examinations and then, as a group, listen to a lecture on reproductive physiology and methods of contraception. The group lecture could be followed by a discussion and a short test to evaluate the women's retention of information and their response to the format. The second group of women would receive the same information, with the order of group/individual interactions reversed. They would have the group lecture on reproductive physiology and methods of contraception first and then would be seen by the family planning practitioner, after which the same evaluative instrument would be administered. The results would then be compared, statistical tests designed to specify significant differences in the two values would be used, and the results would be analyzed to determine which format best meets the program's objectives.

Unit Testing. When a particular unit of instruction or portion of the program has been identified by the staff as problematic or of crucial importance, careful in-depth monitoring of it is required. Any tests of instruments used must be specifically designed to be sensitive to the objectives that unit is to address. Careful sampling of sites and participants can ensure that the groups being measured are representative of the target population and health care providers. Results and recommendations of unit evaluations must be ready in time to modify the program. Using a control group for unit testing often provides more information about the relative effectiveness of the various units, because more than one version can be experimented with simultaneously. When unit testing is conducted with a control group, it is very similar to a feasibility study.

As an example, let's assume that an anthropologist is hired to do a formative evaluation of the relative effectiveness of the unit within the county health department's well-baby clinic that teaches the importance of immunizations. An instrument is designed to assess patient retention of those points of information the staff considers most important to the immunization education program. People representative of the target population are selected and randomly assigned to two or more groups. One is the control group, against which the effectiveness of units used for the other groups is tested. New pamphlets explaining the need for children's immunizations may be used in the experimental groups; the control group may receive either no information at all or the information booklet presently in use in the program. Using a statistical test such as Student's T-Test, comparisons are then made of retention rates of the various groups and relative effectiveness of the units decided.

Periodic Program Monitoring. The third type of formative evaluation to be described here consists of monitoring the program at various intervals during its operation. Periodic monitoring is a useful way to see if the product is on schedule, if short-term goals are being met, and to provide staff feedback. It is a means by which the evaluator can take the pulse of the project as the project is being implemented and to detect problems as they arise. The same people at the same site may be interviewed at monthly intervals, or a single interview schedule may be applied to various sites and different people each time. If the evaluator chooses to visit the same sites, speak with the same people, and use the same unit of measure, periodic monitoring becomes a time-series research design. Such a time series can measure the effect of the program on its target population.

The goal of a formative procedure is to see whether the program is on track, if it appears to be aimed in the direction intended. It can specify problem areas and suggest how to deal with them before they become detrimental to the program itself. Summative evaluation procedures, on the other hand, test the effect the program has had on the target population. They measure its impact, changes in attitudes it causes, and other outcomes of a program. Because evaluators often are not brought in until the end of a project, we will now consider some designs commonly used in summative evaluations.

Summative Evaluation

Summative processes often use one or more of the following research designs: (1) single-group time series, (2) time series with nonequivalent control group, (3) true control group, (4) true control group with posttest only, (5) before-and-after comparisons, and (6) nonequivalent control group.

True control group, true control group with posttest only, nonequivalent control group, and time series with nonequivalent control group designs are often considered to provide the most easily interpretable information. Sampling and timing of the evaluator's introduction into the project are important considerations affecting design selection. That is, in selecting the particular research design, the evaluator must consider his or her access to members of the target population to be able to create randomly assigned control groups or nonrandomly assigned comparison groups. Also, if the evaluator is brought in after the program is implemented, he or she may wish to use nonequivalent-control-group design or a time series with nonequivalent-control-group evaluation.

Single-Group Time Series. This design requires that the evaluator be present before the project is implemented. The object of this type of evaluation is to measure the effect of a particular program on a specified population according to designated criteria. A series of measurements is made before the target population is exposed to the program; the same series of measurements is collected from the same population after the program has been provided to them. The results of a time-series comparison allow the program to be calibrated for effect on that population. A time series can focus on before and after conditions, compare data gathered at the beginning of the project with data collected at the midpoint of the project, or be used for continuous testing of program participants.

Time Series with Nonequivalent Control Group. This design is like the one just described, with the addition of comparison to a group exposed to a similar, regularly measured program. Rather than assessing the impact of a single program on a single population, this design compares two programs administered to two similar groups; these groups are not randomly chosen and are, therefore, nonequivalent. The analysis is a comparison of two programs over time.

True Control Group. In determining the relative efficiency of two programs, the true control group is an excellent strategy. Two equivalent groups are exposed to two distinctive programs, using pre- and posttests to determine the relative value of the programs. For both programs, a single target population is used that is similar in age or other variables. A pretest is administered to this single group and then the members are randomly assigned to participate in the two programs being compared. After the groups have been exposed to separate programs, the posttest is administered simultaneously to both groups. The research design must control for confounding variables, or else false results may be obtained. Confounding variables are unexpected influences on one group that obscure the differential effects of the programs being tested. To avoid or minimize such con founding variables, the researcher must ensure that the two groups' experiences are as similar as possible, except for the programs being evaluated. Likewise, contamination or information crossover between members of the two groups must be avoided.

True Control Group With Posttest Only. This design follows the same research strategy as does the true control group, except that no pretest is given to the two groups. An evaluator might decide to avoid a pretest for a variety of reasons; in some instances, it might unduly prejudice the target population toward the program's intended effects. It may also be impossible or inconvenient to administer a pretest, although this alone should not preclude the utility of a posttest.

Before-and-After Comparisons. If the investigator has access to only one program, how can it be evaluated? One approach to such a situation is to select a sample, administer a pretest before the members are exposed to the program, and then give a posttest to the same group. Although the evaluator will be unable to compare test results with a control group, he or she can examine how attitudes, knowledge, or beliefs of a single group have changed as a result of exposure to the program. This design can be usefully applied in a processual evaluation of discrete changes among members of a cohort. It can also be used in conjunction with data acquired through some other process, e.g., a national sample of respondents. The evaluation then compares the performance of a specific group to the national norm. The before-and-after design allows comparison with results obtained earlier. For instance, in an innovative project called Improved Pregnancy Outcomes (for teenagers pregnant for the first time), a major component was prenatal care and education. Because the project was new and varied in different locations, access to national norms and comparable groups was not possible. However, the before-and-after design is still applicable to test for changes in the young women's attitudes as they participated in the program.

Nonequivalent Control Group. This design allows comparison of two programs even though the two samples are not randomly assigned and therefore, not equivalent. The evaluation process is much like that just described for a before-and-after model, but the effect of two programs on two different groups of people is compared. The second group is selected on the basis of similarity to the control group—those to be exposed to the test program. For instance, women pregnant for the first time (primipara) might consitute the sample from which both groups are drawn. Each group is given a pretest, exposed to one of the programs, and then given the posttest. In another version of this design, selection criteria for the population are varied while holding the program as a constant. Instead of a population composed exclusively of primiparous women, one group could consist of women pregnant for the first time, the second of multiparous women. The evaluator might give a pretest to both groups, expose them to the same program (e.g., on the care and feeding of a newborn), and administer a posttest. The results would reflect the difference not between two programs, but between two nonequivalent samples that vary by a single major criterion.

Sampling and data-gathering techniques are crucial to effective implementation of any evaluation design. This chapter does not treat these topics; the reader is referred to the texts listed as resources. Two books that should be singled out for attention are H. Russell Bernard's detailed and lucid book, *Research Methods in Cultural Anthropology* (1988), and James Popham's *Educational Evaluation,* a superb book on design and sampling (1975).

How to Obtain a Job in Community Health

A medical anthropologist can enter the field of community health by many different paths, all of which entail some degree of academic training, work experience, and personal fortitude.

Academic Training

The traditional background required for a graduate degree in anthropology is an excellent place to begin. If one chooses to work in community health in the United States, a graduate degree in medical anthropology can provide entrance into a chosen profession. There are a number of excellent programs in medical anthropology, such as the University of South Florida, the University of Connecticut-Storrs, the University of California-San Francisco, the University of Kentucky, Case Western and Michigan State University. Those programs that incorporate internships and community-based experience are most respected by potential employers in community health.

Academic training need not be confined exclusively to graduate programs in anthropology. A master's degree with specialization in either applied or medical anthropology could be usefully combined with a master's degree in public health. Some universities, such as South Florida, offer collaborative programs between anthropology and public health.

Experience

While degrees are important (and impressive) to administrators, community health employers are more interested in experience. They need to be assured that an employee can produce results. A work record that shows competence in management, a capacity to produce clear and succinct documents on time, and an ability to use available resources is the best recommendation.

Some skills that enable one to use resources fully are easily learned: how to use the library efficiently, how to write clearly and without jargon, how to organize time so that deadlines can be met. Other skills require a bit more concentration. A degree of statistical sophistication is often required; one need not be able to do the necessary computations, but it is important to know which statistical tests are available and appropriate to particular types of data. Knowledge of computer operations and programming is also very helpful in disaggregating and understanding the type of data frequently collected by community health agencies. Many of these "secondary" skills can give one applicant an edge over others. Employers also can more easily justify hiring a medical anthropologist with special expertise in a particular topic area, such as health education, issues in mother/child health, crosscultural barriers to health care delivery, hypertension, venereal disease, or AIDS.

Fortitude

Though it may not be considered a skill, fortitude is most certainly required if one is to learn how to get a job and how to work in a community health agency setting. As Angrosino and Kushner have suggested, anthropologists seeking employment outside traditional academic areas need to be creative and experimental in their search (Angrosino and Kushner 1978). This requires endurance and a sense of vision. The anthropologist must be able to see how particular skills and interests are of direct value to the agency's needs. This requires a self-confidence that must come from competence. Therefore, the best way to prepare for a job is to acquire knowledge, skills training, experience, and vision—all of which require fortitude.

Putting It All Together

Putting it all together means combining the academic training with job experience to find the right job. The following suggestions are aimed at helping someone interested in working in community health do just that.

1. Develop contacts with people already employed in health programs.

2. Work with community groups interested in local, state and regional health issues.

3. Turn yourself into a resource by professional exchanges based on academic disciplines or on topical areas.

4. Be familiar with the journals related to a specific interest.

5. Learn about and contribute to regional special-interest groups.

6. Make personal contacts through letters, exchange information, and follow up with a telephone call. The local Chamber of Commerce may have a special health care council composed of task forces whose members are employed outside the Chamber of Commerce but who have a special interest in community health. These people are excellent resources.

7. Channel your special interests, skills, and knowledge into a particular program, concerned citizen group, or professional exchanges. To find others who share professional interests, consult the attached bibliography list of journals focusing on topics of concern to anthropologists.

8. Write to authors whose articles address special topical areas.

9. Develop and maintain contacts at local and regional levels of community health, both within and outside academia.

Conclusion

Medical anthropologists are deeply involved in assessing levels of community health both in the United States and in the international arena. Some applied medical anthropologists work abroad; for example, Claire Cassidy assessed the nutritional status of children in AID-funded projects in Mauritania (1988), and Judith Davison evaluated the impact of traditional birth attendant training programs on community health care in Peru (1987). Others, like Robert Trotter and Margaret S. Boone, are applied medical anthropologists who work in the United States: Trotter assessed the level of risk of lead poisoning among Mexican Americans by conducting an ethnography among folk healers and herb shop owners (1987), while Boone evaluated causes of infant mortality in a large metropolitan hospital in Washington, D.C. Boone combined traditional anthropological techniques such as observation and in-depth interviews, with medical chart reviews in a case-control study (1982). This range of activities, from international multicommunity health assessments and program evaluations, to risk assessment of folk medicine in rural United States suggests the breadth of the community health projects in which anthropologists are involved.

The Medical Anthropologist's Contribution in a Community Health Setting

Anthropology has been called the commonsense, holistic discipline. This is not to say that anthropologists have a monopoly on common sense, or the ability to see a program, a practice, or an agency as part of a larger whole, but that the theoretical orientations of the discipline, the research methods, and a background in crosscultural studies *predispose* anthropologists toward certain rare, if not unique, contributions. These predispositions incorporate the following values:

1. To seek information from the target population themselves for their definitions of health, perceptions of health needs, and experiences with health programs.

2. To understand service provision from the clients' as well as the providers' points of view.

3. To view the Western medical model as only one among many possible ways of conceiving of health and illness, and to be aware of the myths and self-reifying aspects of Western medical institutions.

4. To be aware of the potential pitfalls of statistical research: the danger of creating fallacious relationships among variables, and the spurious nature of many statistically "significant" relationships.

5. To mistrust theories that either depart too far from or only reify empirical evidence.

6. To be sensitive to the causal complexities of behavioral phenomena and to the possibility of unanticipated effects of intervention.

Medical anthropologists in community health settings have the advantage of a professional position that Turner has referred to as "liminal" (1970). Taken from the Latin word for "threshold," liminal refers to a temporary condition in which statuses and roles are ambiguous and open to invention. Whether they are employed as culture brokers, program evaluators, administrators, or health planners, the role of anthropologist in community health settings is not constrained by long-standing traditions and expectations, and therefore they have the freedom from structural limitations to invent their own identities and roles, applying their skills in unusual ways. The anthropologist working in a community health setting has several advantages: in this liminal position he or she can assume multiple roles within an agency, or create a new role. Simultaneously, the ability to focus on the health agency as a social system allows the anthropologist to see the interactions between the parts and how they mutually reinforce each other (Hill 1988). Anthropologists are trained to analyze social structures and interpersonal dynamics within communities, and this training can also be applied to local and regional community health agencies.

Similarly, Hazel Weidman, writing from the position of an anthropologist working within a psychiatry department, noted the need to introduce social science into the medical system by applying specialized knowledge and demonstrating the value of social science's qualitative and quantitative research methods (1971). Medical anthropologists no longer need to view themselves as "poor relations" in the medical system, skilled in "soft" (nonquantitative) techniques. Anthropologists now are trained in specialized skills of research design and evaluation that add information otherwise missing from medically dominated agencies. Individuals trained in social and behavioral science, with humanistic, quantitative, and qualitative skills are with increased frequency explicitly requested by program and funding agencies.

Anthropologists are greatly needed in community health. They have skills and training rarely found among other health-agency workers; the crosscultural perspective requisite for understanding today's multicultural health environment. The special role of "resident outsider" gives the anthropologist an opportunity to integrate various apparently disparate agency needs and functions under a single umbrella, efficiently responding to its client's needs. The anthropologist in community health may be an evaluator, a communicator, a facilitator, or a trainer, but first and foremost he or she will bring to community health a sensitivity born of cultural relativism, nurtured in respect for cultural influences on human behavior, and adapted to the most human condition, a concern for health and well-being.

Acknowledgments. I want to express my appreciation to a number of people who helped make the writing of this chapter a rich experience: Mike Angrosino, who encouraged me to write about community health evaluation; J. Douglas Uzzell, Carole Hill, Linda Bennett, and the anonymous reviewers for their immensely useful editorial criticisms. I also thank both Donna Romeo and Steven Gouldman for their editorial assistance. Each of these individuals helped make this chapter better; the responsibility for errors remains that of the author.

References Cited

Anderson, Margaret Ann
    1981   Health and Disease in Southeast Asian Refugees. Master's thesis, University of
        South Florida.
Angrosino, Michael V.
    1981   Community-Based Care of Retarted Adults in Tennessee: An Examination of
        State Policy. Unpublished manuscript, files of the author.
Angrosino, Michael V., and Gilbert Kushner
    1978   Internship and Practicum Experience as Modalities for the Training of the Applied Anthropologist. *In* Social Science Education for Development. William Vickers
        and Glen R. Howze, eds. Pp. 18–34. Tuskegee, AL: Tuskegee Institute, Center for
        Rural Development.
Bernard, H. Russell
    1988   Research Methods in Cultural Anthropology. Newbury Park, Calif.: Sage Publications.
Bohrnstedt, G. W.
    1970   Reliability and Validity Assessment in Attitude Measurement. *In* Attitude Measurement. G. F. Summer, ed. Pp. 80–99. Chicago: Rand McNally.
Boone, Margaret S.
    1982   A Socio-Medical Study of Infant Mortality among Disadvantaged Blacks. Human Organization 41(3):227–236.

Bryant, Carol
1990   Personal Communication.
Cassidy, Claire
1988   A Survey of Nutritional Status in Children under Four and Their Mothers in Four Villages in the Regions of Brakna, Gudimaka, and Gorgol. Tucson: University of Arizona, Nutrition in Agricultural Cooperative Agreement.
Chrisman, Noel
1982   Anthropology in Nursing: An Exploration in Adaptation. *In* Clinically Applied Anthropology: Anthropologists in Health Science Settings. N. H. Chrisman and T. W. Maretzki, eds. Pp. 117–140. Boston: D. Reidel.
Davison, Judith
1987   The Delivery of Rural Reproductive Medicine. *In* Anthropological Praxis: Translating Knowledge into Action. R. Wulff and S. Fiske, eds. Boulder, CO: Westview Press.
Friedman, Gary D.
1974   Primer of Epidemiology. New York: McGraw-Hill.
Hill, Carole E.
1984(ed.)   Current Health Policy Issues and Alternatives: An Applied Social Science Perspective. Boulder, CO: Westview Press.
1988   Community Health Systems in the Rural South. Boulder, CO: Westview Press.
Janes, Craig R.
1986   Migration and Hypertension: An Ethnography of Disease Risk in an Urban Samoan Community. *In* Anthropology and Epidemiology. Craig R. Janes, Ronald Stall, and Sandra Gifford, eds. Pp. 175–212. Boston: D. Reidel.
Long, Patricia
1980   The Use of Needs Assessment Techniques in Planning Community Mental Health Services. Master's thesis, University of South Florida.
MacMahon, B., and T. F. Pugh
1970   Epidemiology: Principles and Methods. Boston: Little, Brown and Company.
Osborn, Barbara M.
1966   Introduction to Community Health. Boston: Allyn and Bacon.
Poland, M., et al.
1990   Quality of Prenatal Care: Selected Social, Behavioral, and Biomedical Factors; and Birth Weight. Obstetrics and Gynecology 75(4):607–612.
Popham, James
1975   Educational Evaluation. Englewood Cliffs, NJ: Prentice-Hall.
Rose, Donna
1981   Planning for Program Deinstitutionalization of Mental Patients. Master's thesis, University of South Florida.
Trotter, Robert
1987   A Case of Lead Poisoning from Folk Remedies in Mexican American Communities. *In* Anthropological Praxis: Translating Knowledge into Action. R. Wulff and S. Fiske, eds. Pp. 146–159. Boulder, CO: Westview Press.
Turner, Victor
1970   The Forest of Symbols: Aspects of Ndembu Ritual. Ithaca, NY: Cornell University Press.
Weidman, Hazel
1971   Trained Manpower and Medical Anthropology: Conceptual, Organizational, and Educational Priorities. Social Science and Medicine 15:15–36.

Whiteford, Linda M.
  1979   The Border Land as an Extended Community. *In* Migration across Frontiers:
         Mexico and the United States. F. Camara and R. V. Kemper, eds. Pp. 127–137. Al-
         bany: State University of New York Press.
  1983   Self-Care and Emergency Room Care: An Analysis of Treatment Regimens. Pa-
         per presented at the World Federation for Mental Health meeting, Washington, DC.
  1984   Staying Out of the Bottom Drawer: The Art of Research Utility. Practicing An-
         thropology 9(1):9–11.
  1990   A Question of Adequacy: Primary Health Care in the Dominican Republic. So-
         cial Science and Medicine 30(2):221–226.
Wood, Juanita B., Robert G. Hughes, and Carroll L. Estes
  1986   Community Health Centers and the Elderly: A Potential New Alliance. Journal
         of Community Health 11(2):137–145.

chapter six

Anthropologists in Medical Education: Ethnographic Prescriptions

THOMAS M. JOHNSON

The involvement of social scientists in medical education is now well into its third decade (Kennedy, Pattishall, and Baldwin 1983). Although the number of medical anthropologists working in medical school settings has never rivaled that of psychologists, the presence of even relatively small numbers has spawned much debate and resulted in profound changes within medical anthropology. For example, the terms "clinical" and "clinically applied" medical anthropology have been thoroughly discussed in the literature (Johnson 1985; Medical Anthropology Newsletter 1980), with the latter now generally taken to refer to medical anthropologists working as teachers, researchers, or clinical consultants in health science center settings *without special training or mandate to intervene in patient care*, and the former referring to those who are *credentialled in both medical anthropology and a recognized clinical discipline* (Chrisman and Maretzki 1982).

There is still no generally recognized role for medical anthropologists in medical education, so working successfully in such settings today demands individual preparation to acquire the necessary specialized knowledge, skills, and temperament. Fortunately, the early involvement of anthropologists in medical school settings, excellent professional socialization studies by medical sociologists, and more recent publications by medical anthropologists now working in clinical settings, provide abundant ethnographic insights into the culture of American biomedicine, and practical strategies necessary for successfully defining and elaborating a rewarding medical school career.

The purpose of this chapter is to draw on each of these sources to provide an ethnographic foundation for anthropologists interested in careers in medical school settings, based on the premise that the ability to work within biomedicine is analogous to being successful in *any* crosscultural endeavor. By taking an ethnographic perspective on biomedicine, this chapter advocates a quintessential anthropological stance which tends to be "forgotten" by many American anthropologists working in their own culture: maintaining objectivity and neutrality about Western medical systems is difficult for most anthropologists, who tend to condemn physicians and identify mainly with patients (Stein 1980). Although critiques of biomedicine from the perspectives of political economy or "critical medical anthropology" should remain a valued perspective within academic medical anthropology, gratuitous physician-bashing and unenlightened patient advocacy are antithetical to successful medical school work.

One major impediment to working in medical schools is lack of insight into the process of medical education and an understanding of the implicit culture—the unconsciously held values, perspectives, and attitudes—of biomedicine. Thus, my goal in this chapter is to help medical anthropologists and others interested in medical school careers to better understand, at a "visceral," rather than merely at an intellectual level, what life in a medical school really involves. The bulk of the chapter is devoted to a discussion of the formal and informal process of professional socialization in medicine, rather than to an elaborate discussion of what medical anthropologists have done in medical schools. Two basic roles for anthropologists are discussed here: teacher and researcher. The chapter contains descriptions of daily life in medical school settings, caveats about the personal and professional stresses facing medical anthropologists who choose to work in them, and suggestions for professionally rewarding anthropological involvement, some of which are distilled into a skills checklist at the end. Reading this chapter is not a substitute for mandatory fieldwork in medical school settings by any anthropologist preparing to work in medical education.

Background

History of Anthropological Work in Medical Schools

Any medical anthropologist planning a career in medical education needs to be aware of the history of such involvement, as well as the roots of tension between social scientists and physicians. The public grants the medical profession license and mandate to control access to practice and define the entire range of medical services, based on their presumed expertise and orientation to the social good. In the last 30 years, however, there has been a growing discontent with the medical profession, as it has been unable to deal effectively with major health problems such as cancer, chronic diseases, and illnesses resulting directly from unhealthy life-styles, despite tremendous increases in health care expenditures. Discontent has also increased with the recognition that medical care is not accessible or available to everyone, regardless of geographic location, social class, or ethnic background. These factors, coupled with a demystification of physicians in the media, a growing resentment of the relatively greater wealth and power of physicians by the general public, and an increasing litigiousness by patients, has led to increasing governmental involvement in shaping the practice of medicine.

Some of the governmental effects to change medical practice has been directed toward medical education. Legislation passed since the early 1960s has encouraged the enrollment of ethnic minorities and women in health profession schools, the growth of primary care to counter trends toward increasing medical specialization, and the expansion of roles for allied health professionals such as nurse practitioners and physician assistants. In addition, major efforts were made through training grants to medical schools to increase curriculum in the psychological and social aspects of medical care.

Early anthropological involvement in medical education was encouraged through such federal training grants. Often, professors with appointments in academic anthropology departments were invited to teach medical students, or to participate in research. Early anthropologists' involvement in the medical arena tended to be serendipitous, temporary, or unexpected. As they entered directly from academic anthropology departments with little formal preparation, they discovered that the traditional styles of academic teaching and methods of anthropological research were alien to physicians and biomedical researchers. Often unprepared for the realities of biomedicine, many early anthropologists in medical education found the activities unrewarding: they participated with mixed results and frequently at some cost to professional identity. Although unanticipated, they discovered what most anthropologists in the field quickly learn: work in an unaccustomed setting can promote culture shock in the form of sensory assaults, intellectual isolation, and other forms of personal and professional stress.

Thus, while there has been recognition of the importance of social science for medicine, at another level social scientists have been considered interlopers thrust upon medical schools. Moreover, members of the medical profession are generally aware of academic social science critiques of biomedicine, and so tend to be somewhat skeptical of the motives of medical anthropologists and others of the social science ilk in their midst. Medical anthropologists anticipating a career in medical schools should remember that, although it can be fairly easily overcome, an antiphysician bias will tend to be attributed to social scientists, even if it is not manifest.

Ethnographic Literature on Medical Education

An essential part of preparation for a career in medical school settings is reading the abundant literature on medical education and practice. Studies of medical student socialization date to the late 1950s and early 1960s. Perhaps the classic is *Boys in White: Student Culture in Medical School* (Becker et al. 1961), in which several medical sociologists immersed themselves in the daily lives of medical students using traditional participant-observation methodology in addition to questionnaires. Robert Merton and colleagues (Merton, Reader, and Kendall 1957) also described medical education as professional socialization in an edited volume, *The Student Physician: Introductory Studies in the Sociology of Medical Education*, in which there appeared the seminal chapter by Renee Fox, "Training For Uncertainty."

In the 1970s and 1980s, several other books of note about medical education as professional socialization appeared. *Mastering Medicine: Professional Socialization in Medical School* (Coombs 1978) was, in a sense, an updating of *Boys In White*, in that an entire medical school class was followed longitudinally from acceptance into medical school through involvement in residency training. Significantly, this book describes socialization as a "status passage," sees the process as both social and individual, and discusses the changes in attitudes and values of medical students as they progress through training. *Becoming Psychiatrists: The Professional Transformation of Self* (Light 1980), is simultaneously a study of the professional socialization into a specialized, marginal branch of medicine, and a discussion of what is revealed by that process of psychiatry's ideas about itself, and its relationship to the public and the rest of medicine. More recently, in a book entitled *The Private Lives and Professional Identity of Medical Students,* Broadhead (1983) has described how medical training delivers a "jarring blow" to the sensibilities and private lives of students. *Becoming Doctors: The Adoption of a Cloak of Competence* (Haas and Shaffir 1987), is also an ethnographic study of medical students. It defines professionalization as a process of the social legitimization of authority and focuses on the anxieties of medical students, who desperately strive for a sense of competence in the face of tremendous uncertainty. These and other recent publications discuss how medical education demands a slavish devotion to professional work, often at the expense of personal health.

Indeed, in the last two decades, the literature on medical education increasingly has dealt with the psychological traumas which result from the rigors of medical training. This literature has taken the form of advice for medical students written by physicians, such as *So You Want to Be a Doctor: The Realities of Pursuing Medicine as a Career* (Bluestone 1981) and *Why Would a Girl Go Into Medicine?* (Campbell 1973). Another type of publication which should be read by anthropologists interested in medical school careers is "kiss-and-tell" or "confessional" books about medicine, many authored by physicians, which are not always flattering, such as *Forgive and Remember: Managing Medical Failure* (Bosk 1979), *Confessions of a Medical Heretic* (Mendelsohn 1979), *Intern* (Dr. X 1965), *Medical School* (Drake 1978), *Medical Student* (Knight 1973), *The Making of a Surgeon* (Nolen 1970), and *Gentle Vengeance* (LeBaron 1982). One recent book, *Becoming a Doctor: A Journey of Initiation in Medical School* (Konner 1987), is of special interest, both because it was written by an anthropologist who decided in mid-career to go to medical school, and because it is exceptionally revealing of the foibles of medical students and their mentors.

Several recent anthropological publications, while somewhat theoretical, contain important insights into biomedicine. *American Medicine as Culture* (Stein 1990a) and *The Psychodynamics of Medical Practice* (Stein 1990b) are authored by a medical anthropologist who has immersed himself as a teacher in medical school settings. The former is particularly revealing, and should be required reading for any course in medical anthropology. *Biomedicine Examined* (Lock and Gordon 1988), *Encounters with Biomedicine: Case Studies in Medical Anthropology* (Baer 1987), and *Physicians of Western Medicine* (Hahn and Gaines 1985) are all edited volumes containing many ethnographic insights and practical strategies for working in biomedical settings, although not all selections specifically address medical education. Two other articles address specifically the issue of working clinically in medical education (Johnson 1981) and hospital settings (Johnson 1987).

Three perspectives from the literature are particularly important. First, the early sociological studies frequently referred to the formation of a "student culture'' in medical schools, an adaptive response to the rigors of medical training in which the student group is structured, albeit informally, to provide mutual support and to regulate the amount of work that students actually do. They also recognize that socialization is both a *social* and a *psychological* process. Second, many studies imply an even more traditional anthropological perspective, the ''rites of passage'' model, from which medical education is seen as a liminal (transitional) period in an elaborate social status transition from layman to professional. Indeed, the terms ''initiation,'' ''transformation,'' ''symbols,'' and ''enduring changes,'' which appear in the many books about medical students, reflect the profound changes which occur in the process of becoming a physician. Finally, it is important to realize that medical students are not passive in the process: many of the ethnographic studies clearly focus on how individuals going through the process *actively* participate in the negotiation and construction of their identities.

Recruitment and Selection for Medical Training

Anthropologists who anticipate working with medical students need to understand the personal deprivation and profound professional molding of students undergoing medical training. This is important because we deal with students who may be uninterested or unsophisticated in the social sciences, who are often quite angry at authority figures, and who are often unable to ''step back'' and critically examine their own professional and personal growth.

At the time when the earliest sociological studies of medical education were being published, students planning to attend medical school were a relatively homogeneous group. Overwhelmingly white, male, and upper-middle-class, college students of the 1950s and 1960s followed a rigidly prescribed premedical curriculum dominated by natural science courses. Compared to students headed for law school, premedical students tended to have made their career decisions earlier, even as early as junior high school. They also were less likely to have considered other career options, thus being exquisitely vulnerable to fears of failure and doggedly (some would suggest blindly) committed to the profession of medicine, despite tremendous personal sacrifice. Since this was a period of increasing competition for places in medical school, a premium was placed on ''getting a good cume'' (cumulative grade point average) and scoring well on the MCAT (Medical College Admissions Test), the two most important criteria for admission at the time.

Competition for grades among premedical students was so fierce in the 1960s that rumors of students sabotaging each other's laboratory experiments were rampant. Stereotypes of premedical students were largely negative, with fellow undergraduates viewing them as grade-conscious and unsociable (Conrad 1986). Premedical students typically succeeded through compulsive study habits and those who successfully negotiated their way into medical schools were usually in the top five to ten percent of their graduating classes. Nevertheless, these students were likely to have been exposed to very little in the social sciences.

During the late 1970s and 1980s, however, many changes occurred in premedical education. Many more women and minority students began to be admitted to medical schools, the number of "slots" increased dramatically as new medical schools were opened, and the number of applicants to medical schools dropped dramatically. Fewer students now find it necessary to follow strict premedical curricula. In addition, premedical majors in biology or chemistry are now frequently enhanced by courses, or even double majors, in social sciences. Today, many medical school applicants have prior experience in allied health professions such as nursing or occupational therapy. Thus, medical school applicants have begun to have more diverse educational backgrounds, appear to be less unquestioningly committed to medical careers, are more likely to object to the personal deprivation involved in medical training, and are often more interested in the psychosocial dimensions of medicine.

Despite these changes, the process of "becoming" a medical student continues to involve profound alteration of personal and social identity. In many respects, the status of young people who express an interest in being a physician begins to change as soon as they declare such an intention to family and friends. Pursuing a medical career, in decades past at least, was held in such esteem that parents often became extremely invested in the fantasy plans of their young "doctors-to-be," even to the point of introducing their 13-year-olds as "the one who is going to be a doctor." Indeed, medical students sometimes inexplicably began to fail exams early in medical school, only to realize (usually with great relief) that they did not really want to be in medical school at all, but only were following that course to "please their parents." "Failure," in such cases, is a way of getting out of medicine without having to admit the truth about their ambivalence to themselves, parents, or others.

The intensely dehumanizing or depersonalizing character of medical education may be foreign to medical anthropologists who have gone through graduate training. Broadhead (1983:19–27) writes that, although medical students today are really a diverse group, the admissions process forces them to act as though they have a single identity: medical student. This identification starts many years prior to formal application with the learning of criteria for being an attractive medical school applicant, the deliberate and well-organized assimilation of skills through formal training, and the presentation of credentials (GPA, MCAT, interviews).

In presenting oneself on paper, medical school aspirants tend only to include those attributes stressed as important by the medical school and to ignore idiosyncratic attributes. Selective revealing of personal identities first occurs during the admissions interview, when there is a need to dissociate oneself from the aggregate and to emphasize individuality, deeper character, stability, and forcefulness. Even while stressing "uniqueness," however, applicants "normalize" their individuality—demonstrating how it actually "fits in" with becoming a physician. Tellingly, many applicants express fear that they "revealed too much" in admission interviews, recognizing that there is a fine line to be walked between assertion of personal characteristics and conformity to expectations of the profession.

In short, in order to gain admittance to medical training, students' personal identities are sacrificed early in order to appear "professional." Most students feel that they will be able to resume more personal roles and goals after training but many of their personal talents, interests, and relationships will be permanently altered.

Basic Science and Research

Medical school is traditionally a four-year program, with the first two years—termed "preclinical"—devoted to classroom education in the "basic sciences," such as biochemistry, physiology, anatomy, pharmacology, and pathology. The third and fourth years consist of "clinical clerkships," in which medical students learn by working in the hospital. The preclinical–clinical education dichotomy defines a basic division in medical school social organization: research versus clinical medicine. Much of the research in medical school settings is conducted by members of basic science departments. Courses in the preclinical years usually are taught by faculty who are typically Ph.D.'s and, thus, are differentiated from the M.D. "clinical faculty." This section discusses research in medical schools, focusing on the perspectives and skills needed for medical anthropologists who desire to conduct research in such settings.

Most basic science departments have no clinical involvement and only teach preclinical lectures or labs and do research. In fact, in many medical schools, these departments are physically segregated from the clinical departments, and there is little opportunity for informal interaction between faculty. Biomedical research is highly lucrative, however, representing one area of federal funding which has not been drastically reduced during recent Republican administrations. Basic science faculty typically sustain themselves by bringing in large research grants and studying highly specialized areas, but much of their research is viewed by medical students as esoteric and irrelevant to the eventual practice of medicine.

There is also increasing pressure on medical school faculty in *clinical* departments to conduct research and publish. Unlike university academic settings, most medical school faculty can choose one of two career paths: tenure track (academic) or "clinical" track. Indeed, physician faculty members may start on tenure track and later move to clinical track, where they devote much of their efforts to teaching and patient care, if their publication records do not bode well for being granted tenure. Whereas tenure-track faculty are expected to generate a portion of their salaries from research grants, clinical faculty generate salary dollars from patient care.

Many medical anthropologists have discovered niches as researchers in clinical departments such as pediatrics, psychiatry, or family and community medicine, whose physician faculty members may not have strong research methodology or grantsmanship skills, and who welcome social science collaboration. Some health science center settings include schools of public health, where anthropologists may secure faculty appointments and develop collaborative research projects with clinical departments. In order to be hired by a clinical department, an anthropologist must make personal contact with the department chair or principal investigator of a major research project, and must also be familiar with the research and clinical priorities of the specialty.

There are specific role requirements and adaptations for medical anthropologists working as basic researchers in medical school settings (Barnett 1985). First, as mentioned earlier, medical anthropologists conducting research in medical school settings must not be overtly critical of biomedicine. Much as any anthropological researcher will be reluctant to criticize or recommend major changes when studying a foreign culture, anthropological researchers in medical settings must suspend judgments about *either* patients or practitioners in order to ensure continuing access to all parties. Applied medical anthropologists in either setting, however, must make judgments and recommend changes understanding that this entails unusual burdens and risks, realize from the outset that they can never be wholly successful, and be willing to accept some of the blame for problems (Tax 1964:237).

Second, medical anthropologists must develop facility in a broad range of research paradigms and data-analysis strategies, and must be able to demystify participant observation. In biomedicine, the gold standard for research is the double-blind, placebo-controlled drug trial; research without a ''control group'' of some sort is virtually unthinkable. Familiarity with case-control designs, quasi-experimental designs, and other strategies not normally taught to anthropologists is most important. Quantification and replicability of research results are the rule, and qualitative data analysis is often misunderstood or dismissed as unscientific. Thus, a good background in quantitative strategies and biostatistics is imperative.

Third, anthropologists must be able to carry out *collaborative* research. Whereas academic anthropology teaches individual ethnographic research, almost all medical school research involves multidisciplinary research teams. Academic anthropology places a premium on single-authored publications, while medical publications are almost always multi-authored, including in the list of authors nearly everyone even remotely connected to the research effort. In the actual conduct of collaborative research, medical anthropologists are in a unique position to facilitate the team effort, since we are trained to understand and interpret the diverse views of the professionals comprising the research team. This generic anthropological research strength should be supplemented by formal interdisciplinary health care team development strategies (see Rubin, Plovnick, and Fry 1975) which can be learned and profitably utilized to increase the value of an anthropologist.

Fourth, research positions in medical school demand grantsmanship skills: anthropologists aspiring for such positions should develop a track record of successful grant writing.

Fifth, research should have relevance to the clinical mission of patient care. In the most valued studies, findings lead to changes in clinical prctices.

Finally, dual training in anthropology and another field more widely recognized in medical school research settings (such as psychology, public health, or biostatistics) can add legitimacy.

Preclinical Teaching

Student Solidarity and Medical Student Culture

Medical students in the preclinical years are largely unaware of research activities except when Ph.D. researchers present their data in lectures. Typically, preclinical students spend six to eight hours each day in lectures, several more hours in labs, and the remainder of the evening studying. In recent years, social scientists have been asked to lecture to students about the broad range of psychological and social features of patient care. In order to teach effectively, however, it is necessary to understand how medical students view their preclinical coursework, as well as to appreciate the student culture that develops during these years.

Medical students in the preclinical years tend to be an isolated and close-knit group. Isolation and exclusivity can be understood, anthropologically, as one aspect of medical students beginning a rite of passage. It is a period in which initiates are literally ripped from their former position in the social structure. Few medical students are fully aware of how profound this separation and isolation really is: essentially, once accepted to medical school, relationships to others are forever altered. For example, most medical students are shocked when, at Thanksgiving vacation (the first trip back home since entering medical school), for example, their usually very straightlaced and proper great aunt asks them the most personal questions about her bowel functions or the like.

Not only is it a shock to be asked for medical opinions after only two months of school, but it is also troubling to have role relationships with others be so dramatically altered. As old friends and former college classmates get together at vacation times, those who chose not to go to medical school are often appalled by the workaholism and constriction of interests that characterizes first-year medical students. Perhaps the most salient comment about medical student isolation comes from medical students themselves, who note ruefully, "All we ever do is go to parties with other medical students . . . and all we ever talk about is medicine."

The exclusivity of medical student status is typically reinforced from the first day of orientation when they are told by the Dean or President that they are "among the chosen few" who should be grateful for having been selected. The sense of being special is an effective way of dealing the anxieties faced by medical students. Like many professionals who must deal with death, pain, danger, and personal deprivation (nurses, soldiers, police) medical students typically adopt the attitude that "nobody can really understand what we do," thereby finding personal strength in group solidarity, referred to as "elitism as a defense."

Most important, the message given to entering medical students is that they now "owe something to the profession" which has "chosen" them, and that they *cannot* fail. This ethos is so strong that there is a veritable "conspiracy of silence" between medical students and most of their M.D. faculty members: to even admit to doubts about choosing medicine as a career or about ability to succeed is taboo. One highly rewarding and needed role for a medical anthropologist on a medical school faculty is to act as a counselor for medical students who are having difficulties in their preclinical years. Medical students feel much more comfortable discussing their ambivalence about medicine with non-M.D. faculty, or the rare M.D. faculty member who is considered approachable. In fact, those M.D. faculty who are known to the students as sympathetic and who are sought out for advice usually make excellent colleagues to serve as "key informants" for medical anthropologists on the teaching faculty of medical schools.

Preclinical Pedagogical Challenges for Medical Anthropology

As difficult as the subject matter can be, and as negative as the students may become toward coursework, some are quite interested and appreciative of the subject matter. For many students, the source of their antipathy is not in the coursework itself, but rather in the fact that they are *told* what they have to do. Medical students are clearly physical adults but social adolescents. In a period of enforced, prolonged dependency, they simply resent being told to do *anything*. Thus, negative medical student attitudes toward curriculum reflect as much an attitude toward authority as it does toward the material itself. Teaching in medical school requires a *consistent* approach to students with regard to advocacy and authority. Shared attitudes toward faculty and coursework are an important ingredient of an adaptive "cement" solidifying the student culture, and faculty who are inconsistent in their dealings with students risk ostracism despite their good intentions.

Although shared attitudes toward coursework are a source of student solidarity, grades are a source of potential friction. Although students are told that they *all* are *expected* to pass and that they should not compete, the success of one student still raises the specter of failure for another. Many medical schools have adopted a pass-fail grading system in an attempt to minimize grade consciousness, but there is still a reluctance on the part of some students to talk too openly about grades. Surprisingly, "success fears" often become more salient than failure fears. It is almost as if there is an "image of limited good" with grades: an assumption that if one person does well, someone else—perhaps a best friend—will do poorly. The issue of grades also complicates relations between majority and minority students. Minority students have been known to comment with chagrin that nobody ever asks them what grades they receives on tests, a reflection of the presumption that minority students inevitably will do worse.

The exclusive bonds that powerfully link medical students are forged by many forces, but perhaps none more powerful than confronting an enormous amount of work. The average medical student learns over 6,000 new words in the first two years of medical school and pressure to "learn everything" is great (Association of American Medical Colleges (AAMC) 1976:9). As an aside, I recommend that any medical anthropologists anticipating working in a medical school study medical terminology systematically (there are many self-instructional texts available) as well as learning this specialized language through exposure in mandatory fieldwork in hospitals and medical schools. At some time during the first several months of medical school, however, all medical students must confront the fact that "you can't learn it all."

This situation presents several pedagogical challenges to anthropologists who teach in preclinical classes. First, medical anthropologists are seldom asked to teach medical anthropology, per se. Medical education has little particular use for such discipline-specific social science information but demands practical information on health behavior that crosses the academic disciplines of behavioral biology, medical psychology, sociology, and anthropology. Anthropologists who want to teach in medical schools today need to be broadly educated in what has come to be known as "medical behavioral science," including in their graduate coursework training in psychology and sociology.

Second, it is uncommon to be asked to teach a "course" in medical school, as most preclinical courses tend to be a coordinated series of lectures by multiple experts. For preclinical presentations, anthropologists must develop a number of self-contained lectures. Although for medical anthropologists lecturing has the advantage of being a familiar format, by being part of the "basic science" curriculum their teaching likely will be viewed somewhat critically by students. Attitudes toward basic science curriculum is a shared feature of the student culture. Beginning students quickly learn from older students already in clinical rotations that "all the basic science stuff *could* be boiled down into a couple of months, for all you use the material clinically!" This type of statement leads the students to hold negative attitudes toward many preclinical professors, whose courses are perceived of as difficult or repetitive, and who often are perceived as having contemptuous attitudes toward medical students. These attitudes are believed by the students to be caused by jealousy, because they "really wish they were physicians, too."

Third, the sheer volume of material presented in preclinical medical education causes great anxiety among students. Most initially attempt to deal with this anxiety by simply studying longer hours (obsessive-compulsive studying is, after all, the technique that always worked before for most medical students). In an effort to define a concrete, finite corpus of material to learn, medical students typically insist on being "spoon-fed" facts they can memorize, and have little interest in conceptual material. Medical anthropologists who lecture in the preclinical years must attempt to distill some of their presentations down to small "nuggets" of factual material that can be memorized. This can be a source of great frustration, as much of the material we teach falls more into the domain of "perspective" than "fact." Indeed, graduate education rewards us for conceptual *understanding* of the subtleties of *complicated* phenomena, while medical decision making demands factual *explanation* of *simplified* situations: achieving a level of "optimal ignorance" is essential to making clinical decisions, for complexity only makes decision making more difficult.

The subject matter taught by basic scientists who are not themselves physicians also is often trivialized because the students do not see them as "role models." The most respected teachers are termed "mud-fuds," referring to faculty members who hold both M.D. and Ph.D. degrees. Such lecturers are able to demonstrate the *clinical relevance* of the material they present. Indeed, the most powerful teaching mode in medical education is the "clinical case," sometimes factual and sometimes apocryphal. Clinical cases are welcomed by medical students because they are seen as examples of "real medicine." Medical anthropologists who lecture to medical students should employ clinical examples to illustrate conceptual points. In order to acquire such examples, ongoing participation in clinical activities such as hospital bedside rounds or observing in outpatient clinics is essential.

Regulation of Workload by Medical Students

Even when material is presented factually and students try simply to study harder, this obsessive-compulsive strategy is doomed to failure. Gradually, students learn to control the workload in more covert ways. One strategy is to informally punish students who attempt to "look too good." A favorite target in most medical school classes is the "gunners"—students who are generally thought to overprepare and "ask questions in lectures to try to show off how much they know." In response, fellow students may actually boo or hiss when identified "gunners" so much as raise their hands. "Gunner Bingo," in which pictures of gunners are pasted on bingo cards and crossed off whenever they raise their hands in class is another technique for sanctioning "deviant" members of the student group. This type of activity in lecture halls can be disconcerting to a medical anthropologist who is a neophyte medical school lecturer.

Perhaps the most provocative example of medical students trying to regulate the level of effort takes place in the cadaver lab during gross anatomy. Anatomy is a particularly difficult course, if for no other reason than the sheer volume of material to memorize, the long hours needed to carefully dissect out all the features to be learned, and the need for teamwork among students. In cadaver lab, students pay careful attention to the speed and precision with which neighboring teams of students dissect. If one group is dissecting particularly quickly, this represents a threat to those going more slowly, so one member of the slower group will walk over and comment, "You had better slow down or you'll miss many of the structures you're supposed to identify!" Similarly, a group dissecting too slowly will be a threat, in that they will be perceived of as trying to memorize too many details. Such a group will be admonished, "You're dissecting so slowly . . . you'd better speed up or you'll have to stay here all night!" Such statements, repeated frequently around the cadaver lab, serve as a mechanism for "leveling" the amount of work done by the students, and operates quite independently of the official assignments by the professor.

Dealing with Sensitive Issues

The cadaver experience is significant for a more critical reason, however: death is a major issue for medical students. Many have never before been in the presence of a corpse, yet psychological "life histories" of medical students reveal that many have had traumatic experiences with death or debility in a family member early in their lives. Some theorists believe that medical school, for some, is a way of dealing with the unresolved anxiety and fear about death or disease, through a psychological defense known as "control by knowing." The cadaver experience, then, forces students to confront death—the enemy—from the first months of medical training.

Most medical schools make no special effort to anticipate emotional reactions to the cadavers by students, instead using the "baptism by fire" method which is characteristic of medical education. Informally, however, the medical student culture helps students through this period. In one medical school students have a ritual (rituals clearly serve an anxiety-allaying function) in which, on the first day of gross anatomy, each student has to enter the dissection lab, walk over to a cadaver, lift the towel off its face, and literally say "hello" to the cadaver. All of this occurs in the presence of other students, who invariably laugh. Students who balk at the idea are forced to do it, either by being physically led over to the cadaver, or ridiculed until they go reluctantly by themselves. Such informal peer support and shaping of behavior is a major function of the student culture.

What is the long-term effect of the cadaver experience on students, however? Because there are seldom structured programs for students to talk about their feelings toward death, or about the immediate anxiety of "cutting on" a cadaver, the student culture is perhaps the only recourse. Often, however, the cadaver lab is the first opportunity for medical students to demonstrate the confidence or bravado which is demanded by medical studies, and the denial of anxieties is powerful. In one medical school, however, students were asked at the end of their four years to write an essay about the most significant event or patient during their four years (Lella and Pawluch 1988). A majority of students wrote about gross anatomy and the cadaver, demonstrating the power of unresolved feelings about death and the cadaver, despite the intervening years.

Participation in gross anatomy by any medical anthropologist interested in medical school teaching is rewarding, and is an opportunity to engage students in cathartic discussions about death at this time. Cadaver lab is not only a laboratory for understanding gross anatomy: it is a unique laboratory for understanding professionalization. Completing a course in gross anatomy also is a highly symbolic accomplishment that forever cements relationships between medical professionals and differentiates them from "outsiders." My own status with medical students frequently has been enhanced by being able to empathize with, and commiserate about, cadaver experiences, which are repeatedly discussed throughout the four years of medical school.

One other source of tension during the preclinical years is the beginning of courses in "physical diagnosis." This type of course is designed, in most medical schools, to teach students how to do H&Ps (histories and physicals). Students not only learn interviewing skills, but also how to conduct examinations using instruments such as stethoscopes and ophthalmoscopes. Indeed, purchasing "black bags" containing instruments is a time of high excitement for medical students, since they are the clear symbols of the profession, but learning to use them presents two major conflicts.

Some medical schools expect students to practice physical examinations on each other, including the more sensitive pelvic and rectal examinations, which causes extreme anxiety. Others send students as early as the first year to hospitals or clinics to practice H&Ps on actual patients. In addition to the usual awkwardness in first using instruments and conducting physical exams, students often express guilt at "experimenting on sick patients" without "having anything to offer in return." As a compromise, many medical schools utilize "pseudopatients"—paid volunteers on whom students practice, but the violation of usual societal injunctions against physical intimacy between strangers is still a source of stress for students.

Medical school anthropologists often participate in teaching interviewing skills, but they really should participate fully in physical diagnosis courses, including experimenting with use of medical instruments. This not only conveys to the students an appreciation for their fascination with them, but also aids in personal understanding of the difficulties associated with their clinical use, including both the technical limitations of various instruments, and the anxiety that using them on actual patients often engenders.

A final preclinical phenomenon deserves mentioning: "medical student syndrome." During the first two years, medical students learn about many different disease entities in courses such as microbiology and pathology. Inundated with the details of diseases, their symptoms, pathophysiologies, and prognoses, medical students often get the symptoms of the diseases they study; a significant number of them actually seek a professional opinion or laboratory confirmation that they do not have some dread disease. Although medical student syndrome is commonly joked about among students and faculty, the joking betrays an anxiety. In essence, medical students are learning a critical aspect of becoming a physician: overcoming fear of disease and cultivating a sense of invulnerability and confidence. Without such confidence, which is magnified even further in the clinical years, and which often gets interpreted as physician arrogance by the lay public, students would be paralyzed by uncertainty. Medical anthropologists must learn to recognize symptoms of medical student syndrome, not only so that they can help students cope with it, but also so they can diagnose it in themselves. Just as traditional ethnographers typically get dysentery when studying in the field, medical school anthropologists are at high risk for medical student syndrome.

Clinical Clerkships:
A Day in the Life of a "Scut Puppy"

Teaching and Learning in Clinical Settings
The third and fourth years of traditional medical schools are designated the "clinical" years, devoted to a series of four- to eight-week rotations through the clinical specialties, such as medicine, surgery, obstetrics and gynecology, psychiatry, etc. The student culture that was so helpful in buffering the stresses of preclinical training weakens considerably during clinical clerkships, as students who formerly spent as many as 16 hours per day together are scattered all over the hospital in groups of two or three. Establishing a teaching presence in clinical settings is potentially one of the most powerful positions a medical anthropologist can attain in medical education, because medical students begin to identify what they are

being taught as relevant or professional as they enter clinical settings and actually begin to interact with patients and physician-teachers.

Although medical students learn a huge technical vocabulary in the preclinical years, the day-to-day language they learn and use during clinical training reveals much about how professional socialization literally shapes the way medical students view the world of patients, nurses, fellow students, and teachers. While learning formal medical terminology is important because it is essential to interacting effectively in clinical settings, in some ways learning the informal language of medical culture is the most significant yet traditionally ethnographic endeavor that a medical anthropologist can undertake in clinical settings. This section focuses on the socialization process that takes place during clinical clerkships, paying particular attention to the "house officer slang" that is learned by medical students during clinical rotations, and that reveals so much about the perspectives, attitudes, and structures of relevance for the profession of medicine. The section also makes suggestions for successful teaching or consulting in the clinical setting.

During clinical rotations, medical students (termed "clerks," and referred to derogatorily as "studs," "scut puppies," or "drones") move through the various clinical specialties working largely under the tutelage of residents (physicians doing specialty training after the four years of medical school). Although residents are supervised by "attendings" (physicians on medical school faculties), they have the primary responsibility for the day-to-day care of hospitalized patients, and medical student clerks act as their assistants. Medical students do much of the routine, undesirable work (termed "scut" or "scut work"), such as admission histories and physicals (H&Ps), collecting and transporting various specimens (blood, urine, sputum, feces, etc.) to the laboratory for analysis, recording all laboratory results in patient charts, and doing whatever patient care tasks they can legally do—and that others do not want to do—such as treating bedsores, removing fecal impactions, and the like. The derivation of the term "scut" is unclear, but may be a sarcastic acronym for "some clinically useful training."

More than anything else, medical students are responsible for conducting good admission interviews and physical examinations on patients. In this work, they are in the difficult position of being able to ask, but not being able to answer, many questions. As they did when interacting with patients in their physical diagnosis classes, students on clinical rotations initially feel that what they do with the patient is of little value: during the clinical clerkships, students see clinical activities primarily as an opportunity to learn medicine, rather than to help patients. Yet the chart notes they write may be the most extensive and pertinent written records on patients, and medical students are usually not expected to work as quickly, so that they can spend more time with each patient.

Although this means that there may be more time to investigate psychosocial issues in greater depth when supervising students, a medical anthropologist in such a position must be exquisitely sensitive to the time demands and conflicting expectations of others in the clinical setting. Time is always in short supply in hospitals, and time management efforts by physicians and medical students permeate daily life. The presence of "beepers" and the fact that they constantly interrupt personal activities profoundly shape the behavior of those who must respond to their call (for example, medical students and residents, in general, fear interruptions at mealtime, leading them to eat very rapidly).

Time pressure is also manifested in something that can be termed the "clinical imperative": the fact that certain basic clinical functions *must* get done no matter what. Until these activities are completed, no applied anthropological activities will be tolerated unless they contribute directly to the clinical task at hand. Medical anthropologists must be sensitive to this ill-defined clinical imperative—to become so sensitive to the rhythms of clinical activity that brief "teaching moments" can be seized, while never intruding at times when input would be unwelcome.

In clinical teaching, we also must be careful to realize that, in encouraging medical students to incorporate psychosocial data into their patient presentations and chart progress notes, we may be putting them in direct conflict with the residents immediately responsible for their clinical education. Isolated from each other, students are dependent upon their residents for guidance, but are frequently chastised for writing "stuff that isn't important." A typical comment by residents, responding to a student's discussion of a patient's psychological reactions or family dynamics is, "skip the soft stuff . . . just gimme the numbers [laboratory results]."

Unfortunately, residents are sometimes the worst possible role models. This is especially true of "terns" (after the term "intern," which used to be the designation for first year residents), who are given the most responsibility but who have the least experience of anyone in the hospital. Typically, interns and their medical students spend every third night "on call" (invariably awake all night in the hospital taking care of patients), encouraged not to call their senior residents for help. Internship has been described as a "brutalizing" and "inhumane" experience in which young physicians are asked to perform well beyond their knowledge and abilities, to cope with incredible workloads, and all the while suffering from sleep deprivation. Usually, the resident's primary goal will be to *avoid* interacting with patients as much as possible, since there is never as much time as is needed to complete all the "technical" aspects of patient care.

One role that can be adopted by medical anthropologists supervising students clinically is to listen carefully to, and comment upon, medical student critiques of their residents and physician attendings. Unfortunately, students are assigned to residents and attendings "by the luck of the draw," so that the type of physicians they are socialized to become is more a matter of chance exposure and selective assimilation than it is the result of a conscious educational program. To counter this, student clerks can be complimented for consciously evaluating the professional behavior to which they are being exposed, but residents should never be criticized in an *ad hominem* fashion. Instead, poor patient care by residents can be discussed with sympathy as a reaction to the stresses inherent in our system of medical education. In addition, things that the residents and attendings do *well* can be pointed out explicitly, so that students have an opportunity to examine and assimilate positive medical practices whose value might otherwise go unnoticed.

Daily "Rounds"

A typical day for medical students during the clerkship years starts between 6:00-7:00 AM, when they meet residents for "work rounds," going from room to room assessing the progress of hospitalized patients, making decisions for treatment and writing orders, updating charts, and other routine patient-care functions. Students are responsible for "presenting" patients they have "worked up" to residents, who ask them questions about the clinical reasoning behind their tentative diagnoses or treatment plans, instruct them in procedures, and assign them further work to do. Following work rounds, students may try to consult textbooks and journal articles about particularly interesting patient problems in preparation for "attending rounds" later in the morning.

Attending rounds (sometimes sarcastically termed "offending rounds") are formal ritual events on most clerkships, in which residents and their medical students present new patients or patients of particular concern to faculty attending physicians. Depending upon the attending's style, these rounds can be exceptional learning opportunities, or they can be lengthy, painstaking rituals designed, from the resident and student perspective, to allow attendings to "show off" their greater expertise, while really not having to do much work. Although some medical anthropologists working clinically only participate in attending rounds, work rounds are much more informal, and participating in them makes a powerful symbolic statement to residents. Participating in early morning rounds signifies willingness to "really do the dirty-work" rather than coming in after the fact and pontificating about the esoteric points of a patient's case. A powerful bond is created among those who are perceived of as truly involved clinically, and this activity also provides access to informal information that would never flow across the status boundary between residents and attendings.

Several points need to be made about such participation. As mentioned earlier, most medical residents initially may be skeptical about a social scientist in their midst. The world of medicine is divided moiety-like into clinicians, on one hand, and patients/lay persons, on the other. In other words, most health care providers assume that people in their midst are either patients (or family members) or practitioners of some sort, and actually go to some length to increase the social distance between patients and practitioners (such as use of specialized language and paraphernalia, clearly delineated "staff" and "public" areas in the hospital, etc.). There also is an expectation that anyone who is not a patient should be instrumental in the healing mission.

Anthropologists will be accepted with surprising ease into the ranks of clinicians, but only if they (1) establish a participation schedule that is regular and then stick with it faithfully, (2) actually *participate* in patient-care activities, and (3) endure "ethnographic tests" that are offered by clinicians to confirm acceptance and interest. Unless one can participate in early morning or late afternoon rounds at least three times each week, acceptance will be much more problematic.

In addition, making rounds on holidays is a very powerful symbolic statement of willingness to "share the burden." Second, never simply stand around. Instead, an anthropologist should help with whatever activity is in progress, even if it is a menial task like discarding used bandages, holding charts, or the like. Tests of interest may take many forms, but they always occur when new residents rotate onto a clinical service. These may entail pointed, caustic remarks about patients or social scientists, or invitations to help remove incisional drains or debride wounds. A medical anthropologist must endure implied ridicule without becoming defensive and must overcome the unaccustomed sensory assaults of clinical settings by assisting with procedures in order to be accepted. This is really no different from being invited to eat unfamiliar food at the home of an informant in a village, and culture shock is a common response to immersion in either situation.

Although the conduct of attending rounds varies with the temperaments of attending physicians, they are typically interrogative in tone, and there is little tolerance for students who respond with "I don't know." In fact, medical students often go to absurd lengths to avoid admitting not knowing answers in attending rounds. Questioning of students by attendings may take the form of a "grilling," termed "pimping the studs": when students take too long to answer, or cannot come up with the correct answer, attendings may comment tersely, "While you've been standing here searching for an answer, your patient just died!" Although this seems gratuitous, and occasionally is mean-spirited and humiliating, the message is one example of covert socialization: reinforcing the idea that medical professionals often must learn to be comfortable making life-and-death clinical decisions, usually quickly, and always with inadequate data. Students and residents alike find attending rounds stressful, for fear of being "shown up" and criticized by attendings. If medical students do a poor job of "presenting a case" or demonstrate inadequate insight into clinical problems, this also reflects poorly on the residents, so that some of the discussions between residents and students on work rounds are often devoted to getting the students prepared for attending rounds.

A less active role in attending rounds is recommended, such as only responding to direct questions, or volunteering information that makes the residents and students "look better" in the eyes of their attendings. Good relationships with M.D. faculty members must be carefully maintained while still being primarily oriented to the residents and students. Curiously, much as traditional ethnographers have discovered while working in tribal societies, being associated with the anthropologist actually imparts a certain status: if some amount of time is not spent with *all* participants in the clinical milieu (including nurses as well as attendings), feelings will be hurt and gossip will likely follow. Medical anthropologists, while aligning primarily with students and residents, must maintain ties with all others in the clinical teaching setting. This can be easily accomplished by establishing collaborative research projects with fellow M.D. faculty members, who are then quite willing to endorse almost any level of clinical involvement as a type of reciprocity. Additionally, spending some time with nurses in the cafeteria, or volunteering to do inservice educational programs for nursing staff, will ensure their good will.

In the daily lives of medical students, attending rounds are followed by lunch (termed "nutrition rounds" or "metabolic rounds" by medical students because of the feeling that they are *always* involved in *some* type of rounds—in the same way, happy hour get-togethers or cocktail parties are referred to as "liver rounds"), which is usually either a hurried cafeteria sandwich or lunch carried out and eaten at a noon conference. Noon conferences are either case presentations or formal lectures, and are referred to as "ischial callosity rounds" or "ass rounds" because participants sit (in contrast to bedside rounds, when participants walk from room to room). In the afternoon, students must either "work up" new patients being admitted to the hospital, or they may be assigned to an outpatient clinic where they do initial interviews with patients, present patients to the residents, and then watch while residents complete patient visits. If students are assigned to outpatient clinic duty, they must then return to the hospital to do admission H&Ps on any patients admitted while they were in clinic, and then attend another late afternoon conference.

Typically, all admission work cannot be completed before afternoon conferences, so medical students will return to take care of patients until 8:00–10:00 PM, and then leave the hospital for home, stopping by the library first to look up relevant information about patients to be presented the next morning. Since medical students and interns are responsible for initial handling of anything that happens to patients during the night, typically on an every-third-night-on-call basis, they simply may not go home to bed, staying instead at the hospital. Depending upon the service (some specialties, like medicine, are considered particularly tough because of the volume of night "hits"; others, like anesthesiology, are less demanding), medical student clerks spend every third night getting less than two hours of sleep, trying to take care of as many patient problems as possible without awakening the first-year resident who is "on call." In short, personal deprivation is great, with seldom enough time for sleep, recreation, or study. As the "lowest on the totem pole," medical students are the first to be called on, and the most likely to be criticized.

Value Orientations in Medical Education

As indicated earlier, the most important feature of medical education is not the imparting of specific scientific knowledge or the refinement of clinical skills, but rather the internalization of value orientations intrinsic to the culture of biomedicine. It is these value orientations that make medical students *feel* like physicians. Initially selecting applicants for traits that are considered desirable, the process of medical education discussed above, which takes place under conditions of extreme stress, then results in profound emotional changes in its initiates. Medical education resembles the most powerful type of indoctrination: group identity is cultivated and personal identity is restructured in a climate in which prior learning and personal identity are excluded from consciousness, students are put under conditions of extreme stress, and new cues are presented and reinforced, often in unconscious ways.

Uncertainty and Therapeutic Activism

In biomedicine, helplessness, vulnerability, uncertainty, and weakness are anathema. Reflecting American core values, the culture of biomedicine encourages instrumentality, optimism, and self-reliance. As an example, one of the most important value orientations in biomedicine has been termed "therapeutic activism": an ethos that demands that practitioners diagnose and treat, despite inadequate data and attendant uncertainty. Medical students, like their residents, learn this value orientation at all stages in their training by being constantly put in positions of being expected to handle more than their actual capabilities permit. Having to make clinical decisions, and then be comfortable with the outcome, is an experience foreign to most anthropologists, but one that must be fully appreciated. Medical students and residents live in a state of almost constant fear that they "forgot something" or wrote an order which will result in a problem. Such feelings are so profound, and the anxiety is so great, that almost every medical student reports losing sleep because of chronic worry. In order to deal with uncertainty, medical students emulate the residents and attendings who supervise them, asserting confidence, being self-reliant, and acting decisively. These value orientations in biomedicine result in physician behaviors that are often interpreted by lay persons as physician arrogance, but are, in fact, desperate attempts by clinicians to feel comfortable in the face of uncertainty.

In addition to attending physicians expressing intolerance of ambiguity and indecision by pimping students, residents also reinforce therapeutic activism in teaching procedures to students (such as lumbar punctures, starting IVs, and the like), using the classic medical school technique of "see one, do one, teach one." This technique, which is also facetiously referred to as "see one, screw one, do one," encourages students to be eager to try new skills, and to become comfortable with feelings of inadequate preparation. Students starting IVs or doing venipunctures worry about "blowing someone's vein," and live in fear of a "horror show" (a patient in a state of rapid physical decline caused by a cascade of one physician mistake after another). Residents also teach students the logic of clinical reasoning, running through the various decision algorithms for analyzing objective laboratory and historical data obtained from patients.

This learning is powerful because it takes place less consciously in the course of daily activities: a type of learning termed "role modeling." Role modeling is powerful because students tend to emulate their residents, often uncritically imitating their behavior toward patients, nurses, and others in the hospital. Students also assimilate biomedical value orientations as they are implicitly encapsulated in the jargon or slang used by residents.

As mentioned earlier, students also are taught professional knowledge and values through the telling of "clinical pearls" and "war stories," major features of the great oral tradition in clinical teaching. Clinical pearls are brief sayings or aphorisms whose simplicity belies the seriousness of their message (examples are: "Headaches that awaken the patient are almost always a bad sign"; "Even if the child isn't really sick, you still have to treat the parents"; "If the chart weighs more than the patient, you know you've got problems"). War stories are told at parties, over lunches, and in private moments, often away from the hospital; they are almost mythological stories about tragic situations, incompetent physicians, or particularly unpleasant patients which almost always contain a moral lesson, instructing students in the "truths" about medicine not taught in journals and books. Medical anthropologists who spend significant amounts of time working in clinical settings will develop a set of "pearls" and "war stories" which can be effectively used in both formal lectures and informal gatherings.

Cynicism and Identification with the Profession

Many lay observers of physician behavior note with a certain sadness (and perhaps even hostility) how idealism tends to be a powerful motive expressed for going to medical school, but how that idealism wanes dramatically during the process. The common cultural stereotype is the well-intentioned medical school applicant who completes medical school hating patients, having no social conscience, and practicing "for the money." Indeed, the fate of idealism, which is almost universally high in the earliest years of training, has been shown to decline rapidly during clerkships, with some suggesting that the curriculum be divided the "precynical" and "cynical" years, rather than the "preclinical" and the "clinical" (Becker and Geer 1958:50).

Cynicism in medical students undoubtedly has multiple manifestations, but is certainly revealed in their changing attitudes toward patients. Other than residents, patients are the most significant "others" in the socialization of medical students. Patients are significant for several reasons, but perhaps no more so than their unwitting role in cementing the special identity of the physician. Typically, group identity is created by defining a group of "others" that are outside the group. By defining patients as clearly "others," physicians define the "self" in an unconscious professional boundary maintenance process.

Student relationships with patients are even more complex, however. Whereas most "precynical" medical students are almost apologetic and guilty for interacting with patients, feeling that they have little to offer in return, in the clinical years anxiety born of chronic lack of confidence and nurtured by the demands from residents and attendings that they be "right" is powerful, leading to resentment of some types of patients by students. Although students early in training will usually not express strong preferences for certain types of patients, that changes dramatically during clinical training, by which time certain types of patients are devalued.

Cynicism is also directly attributable to the unreasonable demands placed upon medical students mentioned earlier, including "pimping" during attending rounds. Medical students in training are deprived of opportunities to explore personal interests and are chronically overtired, uncertain, and anxious. They must deal with patients who are often very troubling and are harassed by attending physicians, residents, nurses, and others. Paradoxically, brutalizing of medical students and residents results in even stronger identification with the profession. An unfortunate but all too common defense is to identify even more closely with persecutors and displace anger and frustration onto those who are natural targets: patients. Although there are those in medical education who advocate "humanizing" the process (a common aphorism is "If we do not treat our students with dignity and respect, how can we expect the students to treat patients with respect?"), there is a powerful tendency to deny that medical students and residents are brutalized. One often hears, "Well, I made it through, so why shouldn't these new students?!" from young attendings and senior residents. As Broadhead notes (1983:101), medical training undermines student's identity as adults. It creates feelings of infantilization, mortification, and dependency; its non-negotiable demands create high anxiety and weaken medical students' commitments to other relationships and interests, such as with friends, spouses, etc. Training engenders feelings of guilt and inadequacy, resentment, hostility, rejection, and stronger identification with the profession.

Understanding these psychosocial dynamics of medical students has a powerful impact on the ability of a medical anthropologist to teach clinically. First, effectiveness increases when a teacher understands the situations in which students are "ready" to learn and how to "package" lessons for maximum benefit. Second, effective teaching activities are not confined to formal curriculum. Simply "witnessing" for the distress medical students feel permits healthy catharsis. When negative comments are made about patients, valuable education takes place by encouraging students to consider that "problem patients" are not inherently problematic, but become so because of personal attributes and professional dilemmas of practitioners. This self-awareness can promote personal and professional growth. In asking medical professionals to examine their own roles in poor patient-practitioner relationships, however, it is essential to bear in mind the aphorism "confrontation without a relationship is an attack": this should only be done in a most gentle way with physicians or students with whom one has an ongoing relationship.

Rationality and Objectivity in Biomedicine

Comments made about patients reveal a great deal about another value orientation of biomedicine: rationality and objectivity. There is an underlying assumption that an ideal state of "health" exists and that deviations from this state can be recognized as specific diseases, caused by specific factors which can be ascertained and treated, and that follow a predictable natural history. Thus, in biomedicine, getting the diagnosis right is a *sine quo non,* and has much to do with medical student attitudes toward patients. The importance of diagnosing, or at least of establishing that something measurable is wrong with patients, is revealed in the practice of "trolling the patient through the lab to see what bites" (this is positive or hopeful) or "going on a fishing expedition" (a more negative statement about "running labs" on a patient who is suspected of being a "crock").

Patients whose organic pathologies are fairly straightforward are valued because it is easier to diagnose and treat them (they may be termed "cheap cases").

Patients with uninteresting problems may be termed "duds." When patients have problems which are vexing, but for whom there is still interest or a diagnostic challenge, they may be said to "have a fascinoma" (something of great interest but which tests have not yet revealed), or "a case of gok" (standing for "God only knows"). Patients who have complaints for which no biophysiological abnormality can be detected are referred to negatively as "head cases," and when patients are perceived to be contributing to the chronicity of problems, or to have caused their problems in the first place, as with drug addicts or "noncompliant" patients, they are devalued. Patients who do not respond to treatment, such as chronic pain patients, are also devalued, and jokes are told around the issue of pain medication. In fact, the use (or nonuse) of pain medication by physicians is often used punitively—if not actually, certainly in jokes—on such devalued patients. The negativity with which patients like these are viewed is revealed by a fertile semantic domain for undesirable patients in medicalese: such patients are termed "crocks," "dirtballs," "MUOs" (marginal undesirable organisms), or "Gomers" (get out of my emergency room).

Difficult patients engender feelings of self-blame and despair in physicians, who then react with even more activism, or by "dehumanizing," or diminishing their status as sick people. For example, patients are referred to as "players" (such as when a resident starts work rounds in the morning with the statement, "Do we have any new players today?"). Particularly difficult or tragic patients, when discussed in conferences, often are referred to as "great cases." Patients are given humorous names, such as when severely burned children are referred to as "crispy critters" or when patients with multiple chronic problems are said to be suffering from "P-cubed" (piss-poor protoplasm"). When confronted with a chronic pain patient for whom diagnostic tests are inconclusive, residents may admonish students to "palpate hard and look for a positive chandelier sign" (push vigorously on the area that supposedly hurts and see if the patient jumps off the bed toward the ceiling). When confronted by patients with presumed or documented psychiatric illness in addition to a medical problem for which they have been admitted to the hospital, residents will often tell students to "Shoot the patient full of 'Vitamin H' [referring to Haloperidol—a powerful antipsychotic medication], buff him [get his lab values as close to normal as possible even if he is not cured], and turf [transfer] him to psychiatry."

In short, the idealism with which medical students enter training gives way to a most biting cynicism in which patients, who are supposedly the objects of care and concern, often become the targets of seemingly sadistic humor. Put succinctly, patients with problems which allow medical students and residents to feel competent as physicians are valued; those who engender feelings of incompetence or failure are repudiated. Medical anthropologists must not react strongly to sadistic medical humor, but must attempt to understand its latent functions of allaying anxiety, revealing "truths" about the medical world, and creating solidarity within the profession by creating an "us-versus-them" mentality.

Dealing with Death

As discussed previously, one of the major issues confronting preclinical students is death as it is manifested in the cadaver. In the clerkship years death becomes even more real as students participate in the care of dying patients. In order to be effective clinical teachers, medical anthropologists must understand professional attitudes toward death and dying, and must clarify their own feelings about death. In fact, struggles against death are a hallmark of medical practice: many physicians see death as the enemy to be vanquished, but of course, it is a battle that all physicians are destined to lose.

I once witnessed a first-year resident on the Burn Unit write two pages of orders on an 83-year-old woman who was hopelessly burned over 85% of her body surface. The nurses were very angry, because they knew from experience that someone of that age with such severe burns cannot survive, and they wanted to focus their efforts on a younger, less severely burned patient, while keeping the elderly woman as comfortable as possible on only a morphine drip (used in the case of intractable pain or imminent death—in fact, most clinicians recognize "the drip" as a signal that nothing more can, or should, be done for a patient). When the nurses questioned the young resident about the wisdom of expending such efforts on a patient who would "likely die before morning," he commented. "I haven't had a patient die on me yet . . . and she isn't going to be the first!"

Sooner or later, of course, all physicians and medical students have a patient who dies: for many, the feelings of impotence in the face of death are overwhelming. Death stirs up anxieties in most of us in American culture, sheltered as we are from the event. But feelings of inadequacy among young physicians can be even more profound. Death and dying, perhaps more than any other topic in medicine, are dealt with in that most common feature of medical social life: the vulgar joke. In the language of medicine, there are so many euphemisms for death that the list is too long to detail here. As examples, however, residents tell students to "watch out for the positive Q-sign!" The "Q-sign" is worse than the "O-sign,": the latter being a patient lying back in bed with mouth open (potentially just asleep), the former in the same position but with the tongue hanging out (a sign of impending death). Related to this is the "positive fly sign," which refers to the unfortunate patient with a positive "Q-sign," but with flies entering and leaving the mouth. Another way of talking about death is the "Nebraska sign," referring to a "flat" electrocardiogram tracing (signaling a lack of cardiac activity). In a similar vein, residents may comment to students that a patient "is about to box" or "is starting to dribble off the court."

If death cannot be defeated, medical students are taught to "manage" it. On the most formal level, students and residents on most services attend weekly "M&M rounds"—morbidity and mortality conferences—in which a careful postmortem attempt is made to discover why a patient died, and how things might have been done differently. Although these conferences have the manifest function of ascertaining the cause(s) of a patient's death, they have the latent function of group solidarity, since they formally channel the informal rumors and innuendos which inevitably follow deaths which were unexpected. They also function to scientifically "sanitize" death: striving to find objective meaning for an event, even after the fact.

Another manifestation of problems in dealing with death on a formal level is the phenomenon of "DNR" (do not resuscitate) status, an order for which may or may not be written formally on the chart of a terminally ill patient, but which is a decision usually reached by the patient's family and all involved in the care to not "code" (resuscitate) a patient if breathing or heartbeat should stop. Normally, such an event would result in "calling a code," which is an exciting event in which members of the resuscitation team are paged, come running from all over the hospital, and attempt, using complex paraphernalia, to stabilize the patient's vital functions. Between the two extremes, however—on one hand the decision not to resuscitate, on the other the decision to do everything possible—is something called the "slow code" or "medical student code" (Neher 1988). Although controversial, even within the medical profession, there are occasions when residents decide unilaterally that a particular patient would be better off not being resuscitated, and they will decide to make somewhat less of an effort than a full code, telling students on the service, "if this guy codes, it's yours!" (everybody understands what this means).

Such maneuverings around the issue of dying are appalling to many, who do not appreciate how difficult it can be to struggle for patients' lives day after day but not be able to cure them. Humor and the more controversial informal orchestrating of death in codes are two ways medical students learn to "control" death—and their own sense of inadequacy. There are other, more positive ways, also taught by residents, such as accepting death and the limitations of medicine: students occasionally are told, "When you cannot cure, you can always care!"

Attitudes toward the Medical Specialties and the Profession

One major function of clinical clerkships is to give students exposure to all of the clinical specialties, so that they can choose what types of residency to enter after medical school. Talking about "biomedical culture" may lead to the false impression that medicine is monolithic. In fact, biomedicine is a complex, "plural" culture, in which not all specialties are considered equally desirable. Beginning students usually are only vaguely aware of these distinctions. As an illustration, 50% of beginning medical students report that they would consider psychiatry as a specialty, yet the number who actually go into psychiatry is around 10%. What happens during the four years of medical school to change students' opinions about psychiatry? The status hierarchy of the medical specialties is something all medical students learn as part of the process of professional socialization, and an understanding of this hierarchy is imperative for a medical anthropologist interested in working in medical school settings.

A message about the relative importance of the different specialties is covertly conveyed in the amount of time allotted to each during clerkships. Medicine and surgery are usually the longest clerkships, each eight to twelve weeks in duration. Other specialties, including psychiatry, are only of four weeks duration. Four week rotations are often described by students as worthless because, "You spend the first week trying to figure out where everything is and how they want it done; the second and third weeks trying to learn everything; and the fourth week on 'cruise control' looking forward to the next rotation.'' As students go through the various specialties, they learn how each specialty views the others, usually through the snide comments made by residents. As neophytes convert to their respective specialties, first-year residents are usually the most zealous proponents of a specialty's worldview, which they convey to students with biting clarity.

In fact, there is rivalry between all medical specialties which must be understood by medical school anthropologists. As ''outsiders'' with no vested interest in a particular specialty, medical anthropologists are in a position to listen dispassionately to medical students' thoughts about their future choice of specialty, helping them to sort through thoughts that might otherwise remain unconscious. Again, the way different specialties are characterized by residents and medical students is informative. Dermatology, for example, is said to be, ''Simple . . . all you have to know is, if it's wet, dry it; if it's dry, wet it.'' Obstetrics and Gynecology is described in many ways, some of which are derogatory: obstetricians are referred to as ''baby catchers''; gynecologists are said to ''hate women.'' Surgeons, who otherwise epitomize the medical profession, are not even exempt from barbs, being included in the ''four laws of medicine'': (1) if it's working, keep doing it; (2) if it's not working, stop; (3) if you don't know what to do, don't do anything; and (4) never call a surgeon.

Just as they often are stereotyped by lay persons, surgeons are also considered ''arrogant'' or ''brutal'' by other specialists. Barbs betraying hostility occur most frequently between specialties which have naturally rivalrous relationships, such as when their work is interdependent. For example, anesthesiologists refer to surgeons as ''technicians'' or ''mechanics,'' while surgeons refer to anesthesiologists as ''gas passers.'' Surgeons refer to nonsurgeons (and particularly neurologists) as ''fleas''—''the last to leave a dying body.'' Pediatricians are said to ''practice medicine on children because they can't get along with adults.''

Rivalry between specialties also is revealed in the processes by which patients are transferred from one specialist to another, or by which ''consults'' (official requests for assistance in the care of a patient from a specialist consultant) are ordered. As discussed earlier, patients who are no longer interesting or who are considered ''undesirable'' to one specialty service will be ''turfed'' as quickly as possible. It is also possible to ''turf'' a patient to a nursing home or to the street, but a ''turf'' to psychiatry is the usual method of getting rid of a patient, which is also referred to as a ''dump.'' Residents often use these terms very matter-of-factly in planning care for a patient—''turfing'' a patient to psychiatry sometimes is a thinly disguised way of saying, ''getting this crock off of our service,'' implying both that the patient's problem is not worthy of continued medical attention and that psychiatry is a devalued ''last resort'' in medicine.

The most profound division within the medical world is between psychiatry and the rest of medicine, with psychiatry almost universally maligned. In fact, I have heard medical school deans telling first-year students who express an interest in psychiatry that they ''will certainly reconsider and change their mind by the end of four years'' (the statement accompanied by a knowing look). Psychiatry is maligned for a variety of reasons, including the fact that many psychiatric conditions are not diagnosed by ''hard'' numerical data nor treated by difficult procedures (talk-therapies are not considered difficult). Residents in psychiatry are perceived of as not having to put in long hours on call like other residents. Patients who have psychiatric disorders are devalued, in part because there is a perception that they ''brought it on themselves'' (such as drug addiction, alcohol abuse, suicide attempts), and in part because psychiatric disorders usually are not treatable with standard medical therapies (the exception, of course, is psychopharmacology).

The relative status of the different medical specialties, as well as the relationships between psychiatrists and other specialists, is of great importance for medical school anthropologists. Typically, nonphysicians are invited to be on the faculties of departments of psychiatry, family medicine, pediatrics, or obstetrics: all clinical specialties in which physicians work with patients in ambulatory care settings where psychosocial factors are seen to be of greater importance, or whose patients are already identified as having ''psychological problems.'' Being employed in these departments, especially psychiatry, does not impart great status in most medical school settings. Additionally, I have discovered that, although other clinical departments are quite sanguine about involvement by nonphysician faculty, psychiatry departments present some specific problems not encountered elsewhere. These are discussed below.

Anthropologists contemplating employment in colleges of medicine must confront problems of professional identity extending beyond the status hierarchy of the medical specialties. First, there is an almost inevitable sense of professional isolation. There is seldom more than one medical anthropologist in any given medical school with whom to share professional accomplishments and emotional traumas. Second, although most medical schools are associated with universities, they may not share the same campus. Even when they do, there are rivalries and jealousies between academic anthropology departments and medical schools, revolving around such issues as a perceived salary and benefit differentials, which may impede collaboration. In addition, the pace of life in academic departments waxes and wanes dramatically around the academic calendar with its semester breaks and vacations; the pace in medical schools stays at a fairly constant level, and vacations are of little importance. These differences in professional rhythms can make collaboration between fellow anthropologists more difficult. Third, individual anthropology graduate students often envy the future job security and high salaries of medical students, which stand in stark contrast to their own rather bleak employment outlook and lower salaries, leading to a sense of relative deprivation and antipathy. Fourth, whereas academic anthropologists are accustomed to being free to come and go at will, medical culture places an emphasis on always being available, even if one is not actually needed. This ''beeper ethos'' must be adopted if an anthropologist is to work successfully in medical schools, but it can destroy the sense of personal and professional autonomy that is so valued in academic settings.

As a social scientist, one might expect to be accepted more easily in a department of psychiatry than in another medical specialty. Although it seems counterintuitive that a specialty devoted to psychosocial issues would be more reluctant to include behavioral scientists, I have discovered over the years of medical school work that my relationship with psychiatry has involved a constant and sometimes tedious process of role definition and redefinition that has not occurred in other specialties. This is particularly true in clinical service and teaching, and less so in the area of research. A medical anthropologist teaching in medical school must be aware that psychiatrists often have even more conflicts about such a clinical presence than other specialists. In order to maintain good relationships with psychiatry colleagues, medical anthropologists must not *assume* collegiality and acceptance, but must monitor how psychiatry perceives itself to be accepted in the medical school as a whole. Since it is already the most marginal of the medical specialties, in many medical schools psychiatry wages a constant battle for status. Thus, at least two different psychiatrists with whom I have worked clinically have perceived other specialists as "using" me rather than consulting a psychiatrist to avoid having to "admit" to the importance of psychiatry in medicine. I have also been criticized for "allowing" myself to be used. In general, I have found that if psychiatry is strong and accepted in a given medical school, there likely will be more ready acceptance of a clinically involved medical anthropologist in their midst.

A final major lesson about the social organization of the medical profession concerns the relationship between academic physicians and those in private practice. Although it is true in many medical programs that local physicians in practice act as preceptors for medical students, in the hospital it is medical attendings— full-time faculty of the medical school—who do the bulk of the teaching. Medical students are taught that there is a status hierarchy within medicine, with academic physicians in a position of higher prestige than physicians in private practice. That message is not stated directly, but through the frequent notation in patients' charts, "patient has been seen previously and referred to hospital by LMD"— being a derogatory reference to "local medical doctor."

"Graduation Follies" and Professional Socialization

Annually, about four months before actual graduation in nearly every American medical school, but after medical students have "matched" (have selected, and been selected) for residency programs, "graduation follies" are held (Segal 1984). It is through graduation rituals that medical anthropologists may come to the greatest theoretical understanding of medical education. These are celebrations of completing medical school, and usually take the form of humorous skits, musical comedy, and other vaudevillian productions, to which medical students, faculty, residents, and families are invited. Follies are noteworthy for their shocking and oftentimes cruel violations of normal standards of decorum, including the most scatological insulting of professors and vulgar exaggeration of their personal and professional foibles, references to patients in sexual, racial, or other ways which violate cultural taboos, and profane or indelicate condemnations of the process of medical education. Although it is possible to view graduation follies as a humorous celebration of the end of medical school, anthropologically they are a ritual of extreme structural reversal, in which students actively and aggressively assert their changed social identity—from subordinated to privileged status.

Graduation follies are a type of collective representation which reveals how medical students come to understand their changing relationships to others over the four years of medical school. The structural reversals played out so overtly in the graduation follies, with students taking license to put themselves in exaggerated superior positions to teachers and patients, is a most dramatic statement of their view of the systematic oppression of medical training. In the overt violation of cultural and professional taboos relating to sexuality, nudity, death, and the like, graduation follies betray the difficulties students have felt in having to deal with such psychologically frightening and culturally taboo issues during training. In the systematic stereotyping and denigration of patients, who are sadistically depicted as vulnerable to diseases, follies are revealing of the attitude of relative invulnerability which not only allows physicians to deal with personal threats of injury and death by sharply contrasting themselves with patients, but also of the professional assumption of a hierarchically superior social position to nonprofessionals.

In short, graduation follies are self-congratulatory rituals which publicly assert medical students' emancipation from subordinate roles as students, and the assumption of superior roles as professionals. They are opportunities to assert certainty, following prolonged struggles with uncertainty: personal, moral, and instrumental. Most significantly, they capture the essence of professional socialization: revealing the profound psychological and social transition that occurs in medical education.

Unfortunately, despite graduation follies, after four years of medical school, professional socialization is only half over, as young M.D.s again become "lowest on the totem pole" as beginning residents. Residency is the last stage in the professional rite of passage which culminates in the reintroduction of initiates to society, albeit with a new role. As residents, former medical students also begin to make decisions about future medical practice based on goals for a private life. Yet it is surprising how little medical residents talk about future practice plans, except only in general terms. Like prisoners, they more typically count the weeks until they will "be finished." Indeed, residency training does not so much as prepare them for life outside of medical school, as it strengthens their resolve never again to be so inundated.

As the culmination of a complex rite of passage, it is unexpected and perhaps even unfortunate that the practice of medicine may actually be a "compensation for, rather than an extension of, the medical school experience" (Broadhead 1983:102). Indeed, some find it ironic that the profession most devoted to the physical and mental health of patients is not dedicated to the same principle for its practitioners and students. The subtle attitudes and styles of residents observed and emulated by the medical students as the cornerstone of medical education are

not those of actual practitioners, but of an overworked, sleep-deprived, fright-
ened, brutalized, and oppressed group of slightly older, but equally liminal people. Much of what the residents teach is not medical practice, but survival skills
for the liminal period. Medical school, if it were a true rite of passage, would
prepare medical students to work with patients, yet it more effectively focuses
attention on maintaining relationships with other medical students, attendings,
and to nurses and other practitioners.

Patients effectively remain outside the medical system into which medical students are socialized—outside a profession which paradoxically has the most intimate access to patients. Indeed, getting too close to patients will be seen as a
betrayal of others in the profession—as Konner (1987:365) puts it, because it conveys, "I care more than you do for patients, therefore you do not care enough."
This is a further argument for anthropologists teaching in medical schools not to
become unbridled patient advocates, because of the potential alienation of physicians. Instead, objectionable behavior in medical students can be viewed as the
effects of victimization by a uniquely totalitarian educational system, interpreted
as compensatory, rather than malicious acts, and taken as an opportunity to suggest alternative coping strategies.

Conclusions

In this chapter, I have attempted to convey an anthropological understanding
about professional socialization and some of the ways medical anthropologists
can find professional satisfaction in health science settings. Some may choose to
conduct clinical research, while others may elect to influence the process of medical education and practice by becoming involved in clinical teaching. Although
guidelines have been offered for such work, which appear in a checklist below,
others may discover new and unique ways of contributing to the health of both
patients and physicians.

The future for medical anthropologists in medical education is difficult to predict, but there likely will be continuing pressure to cut health care costs, which
will also cause financial pressure on medical school faculty. Medical behavioral
science suffered tremendous losses when federal training grants were reduced.
Many medical anthropologists working in medical education and supported by
such grants found themselves increasingly dependent upon research grants for
their salaries. As for teaching, medical schools have recently begun to recruit psychologists and social workers, who can bring in salaries through patient fees. In
the future, any medical anthropologist aspiring to teach in medical settings might
be advised to seek additional training and certification in a recognized clinical
discipline, such as psychology or social work. It is unlikely that medical anthropology will ever become a recognized clinical discipline, not only because of a
historical academic hegemony, but also because there is already professional overcrowding in patient care.

In terms of medical education and research, another ominous trend is the large
numbers of physicians who are getting additional postdoctoral training in a social

science discipline or in epidemiology, in order to better prepare for research. Physicians with such training may obviate the need for nonphysician research collaborators. Similarly, the first generation of physicians formally trained in medical behavioral science now occupies a large number of faculty positions in medical schools. As an unintended consequence of training physicians so well, we may have reduced the future need for nonphysician medical behavioral scientists in medical education.

Nevertheless, medical anthropologists with appropriate training can continue to play important roles in medical schools, as researchers, teachers, consultants, practitioners, coordinators, and even administrators. Graduate anthropology programs should actively encourage such training and involvement in medical school settings, not only for the contribution that anthropologists can make to medical care, but also for the benefit to anthropology as we challenge our discipline to enlarge its traditional emphasis on the non-Western, collective, symbolic, and social levels of analysis to include Western, individual, unconscious, and psychological dimensions in our study of culture. Ultimately, the message conveyed here is that whatever specialized role medical anthropologists seek in medical school settings, our ability to intervene in medicine rests first on our ability to be anthropologists—to genuinely understand and nonthreateningly penetrate the complex world of medical students and physicians.

Medical School Teaching and Research
Professional Development and Skills Checklist

Preparation and Skills for Teaching

1. Structure formal educational preparation to acquire necessary specialized knowledge:

- Study the history of anthropological involvement in medical education settings, focusing on the roots of tension between social scientists and physicians.

- Read literature on medical education and practice. Include medical psychology and medical sociology in graduate coursework to become broadly educated in "medical behavioral science."

- Understand the hierarchy of medical specialties.

- Learn medical terminology.

- Develop interviewing and interpersonal skills for medical/social history taking and crisis intervention.

- Consider dual training and certification in a recognized clinical discipline, such as psychology or social work.

2. Conduct fieldwork in hospital and medical school settings to acquire clinical/ethnographic skills:

- Conduct observational fieldwork in medical school and hospital settings.

- Learn the informal language of medical culture (slang, acronyms, etc.).

- Learn and utilize both formal and informal interdisciplinary health care team development strategies.

- Anticipate and deal with ethnographic challenges regarding loyalty and commitment.

- Avoid overt antiphysician bias and patient advocacy. Develop strategies for dealing with sensory assaults, intellectual isolation, culture shock, and other aspects of professional stress.

- Do not react strongly to sadistic medical humor.

- Always *participate,* even in small ways; make activities relevant to patient care missions.

- Understand professional attitudes toward death and dying, and clarify personal feelings about death.

- Understand how medical students view their preclinical coursework and the dynamics of the student culture that develops during these years.

- Participate in gross anatomy at least once.

- Participate in teaching interviewing skills; full participation in physical diagnosis courses,

- Practice use of medical instruments.

3. Modify teaching activities to suit medical school approach.

Clinical Teaching:

Establish and maintain a teaching presence (rounds) in clinical settings.

- establish a participation schedule that is regular, and then stick with it faithfully,

- actually *participate* in patient-care activities

- anticipate and endure "ethnographic tests" that are offered by clinicians to confirm acceptance and interests (endure implied ridicule without defensiveness; assist with procedures). Be exquisitely sensitive to the rhythms, time demands, and conflicting expectations (the "clinical imperative") in clinical settings.

- Wait for opportunities to educate that arise spontaneously in clinical work ("teaching moments").

- Align primarily with students and residents, but maintain ties with all others in the clinical teaching setting (nurses, attendings).

Lecturing:

1. For preclinical lectures develop a number of self-contained lectures.

- Distill parts of lectures down to small "nuggets" of factual material that can be memorized.

- Always employ clinical examples to illustrate conceptual points.

- Anticipate some unruly activity by students in lecture halls.

- Develop a set of clinical "pearls" and "war stories" which can be effectively used in both formal lectures and informal gatherings.

2. Serve as an unofficial counselor for troubled medical students.

- Seek out and collaborate with those M.D. faculty who are known to the *students* as sympathetic to student issues.

- Maintain a consistent approach to students with regard to advocacy and authority.

- Learn to recognize symptoms of "medical student syndrome."

- Listen carefully to, and comment upon, medical student critiques of their residents and physician attendings.

- "Witness" for the distress medical students feel and thereby encourage catharsis.

- Interpret "problem patients" as not inherently problematic, but become so because of personal attributes and professional dilemmas of practitioners.

- Interpret objectionable behavior in medical students as compensatory, rather than malicious acts, and suggest alternative coping strategies.

- Listen to medical students' thoughts about their future choice of specialty, helping them to sort through thoughts that might otherwise remain unconscious.

Preparation and Skills for Research

1. Structure formal educational preparation to acquire necessary specialized knowledge.

- Develop facility in a broad range of research paradigms and data-analysis strategies.

- Learn how to demystify participant observation.

- Consider dual training in anthropology and another field more widely recognized in medical school research settings (such as psychology, public health, or biostatistics).

2. Demonstrate grantsmanship skills by developing a track record of successful grant-writing.

3. Plan research that has relevance to the clinical mission of patient care.

- Make personal contact with the department chair or principal investigator of a major research project, and must also be familiar with the research and clinical priorities of the specialty.

- Combine anthropological work with existing clinical research projects.

- Learn how to conduct collaborative research with nonanthropological colleagues.

- Do not be overtly critical of biomedicine.

References Cited

Association of American Medical Colleges (AAMC)
   1976   Educational Stress: The Psychological Journey of the Medical Student. Transcript of the OSR/COD Annual Meeting Program, November 11, San Francisco Hilton (Mimeographed). Washington, DC: Association of American Medical Colleges.
Barnett, Clifford R.
   1985   Anthropological Research in Clinical Settings: Role Requirements and Adaptations. Medical Anthropology Quarterly 16(3):59–61.
Baer, Hans A.
   1987   Encounters with Biomedicine: Case Studies in Medical Anthropology. New York: Gordon and Breach Science Publishers.
Becker, Howard S., and Blanche Geer
   1958   The Fate of Idealism in Medical School. American Sociological Review 23:50–56.
Becker, Howard S., Blanche Geer, Everett C. Hughes, and Anselm Strauss
   1961   Boys in White: Student Culture in Medical School. Chicago: University of Chicago Press.
Bluestone, Naomi
   1981   So You Want to Be a Doctor?: The Realities of Pursuing Medicine as a Career. New York: Lothrup, Lee & Shepard Books.
Bosk, Charles L.
   1979   Forgive and Remember: Managing Medical Failure. Chicago: University of Chicago Press.
Broadhead, Robert S.
   1983   The Private Lives and Professional Identity of Medical Students. New Brunswick, NJ: Transaction.
Campbell, Margaret A. (pseudonym)
   1973   Why Would a Girl Go into Medicine? Old Westbury, NY: Feminist Press.
Chrisman, Noel J., and Thomas Maretzki (eds.)
   1982   Clinically Applied Anthropology: Anthropologists in Health Science Settings. Dordrecht, Holland: D. Reidel.
Conrad, Peter
   1986   Roles of Stereotypes in Justifying Failure and Success. Journal of Health and Social Behavior 27:150–160.

Coombs, Robert H.
1978 Mastering Medicine: Professional Socialization in Medical School. New York: Free Press.
Drake, Donald
1978 Medical School. New York: Rawson, Wade Publishers.
Haas, Jack, and William Shaffir
1987 Becoming Doctors: The Adoption of a Cloak of Competence. Greenwich, CT: JAI Press.
Hahn, Robert A., and Atwood D. Gaines (eds)
1985 Physicians of Western Medicine: Anthropological Approaches to Theory and Practice. Dordrecht, Holland: D. Reidel.
Johnson, Thomas M.
1981 The Anthropologist as a Role Model for Medical Students. Practicing Anthropology 4:8–10.
1985 (ed) Symposion—Anthropologists in Clinical Settings: A Matter of Style. Medical Anthropology Quarterly 16(3):59–73.
1987 Practicing Medical Anthropology: Clinical Strategies for Work in the Hospital. In Applied Anthropology in America (2nd edition). E. Eddy and W. Partridge, eds. Pp. 316–339. New York: Columbia University Press.
Kennedy, Donald A., Evan G. Pattishall, and DeWitt C. Baldwin
1983 Medical Education and the Behavioral Sciences. Publication of the Association for the Behavioral Sciences and Medical Education (no. 83–02). McClean, VA: Association for the Behavioral Sciences and Medical Education.
Knight, J. A.
1973 Medical Student. New York: Appleton-Century Crofts.
Konner, Melvin J.
1987 Becoming a Doctor: A Journey of Initiation in Medical School. New York: Viking Penguin.
Lella, Joseph W., and Dorothy Pawluch
1988 Medical Students and the Cadaver in Social and Cultural Context. In Biomedicine Examined. Margaret Lock and Deborah Gordon, eds. Pp. 21 47. Dordrecht, Holland: D. Reidel Kluwer.
LeBaron, Charles
1982 Gentle Vengeance. New York: Viking Penguin.
Light, Donald
1980 Becoming Psychiatrists: The Professional Transformation of Self. New York: W. W. Norton.
Lock, Margaret, and Deborah Gordon (eds.)
1988 Biomedicine Examined. Dordrecht, Holland: D. Reidel.
Medical Anthropology Newsletter
1980 Open Forum—Clinical Anthropology. Medical Anthropology Newsletter 12(1):
Mendelsohn, Robert S.
1979 Confessions of a Medical Heretic. Chicago: Contemporary Books.
Merton, Robert K., George G. Reader, and Patricia Kendall
1957 The Student-Physician: Introductory Studies in the Sociology of Medical Education. Cambridge, MA: Harvard University Press.
Neher, Jon O.
1988 The "Slow Code": A Hidden Conflict. The Journal of Family Practice 27(4):429–430.

Nolen, William
    1970   The Making of a Surgeon. New York: Random House.
Rubin, Irwin M., Mark S. Plovnick, and Ronald E. Fry
    1975   Improving the Quality of Care: A Program for Health Care Team Development.
            Cambridge, MA: Ballinger.
Segal, Daniel
    1984   Playing Doctor Seriously: Graduation Follies at an American Medical School.
            International Journal of Health Services 14(3):379–395.
Stein, Howard
    1980   Medical Anthropology and Western Medicine. Journal of Psychological Anthro-
            pology 3(2):185–195.
    1990a   American Medicine as Culture. Boulder, CO: Westview Press.
    1990b   The Psychodynamics of Medical Practice: Unconscious Factors in Patient Care.
            Berkeley: University of California Press.
Tax, Sol (ed.)
    1964   Horizons of Anthropology. Chicago: Aldine.
Todd, Harry F. and M. Margaret Clark
    1985   Medical Anthropology and the Challenge of Medical Education. *In* Training
            Manual in Medical Anthropology (1st edition). Carole E. Hill, ed. Pp. 40–57. Wash-
            ington, DC: The American Anthropological Association.
X, Doctor
    1965   The Intern. New York: Harper and Row.

● *chapter seven*

Anthropologists in Nursing-Education Programs

Molly C. Dougherty

Increasingly anthropologists look for careers beyond academic anthropology departments to such settings as nursing-education programs. There are opportunities in academic nursing for anthropologists who develop and refine skills appropriate to educational settings in health care. This chapter explores nursing-education programs, characteristics of anthropologists who succeed there, and the skills anthropologists should develop if they desire such employment. I use "anthropologists" to refer to those with Ph.D. preparation in anthropology; "nurse anthropologist" refers to those with a Ph.D. in anthropology and master's degree in nursing, unless otherwise specified.

The Scope of Nursing-Education

Nursing may be defined as "the diagnosis and treatment of human responses to actual or potential health problems" (American Nurses' Association 1980:31). While most nurses today are employed in hospitals, nursing practice historically was public health oriented and based in homes (Leavitt 1984). The community and family perspective of nursing which encompasses the health-illness continuum through the life-cycle distinguishes it among the health professions today.

As an academic discipline, nursing is quite young. The first baccalaureate program in nursing was founded in 1909 at the University of Minnesota. The size and scope of nursing-education is important to understanding opportunities in nursing-education programs. Preparation for licensure as a registered nurse can be obtained by attending one of three types of nursing-educational programs: diploma, associate degree, and baccalaureate. A nursing diploma is awarded after graduation from a hospital-based program, which is usually three years in duration. Basic nursing preparation provided in a two-year community or junior college leads to an associate degree in nursing, and completing a four-year collegiate program results in a bachelor's degree in nursing (American Nurses' Association 1987:32, 35).

Admissions to all three types of initial nursing-education programs totaled to 120,404 in the 1984–85 year and were distributed as follows: 12% to diploma programs, 53% to associate-degree programs, and 34% to baccalaureate degrees.

In 1985, 1,497 programs in the United States prepared nurses for the registered-nurse licensure examination. These figures represent major changes in the relative mix of programs over the past quarter century in that the number of diploma programs has decreased dramatically and the numbers of associate-degree programs and baccalaureate programs have increased sharply. Graduate education has grown rapidly since the 1960s; there were 167 programs leading to the master's degree in 1985 (Rosenfield 1987) and 50 doctoral programs in nursing in the United States in 1990.

Although there has been tremendous growth in numbers of nursing faculty with doctoral degrees, the percentage of nurse faculty with doctorates remains low. A survey of nurse faculty showed that slightly over 8% held doctorates and 78% held a master's degree (American Nurses' Association 1983). Most nurse educators with doctoral preparation have completed their highest degree in education.

In 1965 the American Nurses' Association (ANA) endorsed the baccalaureate degree as basic preparation for nursing. Labor-force demands since 1965 have far outstripped the ability of baccalaureate programs to provide sufficient number of nursing graduates. Increasingly, young women, the traditional source of graduate nurses, select new career options which are now open to them. Demographic trends, which include a growing aged cohort and a relatively small young adult age cohort, indicate that the current nursing shortage will continue well into the 21st century.

Academic disciplines emphasize development of a unique body of knowledge and a research base to support nursing practice. Research to document the efficacy of nursing measures includes generation of knowledge about (1) health and health promotion in individuals and families, (2) the influence of social and physical environments on health, (3) the care of persons who are acutely or chronically ill, disabled, or dying and their families, and (4) therapeutic actions that minimize the negative effects of illness by enhancing the abilities of individuals and families to respond to actual or potential health problems (American Nurses' Association 1985). These focal areas of nursing research fit well with many interests of anthropologists interested in health and complex societies.

While emphasis on knowledge development through research has grown dramatically, most nurse educators are principally practitioners and teachers. Policy-making bodies such as the National League for Nursing (NLN), the ANA, and licensing boards all recognize the importance of social science in nursing curricula. Therefore, every nursing-education program should be considered a potential employer for appropriately prepared anthropologists.

These policy-making bodies consistently stress the importance of educators of nurses *being* nurses. This posture is understandable in a discipline focusing on self-development. The NLN recommends that every faculty member hold a master's degree in nursing and that Ph.D.-prepared faculty hold their final degree in nursing. The recommendations of policy-making groups represent goals for organizations, and in most cases enforcement is limited. Therefore, many programs attempt to follow the recommendations but must employ persons with preparation considerably different than that recommended by NLN.

State laws govern licensure of registered nurses, and departments of professional regulation issue guidelines relating to the instruction of nursing students. Their policies and recommendations have considerable impact on nursing schools. Nursing programs have established formulas specifying hours of clinical contact and classroom instruction and types of patient-care areas for required clinical contact. These formulas are relatively inflexible; boards of professional regulation may decertify programs which do not meet these specifications and prohibit their graduates from taking the state licensing examinations. This is an important form of control. State regulations require that faculty who supervise the clinical instruction of nursing students be licensed as registered nurses. In fact, faculty members are immediately responsible for the acts of their students. Clearly, most of the faculty in a nursing program are nurses, but the content of some courses is not clinical, and not all positions in nursing-education programs are teaching positions.

Anthropology in Nursing-Education

Much has been written on the interconnections between nursing and anthropology (Bauwens 1978; Brink 1976; Dougherty and Tripp-Reimer 1985; Leininger 1978; Tripp-Reimer and Dougherty 1985). Successful blending of the fields (Leininger 1970) has occurred as anthropology has turned attention to the application of anthropology in health settings and as nursing has developed as an academic discipline (Chambers 1981; Donaldson and Crowley 1978).

Nursing Curricula

Nursing curricula are usually based on a broad conceptual framework, often derived from a noted nursing author, or on a constellation of concepts that the faculty believes encompasses the totality of education and nursing (Orem 1985; Roy 1985). One example of such a constellation is the interrelationship among the physiological, affective, and cognitive components of nursing. However, the underlying theory guiding much of nursing-education is the pathophysiological perspective shared with medical education. This perspective reduces diseases to definable, predictable entities with accepted treatment plans. The dominance of this perspective promotes oversimplification of social, family, and health processes encountered in health care contexts. Anthropology, based on more amorphous concepts, risks being reduced and oversimplified to the point of irrelevance.

Several anthropologists with strong ties to medicine have reported on ways to introduce cultural relativity and culture-specific interpretations of disease and symptom management to medical audiences (Johnson 1981; Kleinman 1982; Kleinman, Eisenberg and Good 1978). These represent important advances in the anthropology of health and the techniques work reasonably well. Their effect is mitigated by two factors. First, it remains difficult for students to grasp the importance of parallel and interacting cultural *systems* because illustrative case examples focus on the conditions and diseases of individuals. Rarely is sufficient time dedicated to cultural content such that cultures can be described and comparative analyses of cultures be made. Second, it is clear to nursing students that the focus of nursing care is on individuals. The attention of student nurses is on learning the knowledge and skills they perceive as essential to their immediate success as student nurses and soon thereafter as nurses. Student nurses complain that the psychosocial and cultural course content is redundant and weak. An anthropologist who teaches nursing students may benefit from participant observation and obtain on-site information on which to base teaching strategies.

Most programs produce and will provide on request their philosophy, objectives or competencies, and a curriculum plan. Idealized information on nursing-education programs is found in the catalog of the parent institution. Definitions for specialized terms and descriptions of how they are developed in nursing programs are found in several publications (National League for Nursing 1985a, 1985b). Introductory nursing texts provide definitions and discussion of terms commonly used in nursing-education programs such as nursing diagnosis, process, and outcomes (Carpenito 1987).

Nursing curricula customarily incorporate social sciences, including sociocultural anthropology, in course work and clinical instruction, but they are usually interpreted, abbreviated, and taught by educators with backgrounds in nursing and/or education. At the University of Miami School of Nursing, for example, the curriculum emphasizes transcultural nursing. The rapid growth and variety of ethnic populations spurred the University of Miami's School of Nursing to establish a curriculum in transcultural nursing in 1981. Undergraduate students take 3 semester-hours of general anthropology and 45 semester-hours of transcultural nursing related to traditional content, i.e., nursing leadership, health alternations, rehabilitation, nursing process, and assessment of health status (University of Miami 1989a). Also, the graduate programs focus on transcultural nursing, a concept which recognizes that each ethnic community has unique health beliefs and practices and that nursing-education has the responsibility for preparing professionals who can adapt nursing to specific health needs (University of Miami 1989b).

In comparison, undergraduate nursing students at the University of Washington take coursework on cultural variation and nursing practice, which integrates anthropology and clinical nursing (Chrisman 1982:117–140). Emphasis is placed on the logic of, and need for, an anthropological approach in nursing. First students are taught that to fully care for the client, they should understand his/her goals within a life-style context. Second, the potential dangers of taking only a narrow biomedical approach to patients are stressed. Third, through examples, the epidemiological perspective is presented, discussed, and employed. Building on the pathophysiological theory customary in nursing, the physiological differences among ethnic or racial groups are discussed.

Since 1974, the University of Washington School of Nursing has had a master's program in crosscultural nursing with three components (1) three sequential seminars and summer field experience in the anthropology of health as it relates to nursing, (2) a wide range of anthropology courses that cover the major foci of the discipline, and (3) directed sociocultural research for the master's thesis with a population similar to one served during the field experience (Chrisman 1982:117–140). Many schools of nursing, particularly those in areas recently affected by multiethnic population increases, offer courses to address the needs of nursing students who care for multiethnic groups.

Texts employed in nursing schools to teach crosscultural nursing reflect considerable variation in approach (Branch and Paxton 1976; Henderson and Primeaux 1981; Martinez 1978; Moore, Van Arsdale, Glittenberg, and Aldrich 1980; Orque, Block, and Monrroy 1983; Spector 1985; Stern 1986; van Horne and Tonnesen 1988; Wilson 1989). Some of these texts reduce cultural variation to a constellation of traits or characteristics which first appear to distinguish cultures. Integration of anthropological concepts into the general nursing curriculum can dilute the important relativistic perspective of anthropology.

Nursing programs are accredited by the NLN, which specifies guidelines for curriculum objectives. The accreditation process is criticized for promoting conformity and stifling intellectual curiosity and risk taking. The fact that nearly all programs attempt to conform to the NLN guidelines suggests that in the United States there is strong support for conventional approaches and proven methods in the preparation of nurses.

Socialization

The belief that nursing students learn principally through role models is generally accepted. There is a body of literature on this subject, and faculty consciously attempt to provide patient care that students can and want to emulate. The centrality of role modeling is embedded in the socialization process in nursing programs. Some very insightful research and analysis has been conducted on the socialization process in medical schools and in nursing programs (Becker, Geer, Hughes, and Strauss 1961; Kramer 1974; Olesen and Whittaker 1968). These studies, and others conducted by social scientists who are not nurses, provide information about the values and beliefs that underlie instruction in nursing programs of all types.

Given the changes that have occurred in opportunities for women (and for men) in the past 20 years, another careful examination of socialization of student nurses would be a valuable addition to the literature. A number of nurses have addressed socialization issues, some using quantitative approaches to the study of attitudes and values. Anthropologists recognize how difficult it is to study social processes within one's own milieu. Research on socialization of student nurses would be a worthwhile undertaking for anthropologists interested in women's employment and career socialization.

The social structure of nursing-education emphasizes teaching. Socialization as a nurse is a distinct advantage for a faculty member because the values and beliefs that pervade nursing are transmitted in the basic nursing preparation (Johnson 1981). Although such an understanding may be gained through anthropological field methods, it requires considerable effort. Preparation as a nurse with a baccalaureate—or preferably a master's—degree has a distinct advantage.

Assets of Anthropologists in Nursing-Education

One asset anthropologists bring to nursing-education is the holistic perspective, particularly an emphasis on cultural relativism and the lifeways of subcultures and ethnic groups in the United States. Information about specific cultures is valuable in nursing-education settings in which nursing students provide care to immigrants and refugees from diverse cultures. Anthropology also provides competence in research methods appropriate to field settings and situations in which quantification of observations is not possible or not well developed. Assessing the effect of nursing interventions is central to developing nursing knowledge on the efficacy of nursing measures. Research methods and observational techniques used by anthropologists can be applied to the definition and description of nursing interventions and measurement of outcomes. Publications on research methods by anthropologists help to clarify the contributions anthropologists can make in research settings (Bernard 1988; Van Maanen 1986–88). Refinement of these aspects of nursing are central to the development of nursing and are one application of anthropology in nursing-education settings.

The niche for social anthropologists in nursing-education settings is well developed, but physical anthropologists also have assets of value to nursing-education. Disease ecology, nutrition, adaptation, anatomy, and physiology are subject areas in which anthropologists with appropriate preparation can make contributions to the teaching program in a school of nursing. Nurses and physical anthropologists have a common bond around human physiology. The potential for collaboration around physical health conditions is strong.

Because of the emphasis on documenting the effectiveness of nursing practice and teaching techniques through program evaluation, teacher evaluation, and student evaluation, anthropologists experienced in or prepared to undertake such evaluative research may be valuable to nursing. Persons with skills in this area are employed to design, acquire external funding for, and direct such programs and for client-related research.

Council on Nursing and Anthropology (CONAA)

A growing number of nurse educators hold advanced degrees in anthropology. The Council of Nursing and Anthropology (CONAA), with a membership in 1988 of 241, serves as a communication network for nurse/anthropologists and those with interests in the two disciplines. CONAA produces a biannual bibliography of its members' publications that provides extensive and diverse examples of the literature. Usually symposia sponsored by CONAA are on the program of the American Anthropological Association annual meeting and the Society for Applied Anthropology annual meeting. Membership dues are minimal; membership by anyone interested in the two disciplines is welcomed. CONAA provides an identity for anthropologists employed in nursing-education throughout the United States, Canada, and Europe. Many nurses with interests in anthropology make international contacts during the annual meetings of the Society for Applied Anthropology that are held outside of the United States.

Suggestions

It is recommended that a faculty applicant review information on the program before formally interviewing for a position. An anthropologist applicant should keep in mind that a nurse with his/her highest degree in education will probably evaluate the anthropologist's value to the organization. Anthropologists are advised to read literature on nursing-education to become familiar with its language.

The tenacity of tradition in nursing-education and the reluctance to introduce innovation should be kept in mind by anthropologists who seek employment in nursing-education programs. The potential contributions of anthropologists are generally recognized, but the aspiring anthropologist/nurse-educator must be able to relate anthropology to high-quality patient care, cost containment and patient outcomes. Discussions with faculty in programs which focus on cross-cultural topics would help the anthropologist understand the interpretation of anthropological content in nursing settings. Membership in CONAA or other organizations that include anthropology and health care in their objectives would be beneficial.

Although Ph.D. programs in nursing have been growing in number and importance for several years, there will be excellent career opportunities for nurses who hold doctorate degrees in anthropology, and opportunities for anthropologists will remain good.

International Nursing

International nursing, a rapidly developing area of nursing, encompasses the "application of nursing knowledge and resources within and across national settings by nurses functioning in cultures and countries other than their own." International nursing has important commonalities with crosscultural or transcultural nursing, which may be defined as the integration of culture into all aspects of nursing care, administration, education, and research (DeSantis 1988).

The development of international nursing appears to be following that of nursing in the United States. Initial linkages between educators and administrators established the basis of communication and consultation. Clinical interests such as maternal-infant health and family issues are common to health care systems throughout the world and provide a focus of communication among nurses internationally. Nursing research has recently developed as a vehicle for communication, collaboration, and joint development (Meleis 1987, 1989).

International nursing organizations and U.S. federal initiatives foster and support international nursing in several ways. The International Council of Nurses was founded in 1899. Today it offers help to nurses in many countries to establish the nurse's role, education, and continued development by using materials published by the organizations and the assistance of the executive director and nurse consultants. The Peace Corps is a federal initiative which offers opportunities for international service in a variety of formats (Gudmundsen 1989). National nurses associations (such as the Royal College of Nursing) are formalizing their international relations through associations with nursing organizations with international departments.

The Fogerty International Center of the National Institutes of Health has an annual budget of about $10 million. The center's mission includes strengthening health institutional research capability in foreign countries, research training of foreign health professionals and allied health personnel (Glittenberg 1989).

Several nursing schools have active international programs. At Texas Women's University, Peace Corps fellows are being prepared (Gudmundsen 1989). At Case Western Research University a tripartite partnership is under development: the university, a private volunteer organization (such as Project HOPE), and a local business or religious organization (Segall 1989). At Emory University a Center for International Nursing has been established. Current information about international topics is carried as a regular feature of the *Journal of Professional Nursing*.

There is increasing interest in international nursing as a specialization in nursing. Andrews (1988) argues that international nursing is a specialization because it consists of a body of knowledge with unique problems and issues related to nursing practice not shared with other recognized nursing specialties. These include understanding health care delivery systems in other countries, functioning with limited resources, and functioning within unfamiliar political, social, economic, and cultural systems. International nursing may be studied through baccalaureate, masters, doctoral, or continuing education, but specialization at the master's level is specifically proposed by Andrews (1988). The proposed content is oriented toward the study of other cultures including: (1) general introduction to cultural concepts, (2) health and illness in various cultures, (3) models to analyze health care system, (4) cross-cultural research and issues, and (5) area/regional studies (Andrews 1988).

The similarities and differences between international nursing and crosscultural nursing may be important to an anthropologist interested in a career in nursing-education. In the United States transcultural nursing focuses on a client or group of clients with different cultural backgrounds than the nurse; the emphasis is on the nursing act with patients or clients in a specific setting. International nursing takes into account the socioeconomic, political, educational, and cultural forces shaping the health care system and encompasses education, administration, and research and includes the promotion of the nursing profession and nurses' welfare worldwide (DeSantis 1988). Two thirds of U.S. nurses in international nursing are not engaged in clinical care. They are in public health, administration, teaching, or consultation, as are their counterparts in host countries. The purview of international nursing is national policy making and health planning. The interests of clinically oriented transcultural nurses and policy oriented international nurses are joined by the critical importance of resource allocation in health care delivery. Health care is dependent upon government legislative bodies setting policy and allocating resources for service, education, and facilities. Health care delivery at the local level depends on government support. The commonalities between international nursing and transcultural nursing are reinforced by the traditions and procedures for resource allocation.

Nurses with international affiliations are involved in the United States Agency for International Development, World Health Organization, Project HOPE, church groups, U.S. military and diplomatic missions and U.S. businesses (Mooneyhan, McElmurray, Sofranko, and Campos 1986). An understanding of the missions of these international organizations is recommended. Similar knowledge of such organizations as the Peace Corps and the Fogerty International Center is suggested. Exploring the programs of nursing schools which emphasize international programs may lead to productive professional associations and/or a position with an international focus. Reading the regular feature on international nursing in the *Journal of Professional Nursing* to keep abreast of the developments in international work is recommended.

International consulting is an attractive alternative to many nurses and anthropologists. Nurses who take long-term international assignments are sought after when they have technical skills needed in host countries. Short-term consultations and positions for those without technical skills are more difficult to secure. Interest in international work is increasing in nursing; anthropologists who have lived in other cultures have much to offer nurses who seek international employment. When seeking placement in a nursing-education program, an anthropologist should emphasize the contribution he or she can make to a nursing-education program with offerings in international nursing.

The Tasks of Anthropology within Nursing-Education

The tasks of anthropologists employed in nursing-education are similar to those of faculty in any setting. Emphasis is placed on teaching, research, and community service; each of these is discussed below.

Teaching

Curriculum and Courses   Community health nursing and anthropological community studies reflect commonalities in anthropology and nursing (Chrisman 1982). Community health issues as a focus of study and clinical involvement contrast with the individual focus of study found in most clinical coursework in nursing. Harwood (1981) discusses the differential experiences of various ethnic minorities in the United States, which helps students to understand why some groups assimilate more easily than others and to clarify the assumptions about a "culture of poverty" (Lewis 1966) they may have internalized.

Anthropologists teach social science content at the undergraduate or graduate level, and research methods are taught in many undergraduate programs. Anthropologists commonly teach graduate level courses in theory, research methods, qualitative research methods, and cultural diversity. Recent interest in qualitative research methods in nursing is evidenced by several books on this topic and a recently introduced journal, *Qualitative Health Research*.

Many studies that describe the life experiences of cultural, ethnic, social, or patient groups are available in nursing and health related literature. Some of these studies aim to simply describe the experiences from the perspective of the subjects. Others attempt to develop theory from a relatively limited sample drawn from a narrowly defined population (persons with cancer, for example). These studies are similar to case studies but with additional development and research they could contribute directly to knowledge building. Anthropologists who develop studies from theory and advance theory through research can contribute much to such studies.

For students whose exposure to research has been descriptive or experimental designs, it is difficult to understand research that addresses the influence of the group on the environment (or culture) and, likewise, the influence of the environment (or culture) on the group or individual. The environment under investigation can be as broad as a culture or as restrictive as the hospital or similar institution. Descriptive research leads to understanding diagnostic groups and social forms, but the development of nursing as a discipline with predictive theory requires research that is more sophisticated conceptually.

Suggestions   A combination of ethnographic methods and grounded theory methods is suitable for nursing students (Bernard 1988; Gubrium 1987; Van Maanen 1986–88). The blend of anthropological and sociological techniques introduced in these volumes can be tailored to research problems in nursing and corresponds with experimental designs that nursing students learn in other research courses. Anthropologists can facilitate nursing studies that go beyond within-group analysis and address theoretical issues. Investigations that grapple with the interrelationship between the individual and the environment (or culture) are an example. Anthropological method and theory helps to enrich the context of observations, patterns and interrelationships found in health care settings and in the interface between health care institutions, and cultural patterns found in communities.

A thorough background in research methods and preparation in statistics are valuable, as is an understanding of theory development and its relationship to research. Knowledge of the literature on nursing theory is suggested.

Research

Opportunities   Programs offering baccalaureate and higher degrees expect more research from the faculty than diploma or associate-degree programs. The latter two types of programs have few faculty with extensive research training or experience, but these programs require evaluation and faculty development. In addition, educational material for students and/or clients and reports of projects or grants are needed frequently.

Traditionally, nursing research has taken a practical focus, in some ways similar to the orientation of medical anthropology. In nursing and in anthropology there has been little emphasis on coursework in field methods although both disciplines rely heavily on observation for the collection of clinical and/or research data. Research methods courses are increasingly required in both disciplines and the quality of research is increasing. But nurses with interests in crosscultural nursing or in using field research techniques do not usually have a full year of fieldwork experience and few of them spend significant time in a foreign culture. While foreign fieldwork is not expected of all anthropology students today, nurses are seldom alien to a health care environment in which they conduct research. Issues related to objectivity are very important and anthropologists can contribute to sorting out these issues with nurse investigators. In some cases the outcome of fieldwork in a circumscribed setting can be very good. Wolf's (1988) nursing study is an example in which a full year of observation was used; the study reveals much about the rituals and pace of work on nursing units in hospital settings.

With more emphasis placed on faculty obtaining doctoral degrees in nursing and the need for conceptuallyl sound research, collaboration with experienced anthropologists is an exciting prospect.

Suggestions In baccalaureate and higher degree programs, faculty job descriptions include the expectation of research productivity, and opportunities for anthropologists are many. Most faculty members have a research project they want to implement or are having difficulty writing in publishable form. The anthropologist has an obvious skill to offer.

Anthropologists have found nursing-education rich in opportunities to carry out research on the anthropology of health. Nursing faculty can provide entry into a wide variety of health-care settings, including consumer populations and health-care provider groups. Nurses may welcome collaboration with an anthropologist to prepare material for groups with widely varying educational levels and materials without ethnic bias. Nurses with limited time to pursue research are often willing to provide assistance, and incorporating practicing nurses or nurse faculty in research is recommended. Their involvement should be acknowledged, including coauthorship of publications when appropriate.

Anthropologists should be aware of the usual constraints in research situations. Some nurses are very sensitive to client confidentiality, informed-consent issues, and their responsibilities in protecting client records. Anthropologists may need to carefully and clearly explain their methods, particularly qualitative methods, to nurses. Group presentations and written protocols are a valuable aid. A spirit of helpfulness and collegiality goes a long way in any research setting. The requirement to have approval from an institutional review board for the protection of human subjects is in place in any hospital or health center that receives federal funds. In many cases, hospitals and universities with medical schools have tied steps to avert malpractice suits to the human subjects review. It is increasingly important to have a written research plan.

Anthropologists whose job descriptions specify collaboration in faculty research may need to keep an account of their involvement. Thinking of their total activity as a research program with explicit goals at annual or biannual intervals can be useful. Many graduate programs include a research coordinator or an office for nursing research. Communicating with this person or office in a scheduled way would capitalize on an anthropologist's research skills and activities. The ability to write publishable material, knowledge of research methods, the social organization of health settings, and basic human physiology are all important to anthropologists' success in research programs in nursing-education.

Community Service

Activities   Community service involves continuing education for nurses, consumer services and education, among other activities. Professional development such as participation in professional organizations and consulting is often defined as community service.

Continuing-education programs (usually thematic, one- to three-day conferences) are organized by professional organizations, nursing programs, or service units. Social science topics are often included and anthropologists known to the program organizers are likely to be asked to speak. Nurses are often involved in health-focused consumer groups as educators, counselors, and/or consultants.

Many faculty members engage in consumer education and/or prepare client-education materials for populations with particular health problems (e.g., diabetes, renal dialysis, or childbirth). Two conditions of growing importance are acquired immune deficiency syndrome (AIDS) and use of street drugs. Understanding the distinctions between attitudes and behaviors of ethnic groups with regard to these conditions is important to providing adequate health care to them. Negotiating the health care needs of poor or refugee ethnic groups can be an important role for an anthropologist in a nursing-education setting. Anthropologists can become involved in these activities and contribute to an understanding of ethnic diversity among the participants.

Suggestions   Most anthropologists employed in nursing-education want to be identified with nursing and anthropology, but active participation in professional organizations of both fields can be very time consuming. Developing time management skills can be enhanced by using suggestions from one of several publications available in the popular press, attending programs with time management as a focus, or by restricting involvement to related, relevant activities. Goal setting and periodic self-evaluation are also valuable aids to time management.

Continuing-education programs are a good place for anthropologists to use fieldwork techniques to become familiar with topics, information, and attitudes with which nurses are concerned. An anthropologist can assist consumer-oriented groups to understand the medical system, facilitate access to services, or communicate more effectively with health professionals. In some cases the anthropologists can establish a *quid pro quo* with an organized ethnic or consumer group to the benefit of all. An anthropologist can help nurses understand the cultural influences on health conditions that have a large social component. Community service activities can consume a lot of time. Anthropologists in nursing-education may want to monitor their own goals and determine how much community service is needed to meet them.

Necessary Skills

Basic anthropological fieldwork skills are valuable in nursing-education programs. Understanding the formal and informal structure of the program and its relationship to the larger institution is important. Anthropologists will benefit from personal links to other anthropologists or social scientists in the institution, and these can sometimes be formalized by appointments to anthropology departments. Within the nursing program much informal news and collegiality can be found within standing committees such as admissions and student affairs. The nursing faculty usually welcomes non-nurses and elects them to committee leadership because many committees have amorphous objectives and nurses have other priorities. Anthropologists probably should not expect to be opinion leaders within a nursing-education program because of the bias toward recognizing nurses as spokespersons to the parent institution and to the public. However, anthropologists who assume leadership in community service demonstrate applied anthropology's role in social change and may become opinion leaders.

Problems are encountered by anthropologists who work in nursing-education programs. Any professional employed outside his/her discipline risks feeling isolated, and this happens to anthropologists. In a time of budget cuts they feel particularly vulnerable to having the courses they teach dropped from the curriculum. Remaining in nursing-education for several years, using fieldwork methods to understand the environment of nursing, and building support networks within the program and with national professional organizations are helpful countermeasures to the sense of isolation.

The emphasis on consensus decision making in nursing programs is problematic in two ways. Endless hours are spent in committee and faculty meetings while the objectives, rationale, goals, and philosophy of almost any planned endeavor are worked out, edited, represented, refined, and finally adopted. Second, an emphasis on consensus tends to stifle scholarly debate. This is especially a problem in a discipline establishing a research base and formulating theory. It is also frustrating for an academician trained to refine theory and research techniques through discussion of alternative approaches and intellectual word play.

The emphasis on experimental design and quantitative methods in research may be frustrating also. For many years nurse/anthropologists have had difficulty securing research grants because qualitative research was not sufficiently valued by peer review groups, and at the local level research-based and clinically oriented faculty have not understood qualitative methods. This appears to be changing although there is a clear emphasis on laboratory research in funding from the National Institutes of Health and much internal university funding. Universities have made and continue to support huge investments in the laboratory sciences. This emphasis probably will not change in the near future.

Research based on qualitative methods appears in nursing journals, and the *Western Journal of Nursing Research* regularly publishes qualitative-research articles. *Qualitative Health Research* is a recent addition to the publication outlets for qualitative research in nursing and the social sciences. The qualitative approach taken by nursing faculty is a melding of ethnographic and the grounded theory approaches. They promote a climate in which anthropologically oriented research is better understood.

Research expertise is an asset to those who teach research courses and/or advise student or faculty research. In graduate-level research courses a text such as Polit and Hungler (1987) is employed, and at the undergraduate level, one such as Brink and Wood (1989). Ability to teach the content of such volumes and a knowledge of the nursing-research literature is useful. *Nursing Research* is one source of information on current topics and frequently employed methods. Nursing specialty journals such as the *Journal of Obstetric, Gynecologic, and Neonatal Nursing* often contain research articles directed to a specialized nursing audience. The *Annual Review of Nursing Research* is a valuable description and critique to nursing research in specific areas of inquiry (Fitzpatrick, Taunton, and Benoliel 1990). Library work to familiarize oneself with research is recommended for those who aspire to teach it.

Teaching experience is very important to nurse educators and experience acquired while a student or in any setting should be highlighted. Teaching techniques including videotapes, role playing, lecture, discussion, and more recently compact video disk are all used by nursing faculty and illustrate the time and attention directed toward instruction. Demonstrating versatility and concern for student learning is important. In nursing-education, the skills most needed by anthropologists are teaching and research, including published writing.

How to Get a Job

All programs for nursing-education should be considered potential sources of positions for qualified anthropologists. Given two attractive applicants, one a nurse and the other an anthropologist, most administrators would choose the nurse. And most deans would state that they would not hire a non-nurse. However, this is a statement of the ideal; in reality, non-nurses are hired. When a position must be filled or lost, or when personnel are not available to do a major task, deans resolve such issues expediently. In one southeast school of nursing, two non-nurse faculty members (one an anthropologist) were hired, retained, and tenured even though job descriptions specified that faculty be nurses.

Certain characteristics of anthropologists and nursing-education programs would result in a good career match. Desirable characteristics of anthropologists in order of importance include a productive record of health research, demonstrated ability to write publishable material, familiarity with health-service environments, and a genuine interest in the education of nursing students. Characteristics of appropriate nursing programs, in order in importance, are programs at the master's or doctoral level, administrators who value social science in the curriculum, emphasis on research productivity of faculty, baccalaureate nursing-education, program-evaluation research, affiliation with a major medical center, external research and/or training support, and a need for Ph.D. faculty to serve on graduate students' supervisory committees.

Positions advertised in nursing journals usually specify that nursing preparation is a requirement. Nursing programs are constantly improving and upgrading their offerings as they expand, and add graduate programs including doctoral education. This process requires new faculty with advanced degrees. Naturally, in a discipline that has been in universities only since World War II, it is necessary to hire faculty without ideal preparation. The expansion of nursing within universities will result in new faculty positions for some time to come.

While journals are a worthwhile source of information on position openings, the NLN's 1989 *Guide to State-Approved Schools of Nursing* provides a valuable listing of programs helpful to anthropologists looking for a specific location (National League for Nursing 1989). Sending a letter and a curriculum vitae to the dean or program director is an accepted procedure to initiate an employment application. Highlight important professional characteristics in the letter. If possible, arrange a personal interview to review open positions and to discuss your strengths. Use personal contacts and especially established working relationships with faculty members. Of course, many programs will not have openings appropriate for anthropologists and budgetary constraints are always an issue.

For interviews, be conversant with the philosophy, objectives, and curriculum of the program. Knowing the areas of interest of key faculty is helpful. Try to find out as soon as possible from the potential supervisor what the job entails. Depending on career goals, inquire about eligibility for tenure. Emphasize strengths during interviews and demonstrate knowledge of nursing-education and of the program.

If at first a job is not attained, keep in mind that nursing faculties tend to be fluid and external funds are often received. Keep the application open and updated and check on openings every few months. Some programs are more supportive of social scientists than others, and anthropologists can be more productive in programs with a strong social science base. Experience in one school of nursing facilitates obtaining a position in another.

How to Be an Anthropologist in a Nursing-Education Setting

Several points will help the anthropologist seeking employment within nursing-education.

- Become familiar with the scope of nursing and nursing-education programs nationally.
- Read materials published by the American Nurses' Association and the National League of Nursing to become familiar with what nurses state about nursing.
- Read the research published by nurse anthropologists and anthropologists who are employed in nursing-education.
- Consider the fit between the requirements for teaching, research and service and your interests as an anthropologist.
- Develop versatile teaching skills and gain experience teaching to varied audiences.

- Foster contacts with nursing faculty and develop collaborative research projects.
- Read nursing journals for position openings and send letters of inquiry along with a curriculum vitae.
- Gain experience interviewing and molding your professional and research interests to positions available.
- Join CONAA and participate in their activities at the annual meetings of the Society for Applied Anthropology and the American Anthropological Association.
- Throughout use established field research techniques to sort out the ideal from the real version of activities in nursing-education programs.

Acknowledgments. Many thanks to Toni Sheppard who entered the earlier version of this article onto computer disk and converted the reference format, and to Toni Tripp-Reimer who made helpful suggestions on the proposed revisions.

References Cited

American Nurses' Association
    1980   Nursing—A Social Policy Statement. Kansas City, MO: American Nurses' Association.
    1983   Facts About Nursing 82–83. New York: American Journal of Nursing.
    1985   Directions for Nursing Research: Toward the Twenty-First Century. Kansas City, MO: ANA Cabinet on Nursing Research.
    1987   Facts About Nursing 86–87. New York: American Journal of Nursing.
Andrews, M. M.
    1988   Educational Preparation for International Nursing. Journal of Professional Nursing. 4(6):430–435.
Bauwens, E. E., ed.
    1978   The Anthropology of Health. St. Louis: C. V. Mosby.
Becker, H. S., B. Geer, E. C. Hughes, and A. L. Strauss
    1961   Boys in White: Student Culture in Medical School. Chicago: University of Chicago Press.
Bernard, H. R.
    1988   Research Methods in Cultural Anthropology. Beverly Hills: Sage Publications.
Branch, M. F., and P. P. Paxton
    1976   Providing Safe Nursing Care for Ethnic People of Color. New York: Appleton-Century-Crofts.
Brink, P., and M. J. Wood
    1989   Basic Steps in Planning Nursing Research: From Question to Proposal North Scituate, MA: Duxbury Press.
Brink, P. J., ed.
    1976   Transcultural Nursing: A Book of Readings. Englewood Cliffs, NJ: Prentice-Hall.
Carpenito, L. J.
    1987   Nursing Diagnosis: Application to Clinical Practice. Philadelphia, PA: Lippincott.
Chambers, E.
    1981   Practicing Anthropology 4:5–18.

Chrisman, N.
  1982   Anthropology in Nursing: An Exploration of Adaptation. *In* Clinically Applied Anthropology: Anthropologists in Health Science Settings. N. J. Chrisman and T. W. Maretzki, eds. Pp. 117–140. Boston: D. Reidel.
DeSantis, L.
  1988   The Relevance of Transcultural Nursing to International Nursing. International Nursing Review 35(4):110–112, 116.
Donaldson, S. K., and D. M. Crowley
  1978   The Discipline of Nursing. Nursing Outlook 26:113–120.
Dougherty, M.C., and T. Tripp-Reimer
  1985   The Interface of Nursing and Anthropology. *In* Annual Review of Anthropology, volume 14. B. Siegal, A. Beals, and S. Tyler, eds. Pp. 219–241. Palo Alto, CA: Annual Reviews, Inc.
Fitzpatrick, J. J., R. L. Taunton, and J. Q. Benoliel
  1990 Annual Review of Nursing Research. Vol. 8. New York: Springer Publishing.
Glittenberg, J. E.
  1989   Fogarty International Center: A Resource for International Nursing. Journal of Professional Nursing 5(1):7, 55–56.
Gubrium, J. F.
  1987   Analyzing Field Reality. Vol. 2. Sage University Series on Qualitative Research Methods. Newbury Park, CA: Sage.
Gudmundsen, A. M.
  1989   Building an Infrastructure for International Health Promotion and Disease Prevention· The Peace Corps Fellows Program. Journal of Professional Nursing 5(4):172, 236.
Harwood, Alan, ed.
  1981   Ethnicity and Medical Care. Cambridge, MA: Harvard University Press.
Henderson, G., and M. Primeaux
  1981   Transcultural Health Care. Menlo Park, CA: Addison-Wesley.
Johnson, T. M.
  1981   The Anthropolaogist as a Role Model for Medical Students. Practicing Anthropology 4:8–10.
Kleinman, A. M.
  1982   Clinically Applied Anthropology on a Psychiatric Consultation-Liaison Space. *In* Clinically Applied Anthropology: Anthropologists in Health Science Settings. N. J. Chrisman and T. W. Maretzki, eds. Pp. 83–115. Boston: D. Reidel.
Kleinman, A. M., L. Eisenberg, and B. J. Good
  1978   Culture, Illness and Care: Clinical Lessons from Anthropologist and Cross-Cultural Research. Annals of Internal Medicine 99:25–28.
Kramer, M.
  1974   Reality Shock: Why Nurses Leave Nursing. St. Louis, MO: C. V. Mosby.
Leavitt, J. W.
  1984   Women and Health in America. Madison: University of Wisconsin Press.
Leininger, M.
  1970   Nursing and Anthropology: Two Worlds to Blend. New York: Wiley.
  1978   Transcultural Nursing: Concepts, Theories, and Practices. New York: John Wiley & Sons.
Lewis, O.
  1966   The Culture of Poverty. Scientific American 215(4):19–25.

Martinez, R. A.
    1978   Hispanic Culture and Health Care: Fact, Fiction, Folklore. St. Louis, MO: C.
    V. Mosby.
Meleis, A. I.
    1987   International Nursing Research. Annual Review of Nursing Research 5:205–
    227.
    1989   International Research: A Need or a Luxury? Nursing Outlook 37(3):138–142.
Mooneyhan, E. L., B. J. McElmurray, M. S. Sofranko, and A. B. Campos
    1986   International Dimensions of Nursing and Health Care in Baccalaureate and
    Higher Degree Nursing Programs in the United States. Journal of Professional Nurs-
    ing 2:82–90.
Moore, L. G., P. W. Van Arsdale, J. E. Glittenberg, and R. A. Aldrich
    1980   The Biocultural Basis of Health: Expanding Views of Medical Anthropology.
    St. Louis, MO: C. V. Mosby.
National League for Nursing
    1985a   Educational Outcomes: Assessment of Quality—A Directory of Student Out-
    come Measurement Utilized by Nursing Programs in the United States. New York:
    National League for Nursing.
    1985b   Policies and Procedures of Accreditation for Programs in Nursing Education.
    New York: National League for Nursing.
    1989   Guide to State Approved Schools of Nursing R.N. 47th ed. New York: National
    League for Nursing.
Olesen, V. L., and E. W. Whittaker
    1968   The Silent Dialogue. San Francisco: Jossey-Bass.
Orem, D.
    1985   Nursing: Concepts of Practice. 3rd ed. New York: McGraw-Hill.
Orque, N. S., B. Block, and L. A. Monrroy
    1983   Ethnic Nursing Care: A Multi-Cultural Approach. St. Louis, MO: C. V. Mosby.
Polit, D., and B. Hungler
    1987   Nursing Research: Principles and Methods. 3rd ed. Philadelphia: J. B. Lippin-
    cott.
Rosenfeld, P.
    1987   Nursing Student Census with Policy Implications. New York: National League
    for Nursing.
Roy, C.
    1985   Introduction to Nursing: An Adaptation Model. 2nd ed. Englewood Cliffs, NJ:
    Prentice-Hall.
Segall, M. E.
    1989   Frances Payne Bolton School of Nursing's New Paradigm for International
    Health: Think Globally and Act Locally. Journal of Professional Nursing 5(2):62,
    112–113.
Spector, R. E.
    1985   Cultural Diversity in Health and Illness. Norwalk, CT: Appleton-Century-
    Crofts.
Stern, P. N.
    1986   Women, Health and Culture. Washington, D.C.: Hemisphere Publishing.
Tripp-Reimer, T. and M. C. Dougherty
    1985   Cross-Cultural Nursing Research. In Annual Review of Nursing Research. Vol.
    3. H. Werley and J. Fitzpatrick, eds. Pp. 77–104. New York: Springer Publishing.

University of Miami
  1989a   Undergraduate Studies. Vol. 63. Miami, FL: University of Miami.
  1989b   Graduate School. Vol. 62. Miami, FL: University of Miami.
van Horne, W. A., and T. V. Tonnesen
  1988   Ethnicity and Health. Milwaukee: University of Wisconsin.
Van Maanen, J., ed.
  1986–88   Sage University Paper Series on Qualitative Research Methods. 12 Volumes.
    Beverly Hills, CA: Sage Publications.
Wilson, H. S., ed.
  1989   Research in Nursing. 2nd ed. Redwood City, CA: Addison-Wesley Publishing
    Co.
Wolf, A. R.
  1988   Nurses' Work: The Sacred and the Profane. Philadelphia: University of Penn-
    sylvania Press.

● *chapter eight*

Ethnographic Research Methods for Applied Medical Anthropology

Robert T. Trotter II

Ethnographic research methodology allows medical anthropologists to explore key issues and concepts of health and illness across cultural boundaries and to advance anthropological theory and practice. The ethnographic methods used in medical anthropology include formal techniques for direct observation, participation in life experiences, and informant interviewing. These methods produce data which can be used to construct holistic descriptions of human cultures and to provide detailed information about subsistence, technology, social relationships, health, language, beliefs, family, cultural networks, and the life rhythms of human beings from birth to death and beyond.

A new ethnographic methodological tool kit has improved our ability to understand and predict human behavior within health-related environments. These methods are enhancing the potential for our research to accomplish a dual set of outcomes. They can be directly applied to produce practical changes to health care systems and health beliefs in various communities, and simultaneously can advance the theoretical propositions that the social sciences use to interpret this critical area of human cultures. The practical results accrue as we discover better ways to deliver health education messages, remove barriers to public health projects, change the way people use medical services, or improve the ability of health professionals to deal with patients from a different culture. The theoretical advances result from the opportunities that applied medical anthropology provides for tests of both methods and theories in a real world environment.

Background Information

Ethnographic research methods comprise all of the processes, procedures, and techniques that allow an anthropologist to select, collect, record, manage, and analyze ethnographic data within the framework of anthropological theory. The most common label given to this complex set of research methods and techniques is "participant observation." In fact, the term is so frequently used by anthropologists as a shorthand description of the ethnographic endeavor, it has erroneously come to be considered "the" method of sociocultural anthropology, rather than the general term for all of the processes of ethnographic research. This is an unfortunate situation which makes the ethnographic process appear to be far easier to accomplish than is actually the case.

The classic ethnographic research project involves staying in the field 24 hours a day for a minimum of 12 to 24 months. This provides opportunities for the ethnographer to observe, record, and ask questions about ordinary events, from the time people get up to when they turn in for the night. It allows the researcher to capture cycles of daily, monthly, and annual life. And special events can be recorded in detail as they occur. The 12–24-month research cycle is long enough to insure that most key cultural beliefs and behaviors will be identified, and that no major regularly occurring community events will be missed. Shorter field sessions are possible for groups whose major cultural parameters are already known, or where the object of the fieldwork is an investigation of some special or focused area of behavior.

Ethnographic research necessitates a broader conceptualization of research methodology than is typically found in the experimental or survey-based social sciences where methodological considerations have often been restricted to experimental control, sampling processes, instrument design, and appropriate statistical procedures. In contrast, ethnographic methods encompass all of the critical issues surrounding the direct observation of, interaction with, and interviewing of informants in a field setting. The highly qualitative and socially intimate nature of ethnography demands formal processes. These processes help resolve the difficulties generated by the conditions required for ethnographic research: the opportunity to enter a cultural setting, establish long-term social relationships, be allowed to participate in important community activities, and exit from the setting with data that is defensible, comprehensive, and intact.

The following sections summarize some of the critical methodological elements of classic ethnographic research and introduce advanced ethnographic research methods that are enhancing our ability to investigate and analyze medical anthropology issues.

Review of Selected Methodological Literature
There is a growing literature which describes ethnographic research design, site entry, informant relationships, computer field note management, advanced research techniques, and the personal effects of field studies on the researcher. Older references emphasize practical advice. Newer works assume knowledge of the classics, and expend their efforts refining theory, providing ethnographic training models, describing advanced methods, or defending the descriptive nature of ethnographic techniques in an increasingly quantified world.

Two of the early works describing ethnographic field methods are Kroeber's seminal text, *Anthropology Today* (Kroeber 1953) and the book of recommended fieldwork questions published by the Royal Anthropological Institute, *Notes and Queries on Anthropology* (Royal Anthropological Institute, 1951). However, the benchmark era for the formalization of ethnographic methods is the time period circa 1970. The classic text published during this period which links ethnographic research with larger theoretical concerns is Pelto's (1970) *Anthropological Re-*

search; The Structure of Inquiry. Other period works describe the ethnographic research process, its effects on the researcher, and the practical conditions one could expect to encounter in the field. Examples are Epstein's *The Craft of Social Anthropology* (Epstein 1967), and Spradley and McCurdy's *The Cultural Experience: Ethnography in Complex Society* (Spradley and McCurdy 1972). These publications mark the initial formalization of ethnographic methodological training.

One important edited volume, *Marginal Natives: Anthropologists at Work* (Freilich 1970), links theory, method, and field considerations. Chapters describe how ethnographic knowledge is acquired in the field, the types of approaches ethnographers commonly adopt (passive, adaptive, interactive, and intrusive, to name a few), and comparative descriptions of ethnographic research by some of the most successful fieldworkers of that time period. Each author presents a problem statement (theoretical approach, and research design), describes how they initiated passive or active research processes (fieldwork entry), discusses their methods (the progress of the field research), and describes bowing out (how the ethnographer successfully, or unsuccessfully left their research site behind).

Other books circa 1970 provide behind-the-scenes details about field research; a necessary complement to theory and methodology. The pragmatic classics of this period are filled with practical advice for fieldwork survival: *Doing Fieldwork: Warnings and Advice* (Wax 1971); *Encounter and Experience, Personal Accounts of Fieldwork* (Beteille and Maden, eds. 1975); *Being an Anthropologist: Fieldwork in Eleven Cultures* (Spindler 1970); and *Crossing Cultural Boundaries* (Kimball and Watson 1972). Each contains excellent advice to overcome the problems of doing research in foreign countries. In addition, Frantz's (1972) *Handbook for Student Anthropologists* contains a summary of more than 100 guides for ethnographic research: technical aides; both general and area specific guides to ethnographic questions; manuals for crosscultural research on children, adults, health care, art, food habits; as well as bibliographic references for world areas, such as India, Oceania, and Africa. Another handbook on basic field research is Naroll and Cohen's (1970) *A Handbook of Method in Cultural Anthropology*. While some of the entries in these books have become outdated, each contains a great deal of timelessly useful information.

A subsequent round of ethnographic research texts began appearing circa 1980. These works expand on the earlier texts and bring the field more up to date in terms of methods and procedures. Spradley's two "how-to" ethnographic training manuals, *Participant Observation* (Spradley 1980) and *The Ethnographic Interview* (Spradley 1979) became standard texts for fieldwork training for most of a 10-year cycle. Other works include *The Craft of Community Study: Fieldwork Dialogues* (Kimball and Partridge 1979), and Mike Agar's *The Professional Stranger* (Agar 1980). Agar's book has been frequently cited in the substance abuse literature, due in part to Agar's early drug research, especially his street ethnography of drug use, *Ripping and Running* (Agar 1974). A second edition of *Anthropological Research: The Structure of Inquiry* (Pelto and Pelto 1978) was published in this cycle. A more recent book, *Fieldwork: The Human Experience*

(Lawless, Sutlive, Zamora 1983) is also valuable. These books contain firsthand accounts of the processes of field research and the lessons to be learned.

Revisions in formal approaches to ethnographic research methods seem to appear on about a ten-year cycle. Recent additions to the literature are the two-volume series by Werner and Schoepfle (1987) titled *Systematic Fieldwork*, Bernard's (1988) *Research Methods in Cultural Anthropology*, Fetterman's *Ethnography: Step by Step* (Fetterman 1989), and the advanced methods text, *Systematic Data Collection* (Weller and Romney 1988). These works contain state-of-the-art descriptions of research design and methods for both classic participant observation and the advanced ethnographic data collection necessary in modern medical anthropology.

General Methodological Considerations for Ethnographic Research

The primary purpose of this chapter is to introduce some specific methodologies that are of value to applied medical anthropology. However, since ethnographic research training is less standardized than quantitative research training at the present, this section reviews basic information that should be included in preparation for ethnographic field research; areas of training that medical anthropologists should receive before embarking on ethnographic field endeavors.

Ethnographic research has ten basic stages: (1) Problem definition; (2) field preparation; (3) entry into the community; (4) initial observations and interviews (social mapping); (5) informant selection; (6) intensive and focused interviews on selected topics; (7) general information review and confirmation; (8) exit from individual relationships and, eventually, the community; (9) data analysis; and (10) public dissemination of results. These stages are cyclical, not linear. At any given time an ethnographer is meeting new informants, working with long-standing relationships, and moving out of existing relationships. The ethnographer not only collects new information but also reviews fieldnotes and reinterviews key informants to confirm, modify, or deny previous data. Analysis begins early in the process and continues in conjunction with field data collection, and beyond. Thus, ethnographic field research has a number of predictable activities and types of interactions that are briefly summarized in the following sections.

Planning Field Logistics

The primary concerns for field research planning include survival considerations, field entry permission, research design, and preparations for data management. The latter two involve background research, theoretical considerations, and appropriate methodological design for the initial stages of a project. The other pre-field planning issues are logistics and official field entry permission.

The most important general logistic condition is survival. Survival questions include: What equipment do you need? What supplies are necessary (from toilet paper and computer disks to food in remote or foreign areas, plus clothing and shelter)? Where will you live? What kind of health precautions do you need to take? Have you learned the language sufficiently to allow for entry and survival

needs? Fieldwork involves the researcher living in a field setting (from foreign
rural areas to U.S. urban ghettos) for a prolonged period. Issues of comfort and
basic safety are as important to the completion of ethnographic research as good
research design and data management. It is difficult to collect usable data if you
are sick, injured, or dead.

Another critical element of ethnographic research involves acquiring the appropriate permissions necessary for moving to a field site and beginning the research. The types of permission needed can be divided into official permission
(from governments, agencies, community leaders, and institutions) and informal
permission (from local individuals who control access to information and to others). Expanded discussions of these issues can be found in the literature summarized above.

Field Entry

Once the initial planning has been completed, a number of conditions affect the
entry process. Field researchers are deviants in an ongoing cultural system and
their reasons for being there do not normally match the rules of behavior in the
community. Therefore, ethnographers seek ways to make their presence more
congruent with their surroundings. Research entry involves learning to dress appropriately, to be able to talk, walk, and stand in ways that are compatible with
the cultural environment, to learn how to "fit in," or at least not stand out in a
crowd.

Social Mapping and Successful Roles.   One way that has proven successful
in a wide variety of cultures, both foreign and domestic, is to do a gentle entry.
Most ethnographers follow a multimethod process of entry called "mapping social contexts." It includes observing behavior, following nonintrusive research
leads, and recording copious amounts of observational data. This is often a prerequisite to interviewing, and is certainly a prerequisite to any in-depth (key informant) interviewing or to sustained field research in public environments. Mapping social environments consequently leads to contact with and initial interviews
with local cultural experts.

Informant Selection.   Anthropologists select ethnographic informants on the
basis of expertise in a cultural subject area and the ability of an informant to elo-
quently describe the culture, or to provide "typical" or representative responses
about the culture. Therefore, part of the methodological tool kit of an ethnographer includes techniques for sustaining relationships to keep social alliances open
for future research contacts.

> [T]he ethnographic fieldworker must locate helpful people, win their coopera-
> tion, and establish a close, personal relationship with them. This task is not sim-
> ple, because it involves a basic conflict. On the one hand, the ethnographer es-
> tablishes a relationship of trust with his informants. It is desirable that this be
> productive and beneficial to both parties. Often it is marked by friendship. On
> the other hand, the ethnographer seeks to know things that informants may be
> reluctant to reveal. Indeed, they may perceive that the researcher is asking them
> to tell secrets about other people to whom they are loyal. At the very least, they

will be asked to talk about what they know in a manner that is new to them. Some of the ethnographer's questions may be embarrassing; others are outright stupid. [Spradley and McCurdy 1972:41–42]

Anthropologists also use quantitatively based sampling frames and "power analysis" techniques to randomly select informants when the purpose of their interviewing is to examine dimensions of intracultural variation on subjects that they have already explored through in-depth ethnographic interviews. Several recent articles have explored both the selection of informants and the problems with informant accuracy under various circumstances. Informant selection is always a critical issue, and even more so in the special case of a project that has both ethnographic and quantitative research components and where there is a need to compare and combine data derived from nonrandom ethnographic sampling with randomized quantitative sampling. The dilemmas produced by these often-conflicting sampling conditions is currently being solved in two ways. One is called "targeted sampling," and is being used to deal with the need to study "hidden" populations, such as street studies of drug addicts or the health needs of prostitutes (Watters and Biernacki 1989). The other is to use simulation models to estimate relations and biases that occur due to what is called "snowball" or convenience sampling (Johnson, Boster, and Holbert 1989). A snowball sample is one that begins with an individual who provides the names of other individuals in his or her social networks; those people provide the names of others who can be interviewed, and so on until a sample that is large enough for statistical purposes has been collected. The latter type of sample violates certain statistical assumptions about appropriate sampling, and must be accommodated in some way that reduces the bias created by the lack of randomness in the sample frame.

The sampling articles noted above deal with the problem that a sample not drawn randomly may bias any results derived from it, because it may leave out individuals whose views and beliefs are an important part of the overall intracultural variation in a society. However, anthropologists must also be concerned about bias or misinformation that creeps into their data sets either because of inaccurate memory about events, because of differences or deficiencies in cultural knowledge between informants, or because of differential participation in cultural scenes by particular informants. A series of articles (Bernard et al. 1984; D'Andrade 1974; Freeman, Romney, and Freeman 1987; and Romney and Weller 1984) explore the conditions that affect the precision of informants. Taken together, these articles provide strong support for the accuracy of ethnographic informants, with cautions about the types of data that various types of informants will present either accurately or inaccurately. This allows the ethnographer to select informants with much greater precision and defensibility than was previously possible in medical anthropological research.

The Sustained Research Process

Sustained field research is basically an extension of the entry process. Ethnographers work intensively with relatively small communities or through local social networks where communication tends to be frequent and tight. The researcher develops a reputation which has to be guarded and reinforced, since it will often be deliberately tested. Whether or not the ethnographer is able to overcome these tests normally depends on the types and quality of relationships they develop with the people they interact with in the field. These relationships, in turn, are dependent on the ethnographer learning the tacit knowledge systems of the culture. There are three tacit knowledge areas that are often the key "operating" systems in any culture. These are the culturally defined roles, the reciprocity system, and the taboo knowledge of the culture. Controlling these types of information is a key to sustained research.

Creating Dyads.   Creating dyadic relationships is vital for maintaining a sustained presence in any cultural system. Trust is initially offered through dyads. It is also transferred directly from initial dyads into social networks. An informant who trusts you can introduce you to a member of his or her network, or to a known member of another network and open contacts to further research opportunities.

Once contact has been established, it is important to maintain interactions in the community. Familiarity may breed contempt, but more often it breeds trust. This helps overcome the problem of trying to establish yourself in a social setting where you have no intrinsic membership.

Sustainable Roles.   The next step in sustained entry is to adopt a sustainable role; preferably a role that is already defined by the culture and the community. One circumstance that must be taken into account in developing a sustainable role is that some cultures and subcultures maintain gender roles that are distinctly different from the ones the researcher is accustomed to playing. This can cause discomfort, confusion, and even anger. In some cases the research must be divided among investigators assuming appropriate gender roles for the culture being studied. Any other approach could fail to gain access to key elements within the cultural system and might produce partial, incorrect, or misinformed analyses of the culture under study.

Reciprocity in Fieldwork.   In addition to adopting appropriate roles, all human groups work on culturally constructed systems of reciprocity which must be managed if sustained entry is to be possible. Ethnographers inevitably incur social "debts" that carry return obligations. The more contact you have with an individual, the more complex the obligations are likely to become. Friends owe more social debts than strangers or acquaintances. Family membership compels participation in the most multifaceted set of reciprocal obligations that exist in a culture. If you become the equivalent of "one of the family," you can expect to have tremendous access to intimate information about your informants; you can also expect to have to fulfil all sorts of obligations to them. The strength of reciprocity is that it works. The danger of reciprocity is that it works both ways. The easiest way to destroy a social relationship is to allow reciprocity to become imbalanced. For the ethnographer, the primary danger with reciprocity is that it is almost always based in tacit rather than explicit knowledge systems. It is hard for outsiders to understand and control.

Handling Taboo Knowledge. The other tacit system that is very important to sustained research is taboo knowledge. All cultural systems contain information that is in some way dangerous for outsiders to have, or knowledge that is considered improper for other insiders to know. There are two basic ways that ethnographers protect themselves and their informants from the dangers of taboo knowledge. The first is to avoid learning it. The second protection is to appear to know nothing, even if you have learned the taboo knowledge. Many "secrets" are only secrets because there is a social convention not to divulge them in public. In some of these cases, pretending not to know the information is as socially "appropriate" as not knowing it. As long as there is no need for public acknowledgement that taboo knowledge restrictions have been violated, members of the social group tend to ignore a breach of "cultural security," since these breaches occur within the society itself, through the same process, and are ignored as long as the "violation" is not made public. However, if the knowledge becomes public, the group may be required to move against the offender in order to protect "the secrets" of the group.

In some cases ethnographers deliberately seek out and record taboo knowledge because the taboo knowledge is at the very core of the research problem being explored. This is certainly the case in the ethnographic research being done on street drug use, where taboo information is a such an integral part of the system that learning it cannot be avoided. This creates a number of ethical and individual dilemmas for the researcher, not the least of which is personal safety. Even if this knowledge is not at the core of the study, it becomes dangerous. The ethnographer must be prepared to protect informants and themselves in these types of disclosure conditions.

Once these conditions for sustained research are met, then the ethnographer can proceed to increasingly focused research techniques. Several of these are described in the following sections.

Intensified Research, Advanced Methods, and Rapid Assessment Techniques

An explosion has recently occurred in advanced anthropological research techniques. These new methods do not replace the need for classic ethnographic data collection, but they enhance our ability to confirm basic ethnographic findings from multiple directions and they allow us to produce greater analytical depth and breadth of detail in a number of cultural dimensions. These new methods make rapid assessment ethnography feasible in ways that have not been possible before this time.

The new methods are predominantly focused on three areas of data collection and analysis. These areas are the analysis of culturally defined cognitive systems, the exploration of social relationships and social structure, and the development of decision models based on cultural values and decision processes.

Cognitive Systems

Anthropologists exploring the cognitive dimensions of medical domains have been extremely prolific in creating new methods. Since many of the key issues in medical anthropology require a documentation of cultural domains surrounding peoples' beliefs about health and illnesses, these new research techniques are likely to have a strong impact on theory and practice in medical anthropology well into the foreseeable future. The new techniques can be divided into those that (1) assist in determining the content and limits of health care domains (e.g., free listings), (2) those analyzing the structural elements of cultural domains (e.g., triads, pile sorts, scales), and (3) those that portray a domain from a consensual framework (e.g., consensus theory approach).

Free Listing.   Free listing is a simple technique that is done by virtually every ethnographer who discovers an important cultural domain and wants to do a preliminary exploration of the limits of that area of knowledge, belief, or behavior. Folk remedies are a common example. Since all cultures begin the diagnosis and intervention of illnesses in the home, it is a normal question to ask, "what kinds of remedies and medicines do you use?" This produces a listing for a single informant, which can be rechecked and expanded for that individual, duplicated for other members of the household, then broadened and rechecked with members of the community until virtually all remedies in use in a culture have been identified.

The more sophisticated uses of free listing data treat these qualitative data as variables that can be counted and used in several statistical procedures (Weller and Romney 1988). The free listings generated by individuals, or groups, or even communities can be compared with one another, either in terms of internal variation or variation from one group to the other. For example, questions about the saliency of treatments for an illness can be tested by asking informants for a free listing and then either aggregating the data for the group, or comparing answers within or between groups. One such type of free listing exercise was used by the author to generate a model of the home treatment of illnesses in a Mexican American community (Trotter 1981, 1983). Another use of the free listing exercise is presented in Table 1, below.

The data in Table 1 were generated as part of an applied project to create a culturally appropriate in-school prevention program to reduce risks from alcohol and drug abuse, and AIDS for Navajo youth on the Navajo reservation. The project used several free listing exercises as a rapid assessment technique to establish baseline data on alcohol and drug terminology that could be incorporated into the classroom exercises developed as a part of the project. The Table 1 data were collected by giving a five-by-seven card to informants and asking them to "please list all of the things you can think of, except alcohol, that people use to get high." This rapid scanning technique is useful in groups, such as high school and college classrooms. It works equally well with single individuals and can be done as an interview exercise, one-on-one, where that is necessary. The list in Table 1 was generated by Native American students at Northern Arizona University, as a comparative data set for the free listings generated by high school students on the reservation. We also did a separate free listing of all of the alcoholic beverages

TABLE 1

Native American College Students Free Listing of All the Things People Use to Get High Except Alcohol

Rank	Item	Frequency	Resp Pct
1	Peyote	10	59
2	Crack	10	59
3	Cocaine	10	59
4	Marijuana	9	53
5	Glue	9	53
6	Acid	8	47
7	Gasoline	8	47
8	Coke	7	41
9	Paint	7	41
10	Heroin	6	35
11	LSD	5	29
12	Cigarettes	5	29
13	Speed	5	29
14	Pot	5	29
15	Mushrooms	4	24
16	Weed	4	24
17	Sex	4	24
18	Hair spray	3	18
19	PCP	3	18
20	Paint thinner	3	18
21	White Out	3	18
22	Caffeine	3	18
23	Downers	3	18
24	Uppers	3	18
25	Over the counter drugs	2	12
26	Spray paint	2	12
27	Paint and socks	2	12
28	Angel Dust	2	12
29	Hash	2	12
30	Listerine	2	12
31	Crystal	1	6
32	Stimulants	1	6
33	Oral medication	1	6
34	Prescription drugs	1	6
35	Hallucinogens	1	6
36	Joint	1	6
37	Finger nail polish remover	1	6
38	Xerox correction fluid	1	6
39	Natural high	1	6
40	Dope	1	6
41	Tobacco	1	6
42	Money	1	6
43	Sprays	1	6
44	Elevator	1	6

45	Flying	1	6
46	Birth of baby	1	6
47	Sky diving	1	6
48	Anything thrilling	1	6
49	Anything daring	1	6
50	Cleaning products	1	6
51	AA meetings	1	6
52	Combinations	1	6
53	Ice	1	6
54	Joy riding	1	6
55	Car racing	1	6
56	Aspirin	1	6
57	Indulging in food	1	6
58	IV drugs	1	6
59	Shaving lotion	1	6
60	Sherm smoked with PCP	1	6
61	Depressants	1	6
62	Cool breeze	1	6
63	Hang upside down	1	6
64	Self-satisfaction	1	6
65	Drugs	1	6
66	Nail polish	1	6
67	Exercise	1	6
68	Quaaludes	1	6
69	Freebase	1	6
70	Music	1	6
71	Jog	1	6
72	Opium	1	6
73	Kerosene	1	6
74	Tobacco juice	1	6
75	Rubber cement	1	6
76	Self-righteousness	1	6
77	Pills	1	6
78	Ecstacy	1	6
79	Aerosol spray can	1	6
80	Pure vanilla	1	6
81	Sobriety	1	6
82	Anything toxic	1	6
83	Inhalants	1	6

Total mentions 202; mentions per respondent 11.882 $N = 19$

that people could think of, for comparison with the drug lists and for base line alcohol data for the prevention project. A computer program called *ANTHRO-PAC*, written by Steve Borgatti, was used to generate this summary table of the free listings from the college students. We also created separate and combined alcohol and drug listings for Anglo college students and Navajo youth on the reservation.

There is a large number of ways that this data can be used. In the case of our prevention project, we found it useful to be able to incorporate terminology that was already familiar to the students into classroom exercises. It was also informative to compare the basic lists generated by Anglo and Native American students, and to compare college students with high school students. This gave us a rapid look at intracultural and intercultural variation in the same geographical region. The results demonstrated significant cultural differences in the knowledge of both alcohol and drugs, between Anglo and Navajo students, and between all college and high school students. This has allowed us to more sensitively target the lessons in the in-school prevention program, rather than wasting time talking about drugs that are uncommon or unused in our region.

We collected information on the sex, age, and ethnicity of the informants doing the free listings, to create the opportunity to use the data to analyze relationships between elements in the alcohol and drug cultural domains and other variables such as cultural orientation, intracultural variation, gender differences in knowledge, economic and educational differences, etc. It would be expected that the answers to free listing questions might differ based on the sex, age, income, educational level, and other culturally significant factors that help define current medical anthropology theories.

We have also used the free listings to generate ethnographic questions about alcohol and drug behavior and beliefs, since we noticed some unexpected responses in both the Native American and Anglo groups. These unexpected responses included behaviors that we needed to have described in greater detail in relation to getting high (e.g., joy riding, having babies, thrill seeking, religious experiences), as well as needing better descriptions of substances that were not common to our experience (e.g., whipping cream cans, White Out). Some of the answers had to be explored because they were simply incomprehensible to us. For example, how do you get high from "paint and socks"? It turns out that you spray the paint into the socks and inhale it from them, to hide the paint. The free listings also included jokes, like putting down the word "elevator" as something besides alcohol that gets you high. Following up on these types of answers has been valuable to the overall project.

Free listing techniques, like the ones described, take normal ethnographic questions and responses and open them up to descriptive statistical analysis. These analyses include not only comparing nominal responses, but comparing rank orderings of those responses based on some of the key social and cultural variables listed above. A number of techniques for analyzing free listings, along with their strengths and weaknesses, are described by Weller and Romney (1988:9–16).

Techniques to Define and Analyze Cultural Domains and Their Structures
Several cognitive anthropology research methods were at one time so tedious that they were not much more than clever curiosities or dissertation topics. Recently, they have been transformed into extremely valuable advanced methods and rapid assessment tools through the advent of the microcomputer as a fieldwork tool. These rou-

tines include pile sorts (Boster 1986; Weller and Romney 1988:31–37), and sentence frame techniques (Stefflre 1972; Weller and Romney 1988:55–61).

These procedures allow a researcher to take some or all of the known elements of a cultural domain and to explore the ways that those elements are related to one another, or to the individuals who use them. In each case, informants are asked to make judgments about the similarities and differences of the elements to one another, or are asked the most appropriate response to a particular cultural frame. This information can then by typed into a computer file, which uses an algorithm to create a numerical comparison of the variables. This numerical comparison is called a distance matrix. Distance matrices can be analyzed using statistical techniques which transform the numbers into a visual representation of the relationships of informants to other informants, or of variables to other variables. The two most common statistical techniques associated with the use of these methods in medical anthropology are cluster analysis (Aldenderfer and Blashfield 1984) and multidimensional scaling (Kruskal and Wish 1978).

Cluster analysis is often used in medical anthropology to explore cultural typologies. All human cultures have classification systems. In medical anthropology these range from folk taxonomies of illnesses ad treatments to any other cultural dimension that involves the classification and comparison of people, objects, behaviors, and beliefs. This data is often complex, and the relationships within the data are often difficult to discover. Cluster analysis is one technique that allows this type of data to be thoroughly explored. It can be described as follows:

> "Cluster analysis" is the generic name for a wide variety of procedures that can be used to create a classification. These procedures empirically form "clusters" or groups of highly similar entities. More specifically, a clustering method is a multivariate statistical procedure that starts with a data set containing information about a sample of entities and attempts to reorganize these entities into relatively homogeneous groups. [Aldenderfer and Blashfield 1984:7]

Cluster analysis allows a researcher to explore potentially important hierarchical structural relationships. One technique for taking advantage of the strengths of cluster analysis is to perform a pile sort. A pile sort is a rapid assessment technique that uses visual aides to allow informants to create classifications of elements within an important cultural domain. The most common method is to place pictures, real objects, written labels, or combinations of the three, on cards. Each card represents one element in the domain being studied. The informant is asked to cluster a set of cards or objects (all of the elements of the domain) by stacking them into piles. They are allowed to form as many, or as few, piles as they want. The final groupings represent their classification of elements in the domain. Computer programs, such as ANTHROPAC or SIMPAK, written by James Boster, are available to transform the recorded pile sort data into a distance matrix.

As an example of an applied use of cluster analysis, one of our students (Wong 1990) administered a pile sort to the residents in a shelter for battered women. One purpose of the project was to discover ways to improve the social relationships in the shelter and to reduce friction between staff (who were predominantly Anglo) and clients (who were Native American and Anglo). The cards used in the sorting task each contained a label or phrase that represented one of the important cultural elements that defined life in the shelter. These elements included the most important people and "things" in their lives, and the "things" that were their greatest concerns. Running the data through a cluster analysis program allowed Wong to both visually represent and to better analyze how the residents were related to one another, in terms of the similarity or differences in their responses to this sorting technique.

The resulting analysis produced a dendrogram (a tree shaped visual summary of the data) which graphically identifies relationships in the data. Items (in this case women in the shelter) that are most similar are hooked together, like a kinship chart, by direct lines.

In analyzing this information, Wong stated:

> At an intermediary level there are essentially two clusters present in this dendrogram. One cluster is composed of women one, two, eight, and six. A second cluster is composed of women three, seven, five and four. The main difference between the women of these clusters has nothing to do with age, ethnicity, income, or any other demographic characteristic. These women are separated by severity of abuse they suffered from their batterers. [Wong 1990:79]

This was an important finding for their applied project. Some of the attempts at conflict resolution in the system had been directed at cultural differences, both on the part of the staff and the clients. Finding that people tended to interact differently on the basis of their battering experience, not on cultural orientation, provided information that will allow the organization to redirect some of their efforts into more effective interactions with clients. Thus, cluster analysis summarized and helped confirm conditions that were important in the culture of the shelter.

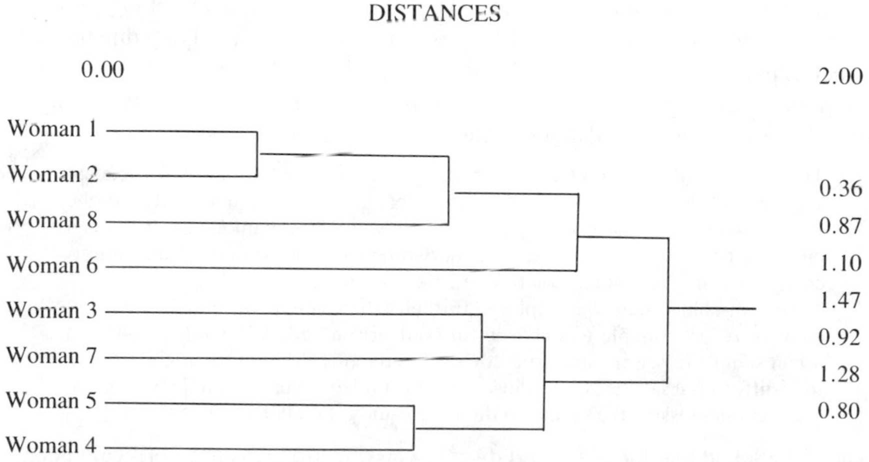

DISTANCES

FIGURE 1

Dendrogram of Eight Informants' Responses to a Pile Sort on Elements of a Women's Shelter

This type of technique, like free listing and the other rapid assessment tools, also has the potential to allow the ethnographer to go back to their informants and ask for additional clarifications of the findings. We have found it to be a very useful research exercise to show dendograms or other graphic representations of the data to our informants, and ask for their explanation of the data groupings from their point of view. This use of thé technique is very likely to identify new issues about how our informants interact with a health care system.

Multidimensional scaling (MDS) is a related analytical technique that has shown significant potential in medical anthropological research. It has been described as a method for uncovering the "hidden structure" of data bases (Kruskal and Wish 1978). MDS allows a researcher to take an extremely complex set of data and analysis it for underlying conditions or principles. For example, Weller (1983) investigated urban and rural Guatemalan concepts of disease classification and causality models. After using ethnographic interviews to determine the conditions that informants used to distinguish between diseases, she created a profile for each illness and compared the illnesses through the use of a multidimensional scaling program. This allowed her to test the relative importance of the hot-cold concept, contagion, and severity of an illness in the Guatemalan disease model. The results are graphically presented in Figure 2.

In discussing this representation of her data, Weller states:

> In the spatial representation, illnesses perceived as similar by the informants appear close together and those perceived as dissimilar are further apart. For example, the gastrointestinal diseases "diarrhea," "intestinal infection," and "dysentery" appear together in the lower-left quadrant of [the figure]. [Weller 1983:252–253]

Multidimensional scaling not only represents the data visually, it provides an estimate of the number of underlying conditions (dimensions) that are organizing informants' classification of the data. The statistic for the analysis of Weller's MDS plot indicated that the most likely solution was two underlying dimensions which explained the information. Weller was testing to determine whether or not the hot-cold concept was one of these. In her analysis of both an urban sample (not shown) and the rural data presented in Figure 2, she states:

> The results of the urban Guatemalan study indicated that the hot-cold concept was probably not as important as the concepts of contagion and severity in the system of disease classification. There was little agreement among urban women on the hot-cold concept, and few of the women's responses correlated significantly with the conceptual structure of illness terms. . . .
> The hot-cold system was explored further with a sample of rural Guatemalan women. A rural sample was chosen for comparison with a previously collected urban sample to see if rural-urban or socioeconomic differences might account for a differential salience of the hot-cold concept. However, the rural results were even less impressive than those in the urban study. [Weller 1983:255]

Thus, she found that the hold-cold disease classification was not a critical underlying element in the classification of common illnesses, or in the model for treatment of those illnesses in Guatemala. The idea of illnesses being spready by con-

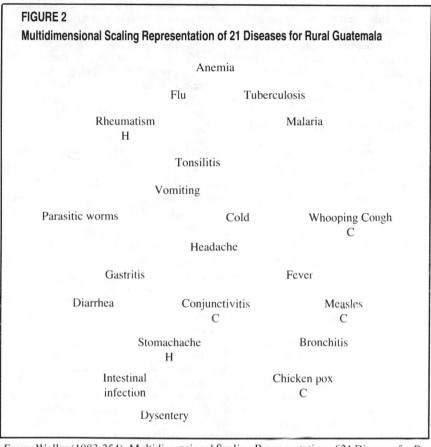

FIGURE 2

Multidimensional Scaling Representation of 21 Diseases for Rural Guatemala

Anemia

Flu   Tuberculosis

Rheumatism   Malaria
H

Tonsilitis

Vomiting

Parasitic worms   Cold   Whooping Cough
C

Headache

Gastritis   Fever

Diarrhea   Conjunctivitis   Measles
C   C

Stomachache   Bronchitis
H

Intestinal   Chicken pox
infection   C

Dysentery

From: Weller (1983;254): Multidimensional Scaling Representation of 21 Diseases for Rural Guatemala.

tagion and the perceived severity of those illnesses were much more important in understanding how Guatemalan women reacted to the illnesses in the home.

In addition to MDS and cluster analysis, there are a large number of other multivariate (and univariate) analytical techniques that can be useful in analyzing traditional ethnographic data sets. Two of the works reviewed above (Bernard 1988; Weller and Romney 1988), provide detailed descriptions on how these techniques can be integrated into ethnographic research.

Consensus Theory. Consensus theory is an interesting new method that allows an ethnographer to explore a consensual description of a cultural domain, while simultaneously assessing individual informants' competence or expertise in that domain. The technique is based on the following theoretical position.

> The assumption in fieldwork has been that the investigator is a valid and reliable instrument and that the informant provides valid and reliable information. We suggest that informants' statements should be treated as probabilistic in character. When, for example, an informant states that the name of an object is "X," we should assume that there is some probability (that we can estimate) that the statement is correct. This probability may be close to 1 in the case of a very knowledgeable informant and close to 0 in the case of an uninformed informant. The more informants there are who agree (when questioned independently) on an answer the more likely it is to be the correct cultural response. [Romney, Weller, and Batchelder 1986:314]

Given this proposition, consensus theory models of culture are developed through a formalized set of questions about a cultural domain, based on the idea that those questions appropriately explore similarities and differences in shared experience and knowledge on the part of informants. Consensus theory melds ethnographic survey questions with a formal mathematical model based on approaches used by psychometricians in test construction, and influenced by signal detection theory and latent structural analysis procedures (Romney, Weller, and Batchelder 1986:316). This method provides a model for deriving cultural "truths" from informants' statements about their beliefs and knowledge. Romney et al. state:

> The central idea in our theory is the use of the pattern of agreement or consensus among informants to make inferences about their differential competence in knowledge of the shared information pool constituting culture. We assume that the correspondence between the answers of any two informants is a function of the extent to which each is correlated with the truth. . . Suppose, for example, that we had a "perfect set" of interview questions (cultural information test) concerning the game of tennis. Suppose further that we had two sets of informants: tennis players and non-tennis players. We would expect that the tennis players would agree more among themselves as to the answers to questions than would the non-tennis players. Players with complete knowledge about the game would answer questions correctly with identical answers or maximal consensus, while players with little knowledge of the game would not. [Romney, Weller, Batchelder 1986:316]

These suppositions suggest that it is possible to develop a model of a cultural domain by taking the most commonly agreed upon answers to questions as having the highest probability of fitting cultural "truth." We are assuming in this case that culturally correct answers are the ones that are most representative of what most people believe to be true; a normative or consensual framework for their world view. The other conclusion from these assumptions is that the people who agree most often with each other are the cultural "experts" for that domain.

One of the important attributes of consensus theory is that it is designed to work with a common condition in ethnography. That is, the situation in which we know the correct questions to ask, but do not know which are the correct, or the most nearly correct, cultural answers to those questions. At the present time, concensus modeling can be accomplished through the use of true-false, fill-in-the-blank, and multiple choice question formats, and is being tested for use with rank order formats. Cultural knowledge that cannot be assessed through these formats (such as open-ended questions) cannot be tested using this process at this time.

Some uses of consensus theory in medical anthropology include measuring intracultural variation in diseases judged on concepts of contagion, severity, hot/cold treatments (Weller 1983, 1984), consensus about the existence of a subculture of corporal punishment (Weller, Romney, and Orr 1986), and a study of hypertension among Ojibwa Indians in Canada (Garro 1987). This model for cultural analysis appears to have a great deal of potential for rapid assessment projects, where the basic elements of specific cultural domains are known, and the researcher needs to confirm cultural models about those domains for policy analysis, intervention, or other forms of applied anthropology.

Focus Groups: Another Rapid Ethnographic Method

Once baseline data on a culture have been established through standard and advanced ethnographic research, it is possible to initiate additional rapid ethnographic assessment techniques at various stages of a project. These techniques allow medical anthropologists to explore some narrowly focused problems in health care delivery, models of belief, and medical problem solving (see Bentley et al 1988, Scrimshaw and Hurtado 1988; Bentley 1986). The actual rapid ethnographic techniques chosen at each stage of a project depend on the goals of the project, combined with what works best in a particular cultural setting. All of the techniques discussed in these sections are excellent for use in collaborative research programs which combine ethnographic and survey approaches with some form of applied intervention or program development strategy.

The preliminary or exploratory stages of an applied project constitute the first area of use of rapid ethnographic methods. The purpose of rapid methods during this time period are to identify key issues, cultural domains, health beliefs, and sociocultural conditions that might act as either barriers to the success of the proposed health project, or to act as supporting mechanisms that would allow the project to succeed. For example, Bentley et al. (1988:110–111) note that their use of rapid assessment in Peru and Nigeria served three purposes. It provided information on people's beliefs about diarrhea, provided facts that improved the language and scope of a multisite survey, and provided data to facilitate the intervention stage of the project.

An example of preliminary stage rapid assessment can be drawn from the in-school alcohol, drugs, and AIDS risk prevention project, described above. We are using focus group interviews as one type of rapid ethnographic technique to help create an AIDS prevention curriculum for junior high and high school students in public and boarding schools on the Navajo reservation and in nearby towns. Focus groups are a social science technique that has been used for some time in marketing research, and is gaining popularity as a rapid assessment technique for applied projects. It is a formal group interview method that allows researchers to simultaneously discover baseline data on targeted issues, as well as providing important information about cultural interactions between informants during the course of the focus group session. Two concise texts provide an excellent introduction to the use of focus groups in applied qualitative research.

These are *Focus Groups: A Practical Guide for Applied Research* (Krueger 1988) and *Focus Groups as Qualitative Research* (Morgan 1989).

Our focus groups bring from 6 to 10 individuals together to investigate knowledge, attitudes, and beliefs about four main issues (AIDS, alcohol use, drug use, and advice about media and other prevention efforts that would be effective with Navajo youth). Within each focus issue, we have between 5 and 8 subsidiary issues that are explored, as well as probes to get greater details, stories, and other forms of natural discourse on the main topics. We are conducting separate male adolescent focus groups, female adolescent groups, and mixed-sex groups of both youth and adults. The adult groups consist of community leaders, teachers, and health professionals working on the reservation (including traditional healers). The focus interviews last about 2 hours each and are recorded verbatim, then transcribed into computer files for coding and analysis.

One type of analysis we are accomplishing with the verbatim focus group data is a combined processual and thematic analysis at a midrange level that allows us to create or modify in-class presentations to fit the cultural conditions identified in our preliminary interviews. The following list includes examples of the process and thematic data collected from the focus groups which are currently being used in the project's design and execution:

1. Girls talk more than boys in the classroom.
2. Older friends, brothers, and sisters commonly buy alcohol for underage youth.
3. There is a high level of exposure to alcohol and drugs from family members and friends.
4. The most common locations where drinking and drug use occur are in cars, at home and in isolated places near town.
5. It is easier for Navajo youth to talk about drugs and alcohol than sex.
6. The individuals that Navajo youth find it easiest to discuss alcohol, drugs, and sex with are older siblings (especially sisters) and aunts. They find it hardest to discuss these issues with parents of either sex.
7. The most common reasons for using drugs and alcohol are: people have probelms they want to forget: wanting to get high; wanting to have fun; wanting to be cool; wanting to keep a friendship; depression or frustration with life; and liking the smell and taste of alcohol.
8. Navajo youth do not like to read, so prevention programs should emphasize other approaches, in addition to reading materials.
9. There is strong respect expressed for elders and authority figures (such as doctors) by Navajo truth.

These focus group findings, as well as many others, are being used in several ways. First, they are helping us identify topics that are easy or hard to discuss, and therefore helping us design the training that is received by the curriculum instructors for this program. In this case, it is easy for both the adolescents and adults to discuss alcohol and drug use, and very difficult for them to discuss anything to do with sexual behavior. Therefore, we have recommended that several different approaches (some visual, some verbal, some passive, some activity based) be used in conveying sexual information to the students, to see which best reduce the existing reluctance to deal with these issues in the classroom. Second, the data is being used to discover how to word questions on the difficult subjects so they can be responded to with reduced embarrassment. This will assist us in developing both the survey evaluation instruments needed by the project (pre- and posttests), and will directly assist in the development of the wording and structure of the curriculum. Third, the information is being used to provide data on typical cultural domains that are germane to alcohol, drug, and high risk sexual behavior (e.g., where, when, and what do people drink, what drugs do they use, does alcohol and drug use increase risky sexual behavior, etc.). This information will be built into the lessons on each of these areas, using natural discourse information from the focus groups to customize the lessons that will be given in the prevention efforts created by the project. We are also getting very useful data on how to structure focus-group based data collection as a type of rapid assessment technique for the Navajo culture.

The entry stage of a health program is not the only valuable time for rapid ethnographic assessment. It can also be used during the middle stages of a project to explore critical topics in greater depth, to maintain good data for process evaluation of the project, and for problem solving in narrow instances. Finally, rapid ethnographic techniques can also be used evaluating the success of the project to determine what worked well and what did not work at the end of the program cycle. In the Navajo youth project described just above, we will be using focus groups in virtually all stages of the research, and will supplement them with other rapid techniques, such as network analysis and decision modeling. We will also use rapid ethnographic techniques to discuss and develop prevention products for the project, such as videos, posters, and demonstrations.

Surveys

Household and community surveys are another type of rapid assessment tool that is becoming popular in medical anthropology. These surveys take advantage of previous ethnographic research, which allows appropriate research instruments to be developed to test the degree and importance of intracultural variability on key medical research issues. For example, when it was discovered that two lead compounds were being used to treat a Mexican American culture-bound syndrome called *empacho,* the author constructed a questionnaire for the Public Health Service that was administered in 36 migrant and public health clinics in the United States (Trotter 1985). The results allowed us to discover how common the use of these substances (called *greta* and *azarcon*) was in several border states, and to help devise an appropriate public education program that reduced the use of the substances without attacking important cultural beliefs about the home treatment of illnesses.

There is a large literature on sampling, survey instrument construction, and the analysis of survey results available in the social science literature that should be consulted prior to the development and analysis of ethnographic surveys. Two

works provide an excellent preliminary exploration of the key issues for this sub-
ject, as well as bibliographic references to more extensive works in the area.
These are *Introduction to Survey Sampling* (Kalton 1983) and *Survey Questions:
Handcrafting the Standardized Questionnaire* (Converse and Presser 1986).

Network Analysis

Anthropologists have always been interested in the effects of social relationships
on human behavior and survival. One of the first formal research methods for
modeling human relationships is Conklin's ethnogeneological method (Conklin
1964), which produces a kinship based model of social networks in a culture.
Following these preliminary explorations, anthropological "network" research
has involved increasingly sophisticated examinations of kinship systems, small
groups, associations, and social systems. Modern network analysis can be seen
as an outgrowth of this trend; a mechanism for expanding our knowledge of the
effects and dynamics of kinship and non-kin networks into all parts of cultural
systems.

Network analysis has been underutilized as a research method in medical anthropology, but shows strong potential for analyzing both formal and informal
health care spheres, as well as healer patient networks. Two primary orientations
to network analysis are available for exploration. One is based on a clique theory
of network formation (Burt and Minor 1983). The other theory approaches networks from a "structural equivalency" model (Killworth and Bernard 1974).

The clique approach to network analysis investigates direct and indirect interaction among network actors. The basis for the analysis is a questionnaire that
allows each individual to identify the rank order of their relationship with each
other individual in their group. This data is then analyzed by computer programs
(e.g., Burt 1987), which identify critical elements about the structure of the social
system. One important characteristic of this type of network analysis is its ability
to locate subgroups in the population. These are called cliques, and designate individuals who have more in common or more interaction with one another than
with other individuals or subgroups in the system.

Network analysis can distinguish between what are called "strong component" and "weak component" cliques. The first are basically tightly knit groups
where everyone can reach one another, the latter are "loose" groups in which
everyone has at least one primary connection with someone in the group, but not
everyone in the group is in direct contact with everyone else. Once subgroups
have been detected, the quality of the relationships within groups and between
them can be explored. One such operation is to look at the "density" of the system, to discover if hierarchies exist in the system and to explore the structural
elements of cliques. This can provide a spatial map of network distances: individuals mapped close together have strong ties to one another, while those further
apart have weaker ties. Another procedure is to determine the ways in which the
structure of a group creates social pressures towards conformity (social contagion
analysis). It is also feasible to study the limits of autonomy of individuals in a
system. This allows an analysis of the "extent to which an individual's relations

provide entrepreneurial oppportunities to pursue his own interests and the extent to which each person with whom he has a relation constrains those opportunities'' (Burt 1987:43). Finally, it is also possible to study the stability of a network (equilibrium network structure), and the different levels of exchange between parts of the system. All of these models of human interaction provide significant opportunities for the analysis of the parts of human cultures that are most concerned with health and healing.

As an alternative to clique analysis, Killworth and Bernard (1974) have promoted network analysis from a structural equivalency model. Structural equivalency analysis identifies individuals who perceive their relationships with others in a fashion that is similar to others' perceptions of them and of each other. The analysis identifies structurally equivalent groups, and the linkage points between those groups and others. As an example, Killworth and Bernard analyzed the subgroups of a minimum security prison. They were able to identify eleven groups within one of the prison ''cottages'' and to show linkages both within and between those groups, providing an in-depth analysis of the relationships that form in a bounded social system. The figure below provides a visual presentation of social groupings identified by this type of network analysis.

The circles with numbers 18, 21, 26, 34 in Figure 3 are the individuals that form one of the eleven small social groups uncovered by the computer program Killworth and Bernard have created for this process, called ''CATIJ.'' The squares associated with each circle indicate individuals who have contact with that individual, but are not a part of this social subsystem. Arrows show either one way, or reciprocal relationships between individuals. Killworth and Bernard state:

> Group five contains white inmates of urban background. The dichotomy between White and Black is shown most tellingly by the fact that only one Black inmate had any member of group five on her first row. [Killworth and Bernard 1974:343]

It is possible for an individual to be part of one or more subsystems, to be outside of all subsystems but to have a strong role in connecting groups together, or to be an isolate. The authors state:

> These eleven groups do not exhaust C-cottage, accounting as they do for only 38 people. Seven other people, serving as between-group intermediaries, are also important to the description of the group, leaving seven people who fall into neither category. [Killworth and Bernard 1974:341]

This type of analysis allows the ethnographer to ask critical questions about an individual's involvement and noninvolvement in both smaller and larger social groups. These questions can include the differential influence of individuals who act as intermediaries, the reasons for the existence of social isolates, the organizing principles for the smaller groups, etc. As with the clique approach, the structural equivalency approach has a great deal to offer in the analysis of group dynamics relating to health care systems.

As an example of innovation in a medical anthropological use of network analysis, one ethnographer used observational data rather than interview data, combined with a network analysis program, to demonstrate power relationships

FIGURE 3
Group 5 from Cottage C

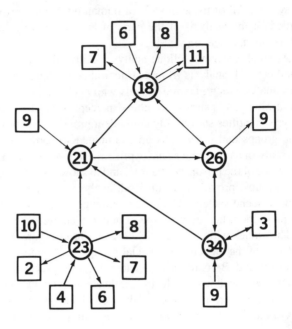

Adapted from Killworth and Bernard (1974)

in an orthodontist's office (Roberts 1990). The office she observed used "joking" to indicate a need for the target of the humor to undertake some kind of behavioral change. Roberts explored the meaning of the relationships defined by this joking social control system, by recording each time a joking interaction occurred between staff (the orthodontist, technician, and receptionist), patients (child patients, adult patients), and parents of child patients. She recorded both the type (content) and direction of all interactions, noting who initiated the action, whether or not it was reciprocated, and the content of the interchange. She was able to vividly portray both symmetrical and the very symmetrical relationships that occur within a medical setting through the use of this form of network analysis.

Figure 4 visually portrays power differentials in the office, as well as role differentiation among the actors. In this case, the content of the "joking" interaction is that someone has not complied with a therapeutic regimen and is being chided for lack of compliance. Single arrows indicate a one-way interchange, from initiator to subject. Double arrows indicate that the joking was initiated from either direction, and was reciprocated in the other direction. A lack of connection

FIGURE 4

Joking Interactions about Compliance

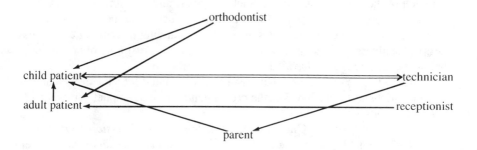

From: Roberts (1990:Appendix): Initiators of Public Humerus Interactions-"Compliance."

between individuals, such as the orthodontist and the technician or the receptionist, indicates a total lack of social interaction on this issue, a condition which helps define some of the role relationships in the office. On other social control issues, such as problems encountered because of "foul-ups" that interfere with scheduling, the network graphic would indicate connections in other directions, because "time problems" can be created by both patients and any staff member who creates a road block in the daily routine. These findings both confirmed Robert's ethnographic data on social relationships in the office, and allowed her to focus questions and other observations in creative and effective directions during a short ethnographic project.

Decision Modeling

The cultural elements that are necessary to make a decision and the choices among competing elements in the decision process are at the heart of a large number of theoretical and practical issues in medical anthropology. All cultures require humans to make decisions. Most of these decisions have measurable consequences for the individual. And in most cases where health and illnesses are concerned, the decision models of one culture will differ from and even conflict with those of another based on the agreed upon values, beliefs, technology, and the symbolic system of that culture.

Decision modeling is more highly developed in market analysis (Plattner 1982), and agricultural decision making (Gladwin 1980, 1989) than in medical anthropology. However, decision modeling has been part of the methodology of medical anthropology for some time. For example, Young (1980) developed a decision model for treatment alternatives in Pichataro, a rural Tarascan community in west central Mexico. He used field records of 323 illnesses and their treatments to construct the primary elements in a decision model. He used these components to create hypothetical cases, then interviewed informants about the choices they would make in those cases. He measured the amount of agreement for each of the answers on the hypothetical cases, and used this information to develop patterns of alternatives. Finally, he constructed the model presented in Table 2, based on the key variables uncovered, including the gravity or seriousness of the illness, knowledge of a home remedy, and accessibility of professional help measured by cost and availability of transportation.

After testing, Young found that this model accounted for 91% of the choices included in the test, which makes the process and the actual model very valuable for understanding this health care system.

The work of Christina Gladwin (1989), *Ethnographic Decision Modeling,* is particularly valuable for this methodological area. It provides an excellent, step by step discussion of the ways anthropologists can create testable decision models in any anthropological area.

Exit From Fieldwork

When a project is over, it is necessary to depart from the community and to attenuate relationships in a way that is ethically correct. Leaving-taking is commonly

TABLE 2
Decision Table for the Initial Choice of Treatment

Rules	1	2	3	4	5	6	7	8	9
Conditions									
1 Gravity	1	1	1	2	2	2	3	3	3
2 Known home remedy	Y	N	N	Y	N				
3 "Faith"		F	M	(F)	F	M	F	M	(M)
4 Accessibility								N	Y
Choices									
a Self treatment	X			X					
b Curer		X			X		X		
c Practicante			X			X		X	
d Physician									X

Key	1 Gravity	3 "Faith"	4 Accessibility
		F = favors folk	Y = money & transportation
Y = yes	1 = nonserious	treatment	available
	2 = moderately	M = favors medical	N = either money or transportation
N = no	serious	treatment	not available
	3 = grave		

Source: Young (1980:116)

the most difficult transition ethnographers make during the research process. The friendships and interactions that form a crucial part of ethnography are intense, and it is always hard to change close personal relationships. Consequently, ethnographers normally maintain at least some contact with people they worked with long after they leave. They keep in touch by visits and correspondence, and they attempt to control their leave-taking to the extent that they will be welcome to return and that it will be possible for other researchers to come in and not have to deal with any "garbage" left behind.

Strangely, there is very little formal literature on field exit methods. Even the anecdotal information more often revolves around reentry into one's own society, rather than identifying the problems of leaving the research setting. Return shock is certainly a severe form of culture shock, and anthropologists experience serious stress when they have to "decompress" from a culturally different set of interactions by rearranging as many patterns of speech, dress, styles of interaction, and thinking back home as was necessary when they entered their field situation. However, the manner in which a researcher clears his or her research site and leaves it with positive relationships is a crucial issue that has been seriously neglected.

One of the only books to discuss field research exit as a formal issue is *Fieldwork Experience*, by Shaffir, Stebbins, and Turowetz (1980). Three chapters provide a preliminary definition of the problem and demonstrate that at the present time there is significant variation in how leave-taking is accomplished by different researchers. The following quote summarizes the conflicting advice received by one of the book's authors:

> Some said that to distance oneself totally was mandatory. Others warned that a total disengagement might prohibit the collection of critical data during the analysis and "write-up" phases of the research project. Still others stated that one never has to leave entirely; social relationships can be maintained after the project has been completed. [1980:260]

The confusion produced by this advice is further compounded by the fact that the ethnographer does not leave one social setting. He or she leaves many, based on a multitude of role relationships that have developed during fieldwork. For some relationships, fading off into the night is both acceptable and appropriate. Those relationships were always defined in both directions as one of stranger or acquaintance. For other relationships, very complex interpersonal roles produce equally complex differences in how leaving will effect the ethnographers and their informants. Exit problems increase with the intimacy of the relationships, with the density of unmet reciprocal obligations (especially those the culture views as permanent), with the probability of hurt feelings, and the need for continuing contacts or future research endeavors. Field exit problems can also be compounded by the type of information the ethnographer has learned. If that information is threatening to the community (taboo in some aspect) field exit can be problematic in direct relation to the threat posed by the knowledge. All of these issues need further systematic exploration by anthropologists.

Dissemination of Results

Applied medical anthropological research is conducted with a view to some pratical end, such as improved program conception, system evaluation, public policy development, or the reduction of risks in specific target populations. All of these outcomes demand some form of dissemination of results to specific target audiences. Burns identifies one of the major considerations that must be accommodated in applied projects.

> The world of policy action demands that research be tailored to the political realities of public decisions and competing interest groups. Public policy anthropology is done in the "real time" of everyday life where research information is needed at critical times to help inform policy decisions. If the information is not ready or fieldwork is not complete when budget hearings come up or elections arise, then these political events take place without social science input. [Burns 1983:129]

This places a condition on applied medical anthropology that projects must be brought to conclusion on time and on budget. Applied fieldwork also includes the predicament of having research information potentially "heard" differently by competing or conflicting social interest groups. Successful applied research involves a need for clear, nonpedantic communication; making science available and understandable within emotionally charged social contexts. Applied research can put both the researcher and the research results at risk of attacks that do not depend on scholarly rigor or truthfulness; attacks that derive solely from emotional appeals to a particular interest group. It is not an arena for research by either the foolish or the faint hearted. At the same time, it is an effective use of the quantities of data that ethnographers collect on the lives of the most unnoticed members of our society.

Applied medical anthropology research normally produces three types of documents for public consumption. These are policy statements (recommendations), scholarly articles (both theoretical and applied), and ethnographies. Each one must be carefully stylistically crafted to communicate a specific message to a targeted audience. Some researchers also produce "popular" articles for mass consumption, which serve a useful purpose of making anthropology accessible to a very broad public. All four of these products differ in style, intent, and audience, but each has a role in the documentation of a particular group and their cultural practices.

Policy Statements

Field research projects collect large amounts of policy-relevant data which can be available as early as the middle to late field sessions, due to the cyclical nature of ethnographic research and analysis. Policy statements created from this data tend to focus on distinctive beavior that relates to an existing program or to national policy. To be effective, these policy reports must propose precise suggestions for alternative approaches to the issues being studied. They must be written in a straightforward style, presenting the data and the recommendations in a jargon-free document.

The common form for documents intended to affect policy is to begin with a short (one to three page) executive summary that contains the most important findings of the project and all of the relevant recommendations. This is followed by the methods, data, and expanded findings and conclusions of the project, often emphasized by bullet statements summarizing key points scattered throughout the text. This is a reversal of the ordering of scientific reports, where the summary and conclusions are placed at the end rather than the beginning of an article, and where theory and methods often receive more attention and space than findings and conclusions. This inversion of emphasis is difficult for some individuals to accomplish, but necessary if the key points of the research are to be "heard." The bulk of a policy report, following the executive summary, presents a concise summary of the methods, the actual data, and expanded recommendations tied back into the data. All of these sections must take into account existing policy for the target organization or issue, and either support that existing policy, or recommend data-based modifications in the existing mission and policies of that institution. These documents must also take into consideration the immutable condition that most policymakers are very busy and are neither familiar with, nor interested in becoming conversant with the more pedantic aspects of medical anthropological research. Most of them are only interested in the potential that the research results have for providing them with recommendations and other tools for improving existing health care systems.

Scholarly Articles and Ethnographies

Medical anthropology projects tend to produce scholarly articles in direct relation to the amount of data collected and to the academic orientation of the researchers. The academic success of a project can normally be judged in terms of the prestige of the journals that accept the articles, and the impact the articles have on the theory and practice of that discipline. Academic articles can be directed at several different audiences, but most commonly they are targeted at a distinctive academic field or subfield, are full of current theory and jargon, and follow a specific academic style, such as that found in the *American Anthropologist* or other anthropological journals. The general purpose of these articles is to inform colleagues about the research conducted, to advance both the theory and the practices of the discipline, and to enhance the credibility and prestige of the researchers.

Any extended medical anthropology field research should also produce holistic studies of the life-styles of the people being studied. This normally appears in the form of a book-length work, called an ethnography, which provides detailed information about the beliefs, behaviors, and the social relationships of individuals and the group. Ethnographic reports describe the group and identify the major social subunits of the population. They typically include chapters devoted to the daily (seasonal, yearly) cycles of the group; typical life histories of people from birth (or from entry into the subculture) to death and into various forms of afterlife, depending on the beliefs of the group; the major belief systems in the culture; and descriptions of group social networks (families, friends, organizations). Ethnographies also commonly provide information on the language, religious beliefs, kinship organization, and subsistence patterns of the group, or any other area that is critical to understanding that cultural system. Any other information provided by the ethnography depends on the cultural parameters of the group studied and the research questions being asked by the study.

Mass Media and Medical Anthropology
Medical anthropologists rarely engage in writing popular articles for mass consumption, although their research is consistently of interest to journalists writing for newspapers, magazines, public radio, television news, and the popular book market. Every year there are dozens of articles in local and national newspapers about traditional healing, AIDS research, domestic violence, new health trends, etc. Many of these contain interviews with anthropologists who have been working either domestically or in foreign countries on these conditions. Our research is also consistently the target of public radio interviews, television special reports, and other forms of public dissemination. This suggests two things. First, a great deal of the research we do is of interest to the general public. Second, we are not well trained to get that information to the public and must normally depend on others to disseminate it through those channels. This suggests two simultaneous courses of action. The first is to cultivate positive relationships with professionals who are well situated and capable of making our research results available to mass communication channels. This means learning to spot when a research finding is likely to be of interest, a judgment call, and then developing the social networks to be able contact someone who can make appropriate use of the information, transforming it into a form that can be disseminated. The second course of action would be to find the means to train more anthropologists in the skills necessary to communicate directly to the public through popular books, articles, TV shows, and other popular media. The former is relatively easily accomplished through minimal training and good personal skills, the latter will necessitate the development of specialists with competence in two professions, anthropology and public communication. Both goals are worth pursuing in the future.

Final Considerations
Ethnographic research cannot be conducted without having highly personal effects on the researchers. Applied medical anthropology appears to take a heavier toll on ethnographers than purely academic research, due to the urgency of the problems studied and their immediate impact on the lives of people the ethnographer has worked with on a daily basis. There is pressure to produce at a rapid pace, and to always be right, since our recommendations can have direct effects on so many peoples' lives. When all things are weighed, the benefits of field research on health issues are enormous. The personal transformations of fieldwork are primarily positive, and the research results are normally both directly and indirectly useful in practical arenas, and in the generation of theories to improve our understanding of the variables underlying health, illness, and treatment. Given the advent of the new methods discussed above, our impact is likely to be even

greater in the future. Consequently, most of us feel the personal costs are balanced by the end results.

References Cited

Adams, Richard N., and Jack J. Preiss, eds.
  1960   Human Organization Research: Field Relations and Techniques. Homewood, IL: Dorsey Press.
Agar, Michael H.
  1974   Ripping and Running: A Formal Ethnography of Urban Heroin Addicts. New York: Seminar Press.
  1980   The Professional Stranger: An Informal Introduction to Fieldwork. New York: Academic Press.
  1986   Speaking of Ethnography. Newbury Park, CA: Sage.
Aldenderfer, Mark S., and Roger K. Blashfield
  1984   Cluster Analysis. Newbury Park, CA: Sage.
Bentley, M. E., et al.
  1988   Rapid Ethnographic Assessment: Applications in a Diarrhea Management Program. Social Science and Medicine 27(1):107–116.
Bernard, H. Russell
  1988   Research Methods in Cultural Anthropology. Newbury Park, CA: Sage.
Bernard, H. Russell, Peter Kilworth, David Kronenfeld, Lee Sailer
  1984   The Problem of Informant Accuracy: The Validity of Retrospective Data. Annual Review of Anthropology 13:495–517.
Beteille, Andre, and T. N. Maden, eds.
  1975   Encounter and Experience, Personal Accounts of Fieldwork. Honolulu: University of Hawaii Press.
Boster, James
  1986   Can Individuals Recapitulate the Evolutionary Development of Color Lexicons? Ethnology 25(1):61–74.
Burns, Alan F.
  1983   Feds and Locals: Strategies of Applied Fieldwork. In Fieldwork: The Human Experience. Robert Lawless, Vinson H. Sutlive, Jr., and Mario D. Zamora, eds., Pp. 129–142. New York: Gordon and Breach.
Burt, Ronald S.
  1987   Structure Version 3.2 Technical Report #TR2, Research Program in Structural Analysis, Center for the Social Sciences, Columbia University, New York.
Burt, Ronald S., and M. J. Minor, eds.
  1983   Applied Network Analysis: A Methodological Introduction. Beverly Hills: Sage.
Conklin, Harold C.
  1964   Ethnogeneological Method. In Explorations in Cultural Anthropology. Ward H. Goodenough, ed. New York: McGraw-Hill Book Company.
Converse, Jean M., and Stanley Presser
  1986   Survey Questions: Handcrafting the Standardized Questionnaire. Newbury Park, CA: Sage.
D'Andrade, Roy G.
  1974   Memory and the Assessment of Behavior. In Measurement in the Social Sciences. H. M. Blalock, Jr., ed. Chicago: Aldine.
Epstein, A. L., ed.
  1967   The Craft of Social Anthropology. London: Tavistock.

Fetterman, David M.
  1989   Ethnography: Step by Step. Newbury Park, CA: Sage.
Frantz, Charles
  1972   The Student Anthropologist's Handbook: A Guide to Research, Training, and
         Career. Cambridge, MA: Schenkman.
Freeman, Linton C., A. Kimball Romney, Sue C. Freeman
  1987   Cognitive Structure and Informant Accuracy. American Anthropologist 89:310–
         325.
Frelich, Morris, ed.
  1970   Marginal Natives: Anthropologists at Work. New York: Harper and Row.
  1977   Marginal Natives at Work: Anthropologists in the Field. New York: Schenkman.
Fried, Morton H.
  1972   The Study of Anthropology. New York: Thomas Y. Crowell.
Garro, Linda
  1986   Intracultural Variation in Folk Medical Knowledge: A Comparison between
         Groups. American Anthropologist 88:351–370.
  1988   Explaining High Blood Pressure: Variation in Knowledge about Illness. Amer-
         ican Ethnologist 15:98–119.
Gladwin, Christina H.
  1980   A Theory of Real Life Choice: Applications to Agricultural Decisions. In Agri-
         cultural Decision Making. P. Bartlett, ed. Pp. 45–85. New York: Academic Press.
  1989   Ethnographic Decision Modeling. Newbury Park, CA: Sage.
Johnson, J. C., J. S. Boster, and D. Holbert
  1989   Estimating Relational Attributes from Snowball Samples through Simulation.
         Social Networks 11:135–158.
Kalton, Grahm
  1983   Introduction to Survey Sampling. Newbury Park, CA: Sage.
Killworth, Peter, and H. Russell Bernard
  1974   CATIJ: A New Sociometric and Its Application to a Prison Living Unit. Human
         Organization 33(4):335–350.
Kimball, Solon T., and William L. Patridge, eds.
  1979   The Craft of Community Study: Fieldwork Dialogues. Gainesville: University
         of Florida Press.
Kimball, Solon, and James B. Watson, eds.
  1972   Crossing Cultural Boundaries. San Francisco: Chandler Publishing Company.
Kroeber, Alfred L.
  1953   Anthropology Today. Chicago: University of Chicago Press.
Krueger, Richard A.
  1988   Focus Groups: A Practical Guide for Applied Research. Newbury Park, CA:
         Sage.
Kruskal, Joseph B., and Myron Wish
  1978   Multidimensional Scaling. Newbury Park, CA: Sage.
Lawless, Robert, Vinson H. Sutlive, Jr., and Mario D. Zamora, eds.
  1983   Fieldwork: The Human Experience. New York: Gordon and Breach.
Lieberman, D., and W. M. Dressler
  1977   Bilingualism and Cognition of St. Lucian Disease Terms. Medical Anthropology
         1:81–110.
Morgan, David L.
  1989   Focus Groups as Qualitative Research. Newbury Park, CA: Sage.

Naroll, Raoul, and Ronald Cohen, eds.
  1970   A Handbook of Method in Cultural Anthropology. Garden City, NJ: Natural History Press.
Pelto, Pertti J.
  1970   Anthropological Research: The Structure of Inquiry. New York: Harper and Row.
Pelto, Pertti J., and Gretel H. Pelto
  1978   Anthropological Research; The Structure of Inquiry. 2nd edition. Cambridge: Cambridge University Press.
Plattner, Stuart M.
  1982   Economic Decision Making in a Public Marketplace. American Ethnologist 9:399–420.
  1989   Commentary: Ethnographic Method. Anthropology Newsletter 30(1):32, 21.
Roberts, Denise A.
  1990   "Why Do You Americans Do Such Things to Yourselves?": An Ethnographic Examination of the Social Dynamics of An American Orthodontic Office. Unpublished ms. in the files of the author.
Romney, A. K., W. H. Batchelder, and S. C. Weller
  1987   Recent Applications of Consensus Theory. American Behavioral Science 31(2):163–177.
Romney, A. K., and S. C. Weller
  1984   Predicting Informant Accuracy from Patterns of Recall among Individuals. Social Networks 4:59–77.
Romney, A. K., S. C. Weller, and W. H. Batchelder
  1986   Culture as Consensus: A Theory of Cultural and Informant Accuracy. American Anthropologist 88:313–338.
Royal Anthropological Institute
  1951   Notes and Queries on Anthropology. 6th edition. London: Royal Anthropological Institute.
Scrimshaw, A., and E. Hurtado
  1988   Anthropological Involvement in the Central American Diarrheal Disease Control Project. Social Science Medicine 27:97–105.
Shaffir, William B., Robert A. Stebbins, and Allan Turowetz
  1980   Fieldwork Experience: Qualitative Approaches to Social Research. New York: St. Martin's Press.
Spindler, George D.
  1970   Being an Anthropologist: Fieldwork in Eleven Cultures. New York: Holt, Rinehart, and Winston.
Spradley, James P.
  1979   The Ethnographic Interview. New York: Holt, Rinehart, Winston.
  1980   Participant Observation. New York: Holt, Rinehart, Winston.
Spradley, James P., and David W. McCurdy
  1972   The Cultural Experience: Ethnography in Complex Society. Chicago: Science Research Associates.
Stefflre, V. J.
  1972   Some Applications of Multidimensional Scaling to Social Science Problems. In Multidimensional Scaling: Theory and Applications in the Behavioral Sciences, Volume 2. A. K. Romney et al., eds. Pp. 211–243. New York: Academic Press.

Trotter, Robert T., II
   1981   Remedios Caseros: Mexican American Home Remedies and Community Health
          Problems. Social Science and Medicine 15:107–114.
   1983   Community Morbidity Patterns and Mexican American Folk Illness: A Compar-
          ative Approach. Medical Anthropology 7(1):33–44.
   1985   Greta and Azarcon: A Survey of Episodic Led Poisoning from a Folk Remedy.
          Human Organization 44(1):64–71.
Watters, John K., and Patrick Biernacki
   1989   Targeted Sampling: Options for the Study of Hidden Populations. Social Prob-
          lems 36(4):416–430.
Wax, Rosalie H.
   1971   Doing Fieldwork: Warnings and Advice. Chicago: University of Chicago Press.
Weller, Susan C.
   1983   New Data on Intracultural Variability: The Hot-Cold Concept of Medicine and
          Illness. Human Organization 42(3):341–351.
   1984   Consistency and Consensus among Informants: Disease Concepts in a Rural
          Mexican Town. American Anthropologist 86:966–975.
Weller, Susan C., and A. Kimball Romney
   1988   Systematic Data Collection. Newbury Park, CA: Sage.
Weller, Susan C., A. Kimball Romney, and D. P. Orr
   1986   The Myth of a Sub-Culture of Corporal Punishment. Human Organization
          46:39–47.
Werner, Oswald, and G. Mark Schoepfle
   1987   Systematic Fieldwork: Foundation of Ethnography and Interviewing. 2 volumes.
          Beverly Hills: Sage.
   1987   Systematic Fieldwork: Ethnographic Analysis and Data Management. Volume
          2. Beverly Hills. Sage Publications.
Wong, Penelope A.
   1990   "Falling Through the Cracks": An Ethnography of a Shelter for Battered
          Women. Unpublished manuscript, Department of Anthropology, Northern Arizona
          University.
Young, James C.
   1980   A Model of Illness Treatment Decisions in a Tarascan Town. American Ethnol-
          ogist 7:106–131.

● *chapter nine*

Research Ethics in Applied Medical Anthropology

PATRICIA A. MARSHALL

In recent decades, social and behavioral scientists have become increasingly concerned with ethical issues surrounding the development and implementation of research. Applied medical anthropologists working in the public or private arena often confront unique ethical challenges because of the special nature of their research. Maintaining confidentiality and insuring informed consent, for example, may be difficult in situations where linguistic barriers exist. Moreover, political, organizational, and financial constraints raise serious questions concerning the advocacy role of the anthropologist. Sensitivity to the moral dimensions of applied medical research facilitates the resolution of ethical dilemmas when they occur and promotes the successful application of research results.

This chapter has three specific aims. First, ethical principles underlying research involving human subjects will be discussed. Second, professional and governmental response to the development of ethical guidelines for conducting research with human subjects will be reviewed. Finally, this chapter will explore the application of ethical principles in research with special attention to the exigencies of investigations conducted by applied medical anthropologists.

Ethical Principles in Human Subject Research

The term "ethical" normally refers to rules of behavior or conformity to a code of principles (Frankena 1973; Kimmel 1988; Reynolds 1979). A *principle* refers to a fundamental theoretical norm. Implicit in the expression of moral principles are judgments about human behavior. Graber and Thomasma (1989:11) define a moral principle as:

> an ought-statement which may express (or yield) a command about (imperative),
> a precept towards (prescriptive), or a description of (descriptive) conduct to be
> done or avoided.

Beliefs about what constitutes ethical and moral behavior are integrally tied to values (Reese and Fremouw 1984); an ethical dilemma occurs when there is uncertainty in regard to which values should take priority in determining a course of action. The importance of values in framing and understanding ethical issues must be considered within the context of social and cultural diversity. In his discussion of ethical relativism and morality, Shweder (1990:208) argues for a version of qualified relativism based on two assertions:

(1) there are genuine and significant differences between the moral codes of different people; a universalistic approach cannot handle all the facts; and (2) there exists more than one rationally defensible moral code; not every significant difference in the moral codes of different peoples can be developmentally ranked.

Although interpretations of moral conduct vary among individuals, communities, and societies, three basic principles have dominated ethical discussions of research with human subjects. These include the principle of respect for persons, the principle of beneficence, and the principle of justice (Agich 1988; U.S. National Commission for the Protection of Human Subjects of Biomedical and Behavior Research 1978; Veatch 1987).

A belief that individuals have the capacity to be autonomous agents is essential in an adequate representation of respect for persons. Free will and self-determination provide the basis for autonomy. The exercise of free will both in thought and deliberation, are important features of autonomy, "The autonomous person is one who not only deliberates about and chooses such plans, but who is capable of acting on the basis of such deliberations" (Beauchamp and Childress 1979:56). However, some individuals are incapable of autonomous action because of immaturity, incapacitation, or incarceration. Thus, infants, children, and the mentally impaired represent persons for whom self-determination is limited; prisoners and other restricted populations also have limited autonomy. The degree of autonomy actually experienced or expressed by individuals may fluctuate with time and vary in different situations (Komrad 1983).

The emphasis on autonomy and self-determination represents a decidedly Western philosophical orientation. Application of the concept of autonomy by applied medical anthropologists working in non-Western settings requires a careful assessment of societal and cultural norms. However, in any cultural setting, the application of self-determination and respect for persons in research with human subjects requires, first, that individuals must have the opportunity to accept or reject participation in scientific investigations, and second, that individuals with diminished autonomy must be protected as research subjects.

Requirements for informed consent and confidentiality in research appeal to and are justified by the principle of autonomy and respect for persons. In the implementation of applied medical anthropological investigations, obtaining informed consent and maintaining confidentiality may be difficult. Informed consent, for example, implies a degree of voluntariness among research participants. Yet, applied medical anthropologists often conduct studies with institutionalized individuals or vulnerable populations with limited autonomy. The voluntary nature of consent is open to question when there exists the possibility of coercion by institutional authorities or because of negative community sanctions exists. Linguistical barriers in cross-cultural studies or research with ethnic minorities present additional constraints to achieving informed consent in applied medical anthropological studies.

In addition to respect for individual autonomy, researchers must consider the health and well-being of human subjects. In everyday language, beneficence commonly refers to acts of mercy, charity, and kindness toward others. Within the

context of research with human subjects, stated simply, the principle of beneficence addresses the obligation of investigators: (1) to do no harm; and (2) to maximize benefits and minimize potential harm (Beauchamp and Childress 1983:108;
Frankena 1973:47). Minimally, the principle of beneficence would dictate that
applied medical anthropological research should be conducted only if some good,
some benefit, could be derived for individuals or society. Investigators must determine whether the benefits of conducting a particular study outweigh the potential risks imposed on research subjects. In the larger context, applied medical anthropologists must take into account the long-term social and scientific consequences that may result from investigations.

Determination of the risks and benefits of conducting research raises two serious issues for the applied medical anthropologist. First, the medical anthropologist working in an applied setting often confronts the problem of control over the
use of research data. This occurs because, rather than working as an independent
investigator, the anthropologist may be employed by an agency or organization
to conduct a specific piece of research. Research contracts with institutions such
as hospitals, or agencies such as AID, PAHO, or WHO (see Pillsbury, this volume), place definite restrictions on the anthropologist's ability to dictate subsequent action in regard to research findings. Ethical dilemmas may occur when the
applied medical anthropologist discovers that study results are being purposely
withheld or are used to manipulate or discriminate against research subjects. In
cases such as these, the risks surrounding implementation of the investigation may
be difficult to anticipate prior to the completion of the study.

A second problem for the medical anthropologists conducting applied research involves the question of allegiance. The applied medical anthropologist is
accountable to individuals and organizations representing diverse interests, including the financial sponsor of the study, the institution or community in which
the study is conducted, and the research subjects. In considering the risks and
benefits at the individual and the societal level, the anthropologist must explore
potential conflicts of interests and determine the most effective way to balance
competing claims for allegiance.

The promotion of human health and welfare is perhaps the most significant
factor in the risk/benefit equation. However, individual and cultural value systems
are influential in determining what constitutes a risk or benefit. Therefore, considerable ambiguity surrounds judgments regarding "minimal" or "serious"
risk. On the far end of the continuum, brutality and inhumane treatment of human
subjects should never be condoned. Assessments of risk are more difficult when
the consequences of research appear to be negligible, as is the case with the majority of studies conducted by medical anthropologists working in applied settings.

In some instances, it is difficult to determine the risks and benefits prior to
conducting the research (Veatch 1987:17–35). Moreover, certain types of research may produce both benefits and harm to individuals or society. Genetic experiments, for example, have the potential of increasing our knowledge concerning congenital diseases and the outcome of such experiments may provide im-

portant information to prospective parents. Alternatively, the results of genetic experiments could have serious social repercussions if knowledge of genetic makeup was used to reinforce or justify discriminatory social practices.

While respect for persons is articulated in the requirement for informed consent, and beneficence is expressed in attention to risks and benefits, the principle of justice is closely linked to issues of equality and fairness in determining who receives the benefits and who bears the burdens of research. Certain populations—racial minorities, welfare recipients, prisoners, hospitalized patients, students, subjects of research in developing countries—are particularly vulnerable to injustices in the implementation of scientific investigations. For example, in clinical investigations conducted during the 19th and early 20th centuries, poor patients attending public clinics were likely to be the subjects of research that largely benefited more prosperous individuals of private clinics (Vogel 1980). The exploitation of Nazi concentration camp victims is another instance of blatant injustice in regard to human subject research.

Although biomedical investigators have been criticized in the past for reliance on the poor or institutionalized individuals as research subjects, applied medical anthropologists often find themselves working with just these populations. The distinction between the two types of research is perhaps best characterized by the nature of the investigative role. While biomedical scientists may or may not have an advocacy relationship with their research subjects, applied medical anthropologists usually have a vested interest in acting as advocates for their clientele, the community, or the subjects of particular investigations.

The need for assessing issues of justice in scientific research is recognized as a fundamental duty of investigators (Beauchamp and Childress 1983; U.S. National Commission 1978; Veatch 1987). Two areas of focus deserve special attention in determinations of fairness:

> the selection of research subjects needs to be scrutinized in order to determine whether some classes (e.g., welfare patients, particular racial and ethnic minorities, or persons confined to institutions) are being systematically selected simply because of their easy availability, their compromised position, or their manipulability, rather than for reasons directly related to the problem being studied. Finally, whenever research supported by public funds leads to the development of therapeutic devices and procedures, justice demands both that these not provide advantages only to those who can afford them and that such research should not unduly involve persons from groups unlikely to be among the beneficiaries of subsequent applications of the research. [U.S. National Commission 1978:9–10]

Taken together, the principles of autonomy, beneficence, and justice form a solid basis for assessing ethical conduct in applied medical anthropological research. Anthropologists are continually challenged to achieve a balance in meeting the requirements of these principles and maintaining scientific rigor and integrity.

Ethical Guidelines for Research with Human Subjects

A major initiative concerning the ethical treatment of human subjects in scientific research grew out of the Nuremberg Trials following World War II (Katz 1972).

The Nuremberg Code of 1947 was used as a set of standards in evaluating war crimes committed by scientists and physicians conducting biomedical experiments with concentration camp prisoners. A key dimension of the Nuremberg Code was its emphasis on and commitment to informed consent in human research. Subsequently, other codes of research ethics were developed, including, for example, the Helsinki Declaration of 1964 (World Medical Association 1978) and the Draft Code of Ethics on Experimentation prepared by the World Medical Association in Geneva in 1961.

Social scientists used these codes as models in formulating codes of research ethics for their individual fields (American Psychological Association 1953, 1974, 1982; American Sociological Association 1971). The American Anthropological Association (AAA) first drafted position papers on anthropological research and ethics in 1948 (Kimmell 1988). These were revised in 1967 and a formal set of rules regarding professional responsibility was adopted in 1971. A revised "Principles of Professional Responsibility" for AAA is currently under consideration (American Anthropological Association 1990a). The principles articulate responsibilities of anthropologists to individuals studied, the general public, students and trainees, employers, sponsors, and host governments. In acknowledging the inherent difficulties of anthropological work, the code of ethics (American Anthropological Association 1990a) states:

> In a field of such complex involvements, misunderstandings, conflicts and the need to make choices among apparently incompatible values are constantly generated. The most fundamental responsibility of anthropologists is to anticipate such difficulties and to resolve them in ways that are compatible with the principles stated here. If such resolution is impossible, anthropological work should not be undertaken or continued.

Ethical guidelines for professional conduct have also been formulated by individual anthropological professional societies. The "Statement on Professional and Ethical Responsibilities" issued by the Society for Applied Anthropology (1983) reiterates similar themes as the AAA code of ethics. Special attention is given to the importance of disclosing research goals, maintaining confidentiality, and obtaining voluntary consent in research participation. The National Association for the Practice of Anthropology (NAPA) has drafted a set of "Ethical Guidelines for Practitioners" that is currently under consideration by NAPA members (American Anthropological Association 1990b). This document addresses specific responsibilities incumbent on the anthropologist in advocacy or nonacademic roles:

> Our primary responsibility is to respect and consider the welfare and human rights of all categories of people affected by decisions, programs or research in which we take part. . . . It is also our responsibility to assure, to the extent possible, that the views of groups so affected are made clear and given full and serious consideration by decision makers and planners, in order to preserve options and choices for affected groups. . . . We should be sensitive to issues related to confidentiality throughout the design of research or other activities involving resource persons. . . . To our employers we owe competent, efficient, fully professional skills and techniques, timely performance of our work and com-

munication of our findings and recommendations in understandable, nonjargonistic language. [1990:6]

Governmental response to increased concern with ethical issues regarding the
use of human subjects in scientific research paralleled developments in professional fields. Review of the Tuskegee syphilis study in 1972 gave considerable
impetus to the movement toward mandatory review of research protocols. The
Tuskegee study, implemented in 1932 in Macon County, Alabama, was designed
to examine the natural course of untreated syphilis (Jones 1981). The subjects,
399 black men, were informed that they had "bad blood," not syphilis; treatments included free spinal taps that were nontherapeutic and painful. By 1969,
28–100 deaths occurred as a result of syphilis-related problems. Nevertheless,
treatment was not provided for the subjects until 1972, following public disclosure of the study.

A panel appointed by the Department of Health, Education, and Welfare reviewed the Tuskegee syphilis experiment and in 1974 the National Research Act
was passed. This Act established the National Commission for the Protection of
Human Subjects of Biomedical and Behavioral Research (Faden and Beauchamp
1986). The U.S. National Commission published several reviews of human experimentation on particular groups including human fetuses (1975), prisoners
(1976), children (1977), and the institutionalized mentally infirm (1978). The
Commission (1978) also published *The Belmont Report*, a document describing
basic ethical principles regarding research with human subjects.

Prior to the existence of the National Commission, the Public Health Service
required some form of committee review for investigations as early as 1965, and
in 1971, the Department of Health, Education, and Welfare (USDHEW 1971)
published a policy on the protection of human subjects in research (Veatch
1987:113). In 1974, human experimentation committees previously in existence
at many institutions were designated as institutional review boards (USDEW
1974). The Department of Health and Human Service (USDHHS 1981) issued
final regulations concerning policies governing research on human subjects in
1981. The government mandates were clear: all research involving human subjects that is funded in whole or in part by a DHHS agency, with certain exemp-
tions, must be evaluated by an institutional review board (IRB). Criteria for IRB
approval include: (1) a sound research design; (2) protection of privacy and confidentiality; (3) equality in treatment of subjects; (4) consideration of risks/bene-
fits; (5) monitoring of data collection; (6) informed consent; (7) documentation of
informed consent; and (8) a statement indicating that participation in the research
is voluntary and that withdrawing from the study will not result in harm or pen-
alty.

The impact of IRB's on the regulation of research with human subjects has
been profound (Agich 1988; Levine 1986; Veatch 1987). There is consensus
about the general purpose of IRB's, that is, they exist to protect individuals from
potential harm that may result from participation in research projects. However,
significant problems remain in the application of the review process and studies
of the nature and function of review committees call attention to the problematic

implementation of this charge (Barber et al. 1973; Gray 1975). Veatch (1987) is skeptical about the lack of definition concerning the task of institutional review boards:

> I will conclude that the ambiguities are so great that, until the theory of the committee is clarified and appropriate structural changes are made in accord with that theory, it is impossible for the experimentation committee to successfully fulfill its tasks. [1987:114]

The problem begins with the selection of committee members (Veatch 1987:109–123). Committees must include representatives from nonscientific fields and from the community but most IRB's are dominated by scientists who are responsible for reviewing the research protocols of colleagues and friends. Two problems become apparent. First, there is the question of professional competence. Who is qualified to judge the professional merit of a particular study? Second, the presence of professional bias may hinder objectivity regarding consideration of harm to research subjects. The high value placed on furthering scientific research among most IRB representatives may outweigh the concerns of a lay representative. Psychological pressure to reach a consensus and the inclination to accept the arguments of a "professional" both influence assessments of studies. A minority voice, while recognized, is not often following in making the final decision about scientific merit and potential harm to research participants. Additional problems center around which studies fall under the guidelines set by IRB's. For example, the 1981 DHHS regulations limit the definition of "human subjects" to living individuals with whom an interaction or intervention occurs and from whom identifiable information is obtained. As Veatch points out, "This has the potential of permitting researchers to gain access to sensitive medical records of deceased persons without the benefit of regulatory protection or IRB review" (1987:98). Additionally, research that involves minimal risk to subjects is exempt from review. The problem is one of interpretation regarding the judgment of "minimal risk."

Anthropologists and other social scientists have expressed serious reservations about the applicability of IRB regulations for basic and applied social research (e.g., Cassell 1978, 1980; Gray 1979; Sieler and Murtha 1980; Wax and Cassell 1979). Critics argue that many ethical issues encountered in social science research, especially ethnographic or phenomenological studies, are not addressed by the federal regulations. Anthropologists, sociologists, and psychologists did not play a role in formulating IRB requirements, and the National Commission for the Protection of Human Subjects of Biomedical and Behavioral Research did not recommend separate criteria for biomedical and social science investigations (Gray 1979).

Applied medical anthropologists working from a university or federally funded institutional base often confront obstacles in meeting standards for IRB approval. For example, in a recent study of patients' fear of contracting AIDS from physicians, Marshall et al. (1990) were required by the IRB to obtain written informed consent from each person interviewed in outpatient waiting areas. Since the study was conducted within the medical center, the IRB insisted that a "boiler plate'' disclaimer, used for all biomedical clinical research within the university, be attached to the informed consent statement. While the investigators' informed consent document was fairly simple and nonthreatening, the university attachment indicated that biomedical or behavioral research in which the subject has agreed to participate involves the risk of injury and that emergency medical treatment for physical injuries resulting from participation would be provided. The language suggested a scope of potential problems considerably beyond the intended purpose of the study. Arguments to have the university "boiler plate" removed for this study were unsuccessful; investigators were informed that any research conducted with university patients must include the disclaimer document.

Ambiguity surrounding the extent of IRB regulatory purview creates additional difficulties for anthropologists (cited in Murphy and Johannsen 1990:131):

> At first these regulations covered only federally funded research. They quickly came to include any research, funded or not conducted at any institution receiving federal monies. [Gray 1979:204; see also Seiler and Murtha 1980:148]

In their detailed account of a failed attempt to conduct unfunded ethnographic student research, Murphy and Johannsen (1990) address two dilemmas regarding the application of IRB regulations. First, there are no clear guidelines distinguishing research conducted by students for the purposes of education and research conducted by faculty and staff. The review process may be particularly problematic in evaluations of short-term participant-observation studies intended as training exercises in anthropological fieldwork methods. Second, while IRB's protect human subjects of research, Murphy and Johannsen found that student researchers have little recourse if they are the victims of ethical misconduct or abuse:

> In the ordinary course of events students and professors . . . have established procedures to follow if they feel that a member of the academic community has acted in an ethically questionable manner or has violated tenets of academic freedom. . . . Yet, we felt constrained not to avail ourselves of these measures for fear of violating one of the provisions we agreed to in seeking IRB approval . . . we promised to avoid placing any "interviewee" at risk of potential damage to their "financial standing or employability" . . . the IRB agreement effectively barred us from recourse to standard grievance procedures. [1990:132]

Objections raised by social scientists to the IRB regulatory process may, in the future, have some impact on reassessing the applicability of guidelines designed primarily for biomedical investigations. Until this occurs, education and advocacy provide the best means of achieving a fair and realistic examination of anthropological and other social science projects. For example, in regard to applied medical anthropological research, members of IRB's must be informed about the nature, purpose, and the unique constraints presented by certain investigations. One step toward increasing awareness among IRB members might be the preparation of a written statement from anthropological associations outlining general goals and methods. This statement could be distributed to IRB members by the IRB chairperson at individual institutions; it might also be included with materials presented to IRB members by anthropological investigators. Disciplinary representation on the IRB, and in lieu of this, identification of an "advocate" for anthropological research among IRB members, may also facilitate the review process. As Veatch (1987) and others (e.g., Murphy and Johannsen 1990) have pointed out, most IRB members are willing to listen to concerns expressed by investigators. The question that remains, of course, is whether or not "listening" will be translated into support and action at the level of regulatory approval.

Application of Ethical Principles in Anthropological Research

The type of research conducted by applied medical anthropologists may involve evaluations of ongoing human behavior or interventions designed to change human behavior. The research context, including the population being studied and the institutional sponsor, significantly influence ethical considerations in the design and implementation of investigations. In this section, difficulties encountered by applied medical anthropologists in the application of ethical principles are considered in regard to three areas: (1) informed consent; (2) confidentiality; and (3) determinations of risks and benefits. Finally, the role of advocacy in anthropology is discussed. Table 1 provides a summary of ethical principles and their application in research with human subjects along with some potential problems faced by anthropologists in applied medical investigations.

Informed Consent

Informed consent in human subjects research consists of three key elements: the provision of information, comprehension of information, and voluntariness in regard to participation. Adequate information for potential subjects includes a description of research purposes and a clear delineation of risks and benefits. Subjects do not need to be informed of technical details. Rather, pertinent information must be communicated in a manner that is understandable, nonjargonistic, and linguistically appropriate.

In the process of obtaining informed consent, it is not enough to simply provide information about a study. In order to make a decision, potential subjects must be able to comprehend the information being communicated. Moreover, as Agich (1988:133) points out, "Ideally, comprehension of the information disclosed should allow the individual's personal beliefs and values to be reflected in any decision." When individuals are unable to adequately understand the meaning of the research because, for example, they are infants, young children, mentally incompetent, or physically impaired, steps must be taken to insure that "proxy" consent is obtained from a legal guardian or family member. In particular circumstances, consent may be assumed because of the minimal risks associated with the study.

Voluntary participation in research depends upon the respondents ability to understand and comprehend the meaning of the research and the impact it may have on his or her life. Voluntariness implies that participation is sought without unnecessary coercion or social pressure. Rewards, bribes, and excessive or unrealistic promises may constitute coercion, especially if the subject is vulnerable

TABLE 1.
Ethical Principles and Their Application: Potential Problems in Applied Medical Anthropological Research

Principles	Application	Problems
1. Respect for persons	Informed consent	• Achieving "voluntariness" in cross-cultural studies, among residents of closed institutions, and staff, patients, clientele of organizations.
		• Linguistical barriers.
		• Meeting criteria for investigational review committees.
	Confidentiality	• Ensuring anonymity of subjects.
		• Protection of research data.
2. Beneficence	Determination of risks/ benefits	• Control over use of research data.
		• Competing allegiances to research sponsor, client, organization, community, study population.
3. Justice	Fairness/equality in selection of research subjects and research design	• Protection of vulnerable study populations (e.g., ethnic minorities, hospitalized patients, institutionalized individuals, mentally impaired, illegal residents).
		• Use of controlled experiments/intervention studies.

in some way to the offers of compensation. The implicit or explicit power of investigators and/or the institutions they represent influences the voluntary nature of participation in research. Thus, social status and social class differences between researchers and subjects may inhibit voluntariness in informed consent.

The elusive nature of obtaining a truly informed consent is complex, both from a psychological and a moral point of view (Katz 1972; Levine 1975). The application of informed consent in social science research is problematic in part, because it is often difficult to assess the degree of risk involved and the extent to which subjects are adequately informed (Adair, Dushenko, and Lindsay 1985). Moreover, in applied medical anthropological studies, especially those involving ethnographic and qualitative methods, it may be difficult to predefine the exact nature and scope of the study. Conversations recorded in field notes and information obtained in open-ended interviews may cover a wide range of topics, not always limited to the specific focus of investigation.

Linguistic barriers can be obstacles to informed consent in applied medical anthropological research with ethnic minorities or in studies conducted with individuals who speak a different language than the investigator. As Coreil (personal communication) notes, an investigation requiring a translator creates a dual problem for the anthropologist. First, the anthropologist must depend on the translator to interpret the research objectives correctly and effectively; second, the anthropologist must depend on the translator to actually follow through with the consent which means relaying the information and requesting participation in the study. In this case, consent can only be assumed if the respondent agrees to participate.

Research conducted in non-Western settings presents the applied medical anthropologist with additional problems in regard to obtaining informed consent. For example, the application of Western ethical standards to medical and social studies conducted in developing countries with divergent cultural norms may be construed as a form of *ethical imperialism* (Angell 1988; Newton 1990). Yet, as Angell (1988) and others (e.g., Barry 1988; Durojaiye 1979; Ekunwe and Kessel 1984; Goodgame 1990) point out, while ethical relativism demands cultural sensitivity to local customs, it does not license an investigator to conduct research without regard to potential harm and without attempts to remain informative at every level of research implementation. In particular, Angell (1988) cautions against an ethical relativism that would foster the exploitation of Third World populations in research that would not be allowed in the investigator's home country.

One problem surrounding informed consent in non-Western settings involves identification of the appropriate person to provide consent. In his discussion of AIDS research in Africa, Barry describes the difficulties in translating and applying the concepts of autonomy and personhood, "Personhood is defined by one's tribe, village, or social group" (1988:1083; see also Goodgame 1990). Therefore, tribal elders or community leaders must often be approached before obtaining consent from individuals. While the notion of personhood may differ in non-Western cultures (De Craemer 1983), the practical aspects of obtaining consent to conduct research from "authorities" is not limited to this setting. The implementation of an applied medical anthropological study, regardless of the cultural setting, normally begins with contacting key persons at the community or institutional level (Bernard 1988; Rylko-Bauer, van Willigen, McElroy 1989; Taylor and Bogdan 1984).

In some cases, investigators suggest that obtaining informed consent can or should be avoided when: (1) it is too difficult to obtain; (2) the study involves negligible or no risks; and (3) if informants knew the true purpose of the research, no one would give consent (e.g., Punch 1986). Sensitivity of the research topic rarely justifies the absence of informed consent and the ambiguous judgement of risk might be best assessed by the subjects themselves (Spradley 1980). For example, in an applied ethnographic study of staff anger toward adolescents on a locked psychiatric ward, Scheinfeld and associates (Scheinfield, Marshall, and Beer 1989) did not encounter problems in obtaining informed consent despite the sensitive nature of the research. Staff participants gave written consent. In addition, because the study involved direct observation of interactions with patients, informed consent was obtained for each adolescent. During the 18-month ethnographic phase of the study, only one patient declined to participate in the study.

However, this particular study calls attention to a problem often confronted by applied medical anthropologists working in an institutional setting. While documented informed consent may be obtained, the question of subtle coercion remains. Staff members, for example, in a hospital environment may feel compelled to participate in a "voluntary" research project if supervisors would look unfavorably on nonparticipation. Similarly, adolescents on a locked psychiatric ward, many of whom are there on an involuntary basis, may feel forced to participate in a study out of fear of repercussions from hospital staff. "Voluntariness" and compliance among personnel, residents, patients, or inmates in closed institutional settings are always open to question.

Studies have shown variable effects of informed consent on participation in research and response to interview questions (Rittenbaugh and Harrison 1984; Singer 1978; Singer and Frankel 1982). In a study of the contents of household garbage, Rittenbaugh and Harrison (1984) found that individuals who knew their garbage was being monitored threw away a significantly lower number of alcoholic beverage bottles than those who were not informed (cited in Bernard 1988:292). Singer (1978) found that providing subjects with more detailed and truthful information in a face-to-face survey interview ahead of time did not effect the response rate or the quality of responses. However, individuals not asked to sign a consent form demonstrated a higher response rate and those who were asked to sign the form following the interview were more self-disclosing about socially undesirable behavior than respondents asked to sign prior to the interview.

One alternative to informed consent is the active use of deception in research. Opinions remain divided in the debate over whether or not deception is an ethically appropriate research methodology (e.g., Barnes 1979; Bernard 1988; Bok 1978; Bulmer 1982; Douglas 1976; Erikson 1967; Punch 1986; Rynkiewich and Spradley 1976; Spradley 1980). The use of covert research in participant-observation studies provides well-documented examples of both the practical and ethical dilemmas encountered by investigators using this technique (e.g., Humphreys 1975; Rosenhan 1973). Humphreys (1975), for example, conducted observations of homosexual acts in a public restroom in St. Louis without informing individuals that he was recording their behavior. Moving beyond the limits of unobtrusive and nonreactive field observation, Humphreys obtained the names and addresses of his subjects by using their license plate numbers. At a later date, he contacted the men, saying that they had been randomly chosen to participate in a health survey.

Humphreys was criticized for his research tactics, especially in the follow-up study. Yet, certain investigators believe that the use of deception or other covert measures is necessary or warranted:

> If the researcher is completely honest with people about his activities, they will try to hide actions and attitudes they consider undesirable, and so will be dishonest. Consequently, the researcher must be dishonest to get honest data [Gans 1962:46, cited in Punch 1989:303]

> The crux of the matter is that some deception, passive or active, enables you to get at data not obtainable by other means. [Punch 1989:303]

Douglas (1976) advocates the use of covert techniques, suggesting that since lies and deception are a part of everyday interaction, investigators must mirror this behavior in order to obtain reliable information. In sharp contrast, Erikson (1967) argues that one is never justified in using deception for research purposes. While Bernard (1988:305–306) condones passive deception in which observations do not involve, "experimental manipulation of informants in order to get them to act in certain ways," he is more cautious about covert deception:

> My own position is that the decision to use deception is up to you, provided that the *risks of detection are your own risks and no one else's*. If detection risks harm to others, then don't even consider disguised participant observation [Bernard 1988:303, emphasis in original text]

Assuming the role of "spy" or "undercover agent" may result in severe consequences for the applied medical anthropologist, the research subjects, and the discipline itself. Deception can foster distrust among subjects of research who inadvertently learn the truth about a study. Subsequently, effective use of research findings may be limited. Distrust may also prevent other applied medical anthropologists from conducting studies in the same locale or organizational setting. Moreover, as Bernard (1988:303) notes, it is not always possible to anticipate the potential harm done by disguised research.

Right to Privacy and Confidentiality

The right to privacy implies that individuals have control over when and how communication about themselves is given to others (Westin 1968:7). In research with human subjects, confidentiality suggests that an agreement has been made which limits access to private information (Sieber 1982). Taken together, respect for individual privacy and the promise of confidentiality are essential in the implementation of ethically responsible research.

Applied medical anthropologists often engage in research involving the collection of sensitive information on the personal life of research subjects, including for example, detailed descriptions of physical or mental problems, social interactions, and political affiliations. Inadvertent *or* intentional disclosure of this information could threaten the emotional and, in some cases, the economic or physical well-being of individual participants. The general welfare of participants is always in jeopardy if theft occurs or when research records are appropriated by governmental, institutional, or organizational authorities (Boruch and Cecil 1979).

The assurance of anonymity for subjects—securing data and concealing identities and locations—represents a research ideal (Bulmer 1982). While a promise of confidentiality may be extended, it is sometimes difficult to sustain as information is made public. This may be particularly problematic when applied medical anthropological studies are conducted in small communities where the behavior of individuals is closely monitored or in institutional settings in which information is obtained from professional colleagues working in close proximity. Additionally, in their discussion of ethical dilemmas in family research, La Rossa and associates (La Rossa, Bennett and Gelles 1981) call attention to the need for confidentiality when interviewing multiple members of one family. Informants must be able to trust the researcher *not* to divulge information that might result in punitive sanctions or cause anxiety for other family members.

Certain types of applied medical anthropological investigations such as research in the area of child abuse, patient abuse, or professional misconduct, involve more serious risks to subjects if confidentiality and privacy are not protected. Studies of illegal behavior or illegal residents present other problems (e.g., Leonard 1990; Stepick and Stepick 1990; Van Maanen 1983). In her investigation of the sexual behavior of male clients of street prostitutes, Leonard placed herself at personal risk in soliciting subject participation:

> To enhance my safety and to prevent interference with prostitute-client transactions, interviews occurred on weekdays between noon and 6:00 PM, when business is slowest. All men who attempted to solicit my services, assuming I was a sex worker, were invited to participate in a "sex survey!" [1990:43]

In addition to herself, Leonard's subjects were at risk if knowledge of their illicit sexual transactions was made public. As Leonard (1990:42) points out, individuals performing illegal activities, "tend to be distrustful of outsiders who probe their attitudes, document their behaviors, and, perhaps most important, acknowledge their 'deviance.' "

An appeal to research confidentiality does not guarantee legal protection for social scientists or the subjects of their research (Van Maanen 1983:276–277). Hopper (1990) describes his difficulties in protecting the confidentiality of his informants when he was asked to be an expert witness for a class-action suit concerning the right to shelter for homeless men in New York. During the trial, Hopper was requested to produce his field notes for examination; his concern was that:

> the notebooks included the names of many informants who worked for the city, and whose jobs I feared would be jeopardized were it disclosed that they had spoken to me freely about their own work and the treatment of homeless men in general. I had, moreover, assured a number of them of total confidentiality as a condition for my being allowed to interview them. [1990:111]

In this case, a compromise was reached in which the notebooks remained under court protection; opposing lawyers could read the documents in the courtroom but were bound to withhold information outside of court. Hopper advised his informants about the situation. In order to minimize problems of confidentiality, he suggests that anthropologists might consider the use of code names in field notes and other research documents that might come under public scrutiny.

The Risk/Benefit Ratio

The assessment of risks and benefits associated with research begins with the selection of a topic and a methodology:

> Remember: The first ethical decision you make in research is whether to collect certain kinds of information at all. Once that decision is made, *you* are responsible for what is done with that information, and *you* must protect informants from becoming emotionally burdened for having talked to you. [Bernard 1988:217, emphasis in original]

Three factors must be considered in weighing the negative and positive outcomes of a study. First, the applied medical anthropologist must consider the overall contribution of the study in terms of its benefit to subjects, to clients, and to the discipline itself. Second, special attention must be given to anticipated consequences of research. One unintended effect of scientific knowledge results from its use in promoting the special interests of individuals with power over more vulnerable groups (Kimmel 1988:118). Medical applied anthropologists face this issue when conducting research with marginal populations or institutionalized subjects. The danger exists that information will be used to manipulate, regulate, or repress the activities of others.

This issue calls attention more specifically to the problem of control over research data and the use of research findings by medical anthropologists working in applied settings. When the anthropologist is hired to carry out a study by an independent organization such as a hospice or mental health center, or an agency such as the World Health Organization, proprietary rights over the use of data may severely restrict the anthropologist's power to influence subsequent action regarding study results. In negotiating the contingencies of research, it is useful to discuss this issue with clients, sponsors, funding agencies, and the beneficiaries of the research before the study begins. Nevertheless, even when discussions occur prior to implementing the study, the anthropologist may face serious ethical dilemmas when study results are subsequently controlled by institutional or organizational authorities. The situation may be particularly problematic if attempts are made to cover up controversial findings or if results are used to justify negative sanctions against or discriminatory practices toward certain individuals.

A third factor in determining the risk/benefit ratio involves consideration of the appropriateness and impact of research design. For example, the use of experimental treatment groups in an intervention study raises several ethical questions. The medical applied anthropologist must decide first, who will be selected to participate in the study, and second, of these individuals, which ones will be assigned to the experimental or the control group. Randomization in social intervention studies is justified when the benefit of the intervention is not fully determined until after the study is completed (e.g., Campbell and Cecil 1982). Difficulties arise if it is known prior to the study that the untreated control group would be denied a potential benefit.

In designing a study of an intervention for IV drug users susceptible to HIV infection, Stall (personal communication) was confronted with the dilemma of withholding a therapy from the control group of subjects. Subjects in the experimental group were to receive a fairly extensive educational program on risk factors for AIDS. One purpose of the investigation was to determine the impact of the instructional program by comparing the subsequent behavior among experimental and control groups of IV drug users. Individuals in the control group were just as much at risk for contracting AIDS as the experimental group. Stall believed it would be unethical not to provide at least minimal education to all subjects at serious risk for HIV infection. Stall resolved the conflict by incorporating a scaled down version of the instructional program for control group subjects; they were provided with an intensive one-day workshop instead of the extended educational intervention.

The Anthropologist as Advocate

In anthropological circles there is an on-going and lively discussion around the issue of advocacy (e.g., Grillo 1990; Hastrup and Elsass 1990; Mathieson 1990; Paine 1985a, 1985b, 1990; Partridge 1987; Singer 1989, 1990). For some anthropologists, there is no dilemma; the anthropologist must be an advocate, particularly in the area of applied research and policy development. Partridge (1987), for example, places the advocacy role squarely within an ethical context, suggesting that our responsibility as practitioners, ". . . requires a commitment beyond narrow professionalism to take action once analysis indicates a course of action" (pp. 230–231). In contrast, Hastrup and Elsass (1990) take a middle-of-the road position, arguing that there are fundamental differences between advocacy and anthropology. "Context" is the purview of anthropology and its goal is the production of knowledge; an advocate must move beyond the limits of his or her profession because "no 'cause' can be legitimated in anthropological terms" (Hastrup and Elsass 1990:301).

The role of advocacy demands a moral commitment for active engagement with others in relation to a specific problem (Henriksen 1985). Quite simply, it means that the anthropologist must take a stand. The difficulty, however, is that advocacy and intervention cannot be considered apart from interpretation, definition, and translation. As Hastrup and Elsass (1990:304) suggest, " 'Speaking for' someone presupposes that one knows who he is."

Paine (1985b, 1990) is unequivocal about the complementarity of anthropology and advocacy. Nevertheless, Paine (1985b:309) raises the following questions: (1) who should be the recipients of advocacy?; (2) what form should advocacy take?; and (3) when should an advocate intervene? Addressing the need for praxis in medical anthropology, Singer (1990) provides some answers to the questions raised by Paine. Singer is broad ranging in his identificationa of advocacy roles and tactics that the anthropologist might use to effect change in the medical arena. In regard to research, for example, he suggests:

Designing health related studies to aid community groups in challenging the medical establishment to: (a) address pressing health issues; (b) develop language and culturally appropriate care; (c) end discriminatory treatment of ethnic populations in the clinic and in employment; (d) change sexist policies and practices; (e) implement prevention programs; (f) share health information with nonprofessionals; (g) demystify medical discourse and practice; (h) radicsally alter the provider-patient relationship; and (i) restructure decision-making bodies to reflect community composition. [Singer 1990:185]

The role of advocacy for applied medical anthropologists is exacerbated by the problem of allegiance to those who often have competing interests in regard to research findings. The tension between accountability and advocacy is situated within the context of the anthropologist's relationship with: (1) the subjects of the research; (2) the beneficiaries of the research; (3) the funding agency; (4) the employer; (5) the research sponsor; (6) professional anthropology; and (7) individual values. The question of allegiance always includes a moral dimension. There are no easy answers for anthropologists faced with the dilemma of choosing between competing interests and conflicting values. As Rylko-Bauer (Rylko-Bauer, Van Willigen, and McElroy 1989:623) and associates point out, recommendations made on the basis of research may conflict with the needs and the goals of the intended beneficiaries, the community, or with the interests of the client group.

Conclusions

Ethical principles governing applied medical anthropological research are not unique to our discipline. Respect for persons, beneficence, and justice are overriding concerns for any scientist. The way in which these principles are expressed in the implementation and design of a study depends, in part, on constraints imposed by the specific context. In this regard, anthropologists are likely to encounter more obstacles than other social scientists, especially those engaged in policy related investigations. The moral challenge for the anthropologist is maintaining a balance in a research reality in which social facts and social values are mystified, reified, and often nebulous (Fluehr-Lobban 1991; Cassell and Jacobs 1987). Under these conditions, the anthropologist must assume a reflexive stance—always with a view toward individuals who may be harmed.

References Cited

Adair, J. G., T. W. Dushenko, and R. C. L. Lindsay
    1985   Ethical Regulations and Their Impact on Research Practice. American Psychologist 40:59–72.
Agich, George
    1988   Human Experimentation and Clinical Consent. In Medical Ethics: A Guide for Health Professionals. John Monagle and David C. Thomasma, eds. Pp. 127–139. Rockville, MD: Aspen Publishers.
American Anthropological Association
    1990a   Memo, March 15, to Members of the Association from Eugene Sterud, Executive Director, containing national ballot for "Revised Principles of Professional Responsibility," pp. 1–4.

1990b   Unit ballot for National Association for the Practice of Anthropology: Ethical
        Guidelines for Practitioners, p. 7.
American Psychological Association
   1953   Ethical Standards of Psychologists. Washington, DC: American Psychological
          Association.
   1974   Standards for Educational and Psychological Tests. Washington, DC: American
          Psychological Association.
   1982   Ethical Principles in the Conduct of Research with Human Participants. Wash-
          ington, DC: American Psychological Association.
American Sociological Association
   1971   Code of Ethics. Washington, DC: American Sociological Association.
Angell, Marcia
   1988   Ethical Imperialism: Ethics in International Collaborative Clinical Research (Ed-
          itorial). New England Journal of Medicine 319(16):1081–1083.
Barber, Bernard, et al.
   1973   Research on Human Subjects: Problems of Social Control in Medical Experi-
          ments. New York: Russell Sage.
Barnes, J. A.
   1979   Who Should Know What? Social Science, Privacy and Ethics. Middlesex: Pen-
          guin Books.
Barry, Michele
   1988   Ethical Considerations of Human Investigation in Developing Countries: The
          AIDS Dilemma. New England Journal of Medicine 319(16):1083–1086.
Beauchamp, Thomas, and John Childress
   1979   Principles of Biomedical Ethics. New York: Oxford University Press.
   1983   Principles of Biomedical Ethics. 2nd edition. New York: Oxford Press.
Bernard, H. Russell
   1988   Research Methods in Cultural Anthropology. Newbury Park, CA: Sage.
Bok, Sisela
   1978   Lying: Moral Choice in Public and Private Life. New York: Pantheon.
Boruch, R. F., and J. S. Cecil
   1979   Assuring the Confidentiality of Social Research Data. Philadelphia: University
          of Pennsylvania Press.
Bulmer, Martin, ed.
   1982   Social Research Ethics. London: Macmillan.
Campbell, D. T., and J. S. Cecil
   1982   A Proposed System of Regulation for the Protection of Participants in Low-Risk
          Areas of Applied Social Research. In The Ethics of Social Research. J. E. Sieber, ed.
          New York: Springer-Verlag.
Cassell, Joan
   1978   Risk and Benefit to Subjects of Fieldwork. American Sociologist 13:134–143.
   1980   Ethical Principles for Conducting Fieldwork. American Anthropologist 82:28–
          41.
Cassell, Joan, and Sue-Ellen Jacobs (eds)
   1987   Handbook on Ethical Issues in Anthropology. Special publication of the Amer-
          ican Anthropological Association, No. 23. Washington, DC: American Anthropolog-
          ical Association.
De Craemer, W.
   1983   A Cross-Cultural Perspective on Personhood. Milbank Memorial Fund Quarterly
          61:19–34.

Douglas, Jack D.
    1976   Investigative Social Research. Beverly Hills, CA: Sage.
Durojaiye, Michael O.
    1979   Ethics of Cross-Cultural Research Viewed from Third World Perspective. Inter-
    national Journal of Psychology 14(2):137–141.
Ekunwe, Ebun O., and Ross Kessel
    1984   Informed Consent in the Developing World. Hastings Center Report 14(3):22–
    24.
Erikson, Kai
    1967   A Comment on Disguised Observation in Sociology. Social Problems 14:366–
    373.
Faden, R. R., and Thomas L. Beauchamp
    1986   A History and Theory of Informed Consent. New York: Oxford University
    Press.
Fluehr-Lobban, Carolyn (ed)
    1991   Ethics and the Profession of Anthropology. Philadelphia: University of Penn-
    sylvania Press.
Frankena, William
    1973   Ethics. 2nd edition. Englewood Cliffs, NJ: Prentice-Hall.
Gans, H. J.
    1962   The Urban Villagers. New York: Free Press.
Goodgame, Richard W.
    1990   AIDS in Uganda—Clinical and Social Features. New England Journal of Med-
    icine 323(6):383–389.
Graber, Glenn C.
    1988   Basic Theories in Medical Ethics. In Medical Ethics: A Guide for Health Profes-
    sionals. John Monagle and David Thomasma, eds. Pp. 462–475. Rockville, MD: As-
    pen Publishers.
Graber, Glenn C., and David C. Thomasma
    1989   Theory and Practice in Medical Ethics. New York: Continuum Publishing.
Gray, Bradford H.
    1975   Human Subjects in Medical Experimentation. New York: Wiley-Interscience.
    1979   The Regulatory Context of Social Research: The Work of the National Commis-
    sion for the Protection of Human Subjects. In Deviance and Decency: The Ethics of
    Research with Human Subjects. C. B. Klockars and F. W. O'Connor, eds. Pp. 197–
    224. Beverly Hills, CA: Sage.
Grillo, Ralph
    1990   Comments: Anthropological Advocacy: A Contradiction in Terms? Current An-
    thropology 31(3):308.
Hastrup, Kirsten, and Peter Elsass
    1990   Advocacy: A Contradiction in Terms? Current Anthropology 31(3):301–308.
Henriksen, George
    1985   Anthropologists as Advocates: Promoters of Pluralism or Makers of Clients? In
    Advocacy and Anthropology. Robert Paine, ed. St. John's: Institute of Social and
    Economic Research, Memorial University of Newfoundland.
Hopper, Kim
    1990   Research Findings as Testimony: A Note on the Ethnographer as Expert Witness.
    Human Organization 49(2):110–113.

Humphreys, Laud
  1975   Tearoom Trade. Chicago: Aldine.
Jones, J. H.
  1981   Bad Blood. New York: Free Press.
Katz, Jay
  1972   Experimentation with Human Beings. New York: Russell Sage.
Kimmel, Allan J.
  1988   Ethics and Values in Applied Social Research. Newbury Park, CA: Sage.
Klockars, C. B., and F. W. O'Connor, eds.
  1979   Deviance and Decency: The Ethics of Research with Human Subjects. Beverly
         Hills, CA: Sage.
Kleymeyer, Charles D., and William E. Bertrand
  1980   Toward More Ethical and Effective Carrying out of Applied Research across
         Cultural or Class Lines. Ethics in Science and Medicine 7(1):11–25.
Komrad, Mark S.
  1983   A Defense of Medical Paternalism: Maximizing Patients' Autonomy. Journal of
         Medical Ethics 9(1):38–44.
La Rossa, Ralph, Linda A. Bennett, and Richard Gelles
  1981   Ethical Dilemmas in Qualitative Family Research. Journal of Marriage and Fam-
         ily 43–303–313.
Leonard, Terri L.
  1990   Male Clients of Female Street Prostitutes: Unseen Partners in Sexual Disease
         Transmission. Medical Anthropology Quarterly 4(1):41–55.
Levine, Robert J.
  1975   The Nature and Definition of Informed Consent in Various Research Settings. In
         The National Commission for the Protection of Biomedical and Behaviors Research,
         Volume I: The Belmont Report. Appendix. Bethesda, MD: Department of Health,
         Education, and Welfare.
  1986   Ethics and Regulation of Clinical Research. 2nd edition. Baltimore: Urban and
         Schwarzenberg.
Marshall, Patricia, et al.
  1990   Patients' Fear of Contracting the Acquired Immunodeficiency Syndrome From
         Physicians. Archives of Internal Medicine 150:1501–1506.
Mathiesen, Per
  1990   Comments: Anthropological Advocacy: A Contradiction in Terms? Current An-
         thropology 31(3):308.
Murphy, Michael Dean, and Agneta Johannsen
  1990   Ethical Obligations and Federal Regulations in Ethnographic Research and An-
         thropological Education. Human Organization 49(2):127–134.
Newton, Lisa H.
  1990   Ethical Imperialism and Informed Consent. IRB: A Review of Human Subjects
         Research 12(3):10–11.
Paine, Robert
  1985a Advocacy and Anthropology. St. John's: Institute of Social and Economic Re-
         search, Memorial University of Newfoundland.
  1985b Anthropology and Advocacy: First Encounters. In Advocacy and Anthropol-
         ogy. St. John's: Institute of Social and Economic Research, Memorial University of
         Newfoundland.

1990   Comments: Anthropological Advocacy: A Contradiction in Terms? Current Anthropology 31(3):309.
Partridge, William L.
1987   Toward a Theory of Practice. *In* Applied Anthropology in America. Elizabeth
M. Eddy and William L. Partridge, eds. Pp. 211–233. New York: Columbia University Press.
Punch, Maurice
1989   The Politics and Ethics of Fieldwork. Beverly Hills, CA: Sage.
Reese, H. W. and W. J. Fremouw
1984   Normal and Normative Ethics in Behavioral Sciences. American Psychologist
39:863–876.
Reynolds, Paul Davidson
1972   On the Protection of Human Subjects and Social Science. International Social
Science Journal 24:693–719.
1975   Ethics and Status: Value Dilemmas in the Professional Conduct of Social Science. International Social Science Journal 27:563–611.
1979   Ethical Dilemmas and Social Science Research. San Francisco: Jossey-Bass.
Rittenbaugh, C. K., and G. G. Harrison
1984   Reactivity of Garbage Analysis. American Behavioral Scientist 28:51–70.
Rosenhan, D. L.
1973   On Being Sane in Insane Places. Science 179(4070):250–258.
Rylko-Bauer, Barbara, John van Willigen, and Ann McElroy
1989   Strategies for Increasing the Use of Anthropological Research in the Policy Process: A Cross-Disciplinary Analysis. *In* Making Our Research Useful. John Van Willigen, Barbara Rylko-Bauer, and Ann McElroy, eds. Pp. 1–26. Boulder, CO: Westview Press.
Rynkiewich, Michael A., and James P. Spradley
1976   Ethics and Anthropology: Dilemmas in Fieldwork. New York: John Wiley.
Scheinfeld, Daniel, Patricia Marshall, and David Beer
1989   Knowledge Utilization Structures, Processes, and Alliances in a Psychiatric
Hospital Study. *In* Making Our Research Useful. John Van Willigen, Barbara Rylko-
Bauer, and Ann McElroy, eds. Pp. 201–218. Boulder, CO: Westview Press.
Seiler, Lauren H., and James M. Muirtha
1980   Federal Regulation of Social Research Using "Human Subjects": A Critical As-
sessment. American Sociologist 15:146–157.
Shweder, Richard A.
1990   Ethical Relativism: Is There a Defensible Version? Ethos 18(2):219–223.
Sieber, J. E., ed.
1982   The Ethics of Social Research: Surveys and Experiments. New York: Springer-
Verlag.
Singer, E.
1978   Informed Consent: Consequences for Response Rate and Response Quality in
Social Surveys. American Sociological Review 43:144–162.
Singer, E., and M. R. Frankel
1982   Informed Consent Procedures in Telephone Interviews. American Sociological
Review 47:416–427.
Singer, Merrill
1989   The Coming of Age of Critical Medical Anthropology. Social Science and Med-
icine 28:1193–1204.

1990   Reinventing Anthropology: Toward A Critical Realignment. Social Science and
Medicine 30(2):179–186.
Spradley, James P.
1980   Participant Observation. New York: Holt, Rinehart and Winston.
Stepick, Alex and Carol D. Stepick
1990   People in the Shadows: Survey Research among Haitians in Miami. Human Or-
ganization 49(1):64–77.
Society for Applied Anthropology
1983   Statement on Professional and Ethical Responsibilities. Washington, DC: Society for Applied Anthropology.
Taylor, Steven J., and Robert Bogdan
1984   Introduction to Qualitative Research Methods: The Search for Meanings. New
York: John Wiley and Sons.
U.S. Department of Health, Education, and Welfare (USDHEW)
1971   The Institutional Guide to DHEW Policy on Protection of Human Subjects.
Washington, DC: U.S. Government Printing Office.
1974   Protection of Human Subjects. Federal Register 39 (May 30): Pt II 18914–
18920.
U.S. Department of Health and Human Services (DHHS)
1981   Final Regulations Amending Basic HHS Policy for the Protection of Human Research Subjects: Final Rule: 45 CFR 46. Federal Register: Rules and Regulations 46
(16, January 26): 8366–8392.
U.S. National Commission for the Protection of Human Subjects of Biomedical and Behavior Research
1975   Report and Recommendations: Research on the Fetus. Bethesda: DHEW Publication No. (OS) 76–127.
1976   Report and Recommendations: Research Involving Prisoners. Bethesda: DHEW
Publication No. (OS) 76–131.
1977   Research Involving Children: Report and Recommendations. Washington, DC:
U.S. Government Printing Office.
1978   Report and Recommendations: Research Involving Those Institutionalized as
Mentally Infirm. Bethesda, MD: DHEW
Publication No. (OS) 78–0006.
1978   The Belmont Report: Ethical Principles and Guidelines for the Protection of Human Subjects of Research. Washington, DC: U.S. Government Printing Office.
Van Maanen, J.
1983   The Moral Fix: On the Ethics of Fieldwork. In Contemporary Field Research.
R. M. Emerson, ed. Pp. 269–287. Boston: Little, Brown.
Veatch, Robert M.
1987   The Patient as Partner: A Theory of Human-Experimentation Ethics. Blooming-
ton, IN: Indiana University Press.
Vogel, Morris J.
1980   The Invention of the Modern Hospital. Chicago: University of Chicago Press.
Wax, Murray L., and Joan Cassell, eds.
1979   Fieldwork, Ethics and Politics: The Wider Context. In Federal Regulations: Ethical Issues and Social Research. Murray Wax and Joan Cassel, eds. Pp. 85–101.
Boulder, CO: Westview Press.
Westin, A. F.
1968   Privacy and Freedom. New York: Atheneum.

World Medical Association
    1978   Declaration of Helsinki. *In* Encyclopedia of Bioethics, Vol. 4. Warren T. Reich, ed. Pp. 1770. New York: Free Press.

Contributors

MARGARET S. BOONE (Ph.D., The Ohio State University) is an applied anthropologist living in the Washington, DC, area, where she provides consultant services mainly for the federal government. Her experience includes evaluation research with the U.S. General Accounting Office and the Census Bureau, and she has made extensive use of computers in policy research. She has 15 years of full- and part-time teaching, and is presently an adjunct professor with the George Washington University School of Medicine. She maintains an active interest in health and population issues of American minorities, and is a member of the Washington, DC, Infant Mortality Review Board. Publications include *Capital Crime: Black Infant Mortality in America* (1989) and *Capital Cubans* (1989).

MOLLY DOUGHERTY (B.S.N., M.N., and Ph.D. in anthropology, University of Florida), Professor and Research Coordinator in the College of Nursing at the University of Florida, is also an Adjunct Professor in the Department of Anthropology. While she maintains an interest in the interface between nursing and anthropology, her research and clinical activities are in women's health, and her National Institutes of Health-funded research is on the behavioral management of urinary dysfunctions in aging women.

CAROLE E. HILL (Ph.D., University of Georgia) is Professor and Chair of the Department of Anthropology at Georgia State University. She has conducted applied research in Costa Rica and in the southeastern United States, concentrating on the appropriateness and effectiveness of primary health care policies in rural and urban areas. She has worked with health care agencies to evaluate interventions in multicultural populations. Her interest also involves teaching and training students to apply anthropology in health settings.

THOMAS M. JOHNSON (Ph.D., University of Florida) is an Associate Professor of Family Medicine in the School of Primary Medical Care of the University of Alabama in Huntsville. He has worked as an applied medical anthropologist in community mental health and medical school settings, emphasizing the teaching of behavioral science in clinical settings, including supervision of students in obstetrics and gynecology, internal medicine, and psychiatry. Johnson has conducted research on strategies to reduce pain in burn care, the process of medical education, physician-patient interaction, high-risk obstetrics, and AIDS.

PATRICIA A. MARSHALL (Ph.D., University of Kentucky) is Assistant Professor in the Department of Medicine and Assistant Director of the Medical Humanities Program at Loyola University Stritch School of Medicine in Maywood, Illinois. She coordinates curriculum on ethical decision making for medical students and she is a member of the Ethics Consultation Service for the Loyola University Medical Center. In recent years, she has conducted research on patients' fear of contracting AIDS in medical settings, and ethical issues in organ transplantation.

BARBARA L. K. PILLSBURY (Ph.D., Columbia University) is a medical anthropologist, specialized in international health and the planning and evaluation of health and family planning programs in the developing countries. She currently heads a consulting group, International Health and Development Associates, and is a Visiting Professor in the School of Public Health, University of California at Los Angeles (UCLA). She has lived, conducted research, or worked with international agencies in numerous countries in Asia, the Middle East, and Africa. Pillsbury has served as Behavioral Science Advisor to the U.S. Agency for International Development (AID), first as a medical anthropologist with AID's policy bureau, then as women-in-development coordinator for Asia, and subsequently as Chief for Research and Evaluation for Asia. She was founding President of the National Association for the Practice of Anthropology.

ROBERT T. TROTTER II (Ph.D. Southern Methodist University) is a Professor and Chair of the Department of Anthropology at Northern Arizona University. He has served as President for the National Association for the Practice of Anthropology (NAPA). His research interests include crosscultural models of alcohol and drug use, Native American HIV/AIDS-related research, Mexican American folk medicine, computer assisted research methods, ethnopharmacology, and migrant farm worker health care programs.

LINDA M. WHITEFORD (Ph.D., University of Wisconsin; M.P.H., University of Texas) is an Associate Professor at the University of South Florida and is the Leader of the Applied Medical Anthropology Track in the M.A. Program. Her current research interests are in international health, particularly in the Spanish-speaking Caribbean, and in issues of maternal and child health. In 1989, she published with co-editor Marilyn Poland, *New Approaches to Human Reproduction: Social and Ethical Dimension* (Westview Press).